UP FROM BONDAGE

DALE E. PETERSON

Up from Bondage

THE LITERATURES OF RUSSIAN

AND AFRICAN AMERICAN SOUL

DUKE UNIVERSITY PRESS   Durham & London   2000

© 2000 Duke University Press

All rights reserved

Printed in the United States of America on acid-free paper ⊚

Designed by C. H. Westmoreland

Typeset in Quadraat by Tseng Information Systems, Inc.

Library of Congress Cataloging-in-Publication Data appear
on the last printed page of this book.

Portions of the prologue first appeared in "Justifying the Margin: The Construction of 'Soul' in Russian and African American Texts," *Slavic Review* 51 (1992): 749–57; chapter 1, in "Civilizing the Race: Chaadaev and the Paradox of Eurocentric Nationalism," *Russian Review* 56 (1997): 550–63; chapter 3, in "Notes
from the Underworld: Dostoevsky, Du Bois, and the Discovery
of Ethnic Soul," *Massachusetts Review* 35 (summer 1994): 225–
47; chapter 4, in "The Origin and End of Turgenev's *Sportsman's
Notebook*: The Poetics and Politics of a Precarious Balance," *Russian Literature* 16 (1984): 347–58; chapter 5, in "Underground
Notes: Dostoevsky, Bakhtin, and the African American Confessional Novel," in *Bakhtin and the Nation*, ed. Donald A. Wesling
et al. (Lewisburg, Pa.: Bucknell University Press, 2000), 31–46;
chapter 6, in "Richard Wright's Long Journey from Gorky to
Dostoevsky," *African American Review* 28 (1994): 375–88; chapter 8, in " 'Samovar Life': Russian Nurture and Russian Nature
in the Rural Prose of Valentin Rasputin," *Russian Review* 53
(1994): 81–96; the epilogue, in "Response and Call: The African
American Dialogue with Bakhtin," *American Literature* 65 (1993):
761–75.

For Lorna, Zachary, and Seth

CONTENTS

ACKNOWLEDGMENTS

This book has a long history, and I have accumulated many debts to those who have nurtured its growth. To the best of my recollection, it started to germinate fifteen years ago in midair over the Atlantic. Stimulated by a memorable conversation with Houston Baker Jr. on a flight to Moscow for a Soviet-American conference on literature and national identity, I began to reflect on the strong affinity expressed by contemporary African American cultural theorists for the dialogic thought of Mikhail Bakhtin. After many years of teaching and thinking about the parallels and contrasts between Russian and American literature, I finally began to appreciate the particular relevance of the emancipation of serfs and slaves for the literary forms and cultural theories created by the most innovative Russian and African American writers.

I could not have dared to explore so vast a terrain on my own without the intellectual encouragement provided by two mentors. My early years of teaching at Amherst College brought me into close association with Leo Marx, who offered me a model of cultural criticism and textual fidelity I shall always hope to emulate. My former colleague, Robert Gooding-Williams, allowed himself to be persuaded to collaborate with me several times in teaching an upper-level interdisciplinary course on the construction of Russian and African American "soul." His patient tutelage and philosophical mind provided much moral support in the classroom and improved many a page of my writing.

Crucial portions of my research depended on access to special collections. I am grateful to the Board of Trustees of Amherst College for making possible a Faculty Research Grant that enabled my travel to the Czech Republic and to Howard University in pursuit of my work on the Russian Eurasians and the New Negro movement. Dean of Faculty Lisa A. Raskin has been especially kind in understanding and accommodating my special requests. I cannot praise sufficiently the professional librarians who have assisted me in locating and utilizing the materials in their vast collections. Milena Klimova, the Curator of the Slovanska Knihovna at the Klementinum in Prague, generously gave me her personal attention, pointing me toward the invaluable Savitsky Archive and issuing the necessary permissions to work in it and make citations from it. I am also grateful to Joellen El Bashir, Curator of Manuscripts at the Moorland Spingarn Research Center, for her courtesy in granting me unimpeded access to the Alain Locke papers at Howard University. Nearer to home and equally gracious, I thank Linda Seidman and her staff at the W. E. B. Du Bois Library of the University of Massachusetts, Amherst, for helping me find exactly the items I needed in the Du Bois Archive.

The individual chapters of my book gradually cohered over a decade and, in many instances, represent significant expansions of published articles. Portions of the prologue first appeared in *Slavic Review,* and shorter versions of succeeding chapters have been published in the *Russian Review, Massachusetts Review, Russian Literature, Bucknell Review, African American Review,* and *American Literature.* I am grateful to the editors and publishers of the above journals and to the American Association for the Advancement of Slavic Studies for permission to reprint in part my previous writings.

No acknowledgment would be complete without expressing my enormous gratitude to my colleague, Kim Townsend, who has read carefully and commented critically on every sentence in the penultimate version of my manuscript. I am ultimately responsible for whatever stylistic infelicities remain, but he has done his best to correct them. My editor at Duke University Press, Valerie Millholland, has been a paragon of patience and a much-appreciated source of constant faith and encouragement; her humane professionalism has helped me persist. Others of my close friends and colleagues at Amherst College have contributed more than they suspect. I am grateful for the superb conversation of Frederick Griffiths and the shrewd perceptions and remarks in response to my work offered by Barry O'Connell, Rhonda Cobham-Sander, Stanley Rabinowitz, and Stephanie Sandler. My greatest debt of gratitude goes to my wife, Lorna, who has literally and lovingly supported every word of this attempt to put two great literary cultures into sympathetic dialogue across racial and linguistic barriers. She has made me feel that this academic book was something worth doing in a life, even if only to justify a marginal position in a world that cries out for more active correction of ignorance and intolerance.

If we call up the most analogous case as a basis of forecast, — the torturous way by which the peasant came into Russian literature and the brilliant sudden transformation his advent eventually effected, we may predict . . . the Great Age.

— Alain Locke, "American Literary Tradition and the Negro"

Every word smells of the context or contexts in which it has lived its socially intense life.

— Mikhail Bakhtin, "Discourse in the Novel"

PROLOGUE

Justifying the Margin:

The Cultural Construction of "Soul"

Twice in the twentieth century, proclamations of a culturally distinct African American literature have been accompanied by generous reference to Russian precedents. What is perhaps even more remarkable than this sensed affinity between modern black and Russian modes of artistic expression is how little the phenomenon has been remarked upon. Despite the amount of attention currently devoted to studies of ethnic and postcolonial literatures, the scholarly world has little noted nor long remembered the significant moments when African American writers and thinkers have called to mind the emancipatory example of nineteenth-century Russia's soulful writing and music.

Clearly, something already present in the cultural self-awareness of African American intellectuals prepared them to respond to the call of Russian literary forms once they became widely available in English translation. What W. E. B. DuBois famously named the "double consciousness" of the Negro American—"this sense of always looking at oneself through the eyes of others, and measuring one's soul by the tape of a world that looks on in amused contempt and pity"—seemed to resonate sympathetically with the psychological and musical polyphony, the "double-voicedness," that could be detected in the words and notes of Russia's best-known authors and composers. Yet the underlying reasons for this powerful gravitational pull between two geographically remote modern literatures have rarely been investigated. In this book I indicate some of the historic forces and cultural dynamics that account for this rather unexpected connection. Each chapter investigates comparable moments in the development of Russian and African American ethnic self-consciousness, with a particular focus on those theorists and artists who have helped define the shifting shape of each people's cultural and artistic identity. Proceeding thematically rather than strictly chronologically, I note analogous phases in the expressive modes by which Russian and African American cultural particularity came to be asserted. More than an influence study, my aim is to demonstrate the larger structures of mentality present in the specific philosophical arguments and literary forms of Russian and African American cultural nationalism and to speculate on the reasons why these separate voices have expressed their historic distinctiveness in words and texts that are remarkably akin to one another.

In 1925 Alain Locke issued the manifesto of the modern Black Arts movement, *The New Negro*. At first glance there could not have been a clearer call for the liberation of authentic Negro speech from prior constraints: "We have lately had an art that was stiltedly self-conscious, and racially rhetorical rather than racially expressive. Our poets have now stopped speaking for the Negro—they speak as Negroes." [1] The first serious movement to assert the aesthetic autonomy of African American culture had been announced. Yet this liberating word of the Harlem Renaissance was uttered with a sideward glance at the accomplished fluency of Russian artists in speaking to the world at large through compositions based on folk idioms. Locke cited the example of his brilliant contemporary, the author of *Cane*—the experimental book of 1923 that poetically distilled the pungent essence of the Southern slave culture: "For vital originality of substance, the young Negro writers dig deep into the racy peasant undersoil of the race life. Jean Toomer writes: 'Georgia opened me. . . . There one finds soil, soil in the sense that the Russians know it—the soil that every art and literature that is to live must be imbedded in' " (51). Originality of substance (later known as black "soul") was understood to reside in the undersoil of rural vernacular culture, that same submerged cultural layer that Russian artists had successfully turned into literate rows of print and musical notation. For the "New Negro" the residue of slavery's songs and tales was a rich loam directly analogous to the earthy peasant roots of serfdom that had nourished the world-renowned literature and music of Russian "soul."

In another essay in the volume, Locke elaborated on the ongoing cultural contact that was encouraging innovative African American variations on forms of Russian artistry. He predicted, for instance, the evolution of a new musical language to orchestrate the expressive force of Negro spirituals: "Their next development will undoubtedly be, like that of the modern Russian folk music, their use in the larger choral forms of the symphonic choir" (202). In retrospect it seems evident that the cultural leaders of the Harlem Renaissance fully shared the ambition of Russian artists like Turgenev or Mussorgsky to make a universally resounding and technically distinctive mode of expression arise from the neglected speech and song of a denigrated peasantry. Cultivated artists who had fully mastered the syntax of cultural literacy hoped to give visibility and audibility to a "marooned" nation of preliterate serfs and slaves.[2] No longer "cultural nondescripts," Locke's New Negro artists, like their Russian brethren, would insist on addressing the world, in a highly literate discourse that articulated its meanings with an emphasis on ethnic inflections and vernacular content.

Alain Locke's aspiration to bring into being a recognizably black aesthetic has largely been realized during the last few decades. Once again, however, a powerful assertion of the particularity of African American cultural expression has been aided and abetted by a Russian precursor. The manifesto of this new New Negro movement is Henry Louis Gates Jr.'s influential 1988 study, *The Signifying Monkey*. The premise of its argument is that African American speech has necessarily constructed itself as a "double-voiced" discourse that signifies covert meanings not recorded in the lexicon and diction of standard literacy: "Free of the white person's gaze, black people created their own unique vernacular structures and relished in the double play that these forms bore to white forms."[3] When properly appreciated, it became possible to hear the oral undertones and rhythmic inflections (the "soul music") that black literary artists had effectively smuggled into their printed texts. Significantly, though, the language that Gates employs to conceptualize the workings of this African American "signifyin'" itself refers to a Russian linguistic theorist: "The process of semantic appropriation . . . has been aptly described by Mikhail Bakhtin as a double-voiced word, that is, a word or utterance, in this context, decolonized for the black's purposes 'by inserting a new semantic orientation into a word which already has—and retains—its own orientation.' . . . Signifyin(g) is black double-voicedness" (50–51).

Why should there be so strong an affinity between Russian artistic and linguistic precedents and African American aesthetic and cultural ideologies? The felt imperative to insert subversive inflections into the dominant forms of literacy is an impulse common to all denigrated and colonized populations. One can speculate, however, that it is felt with special urgency by groups that have literally been the bound servants of the master's civilization. Russians and African Americans have battled for years to assert the existence of an authentic cultural particularity and to create decolonized modes of ethnic self-expression. Their struggle has been complicated by the need to be acknowledged by a dominant civilization that has historically denied cultural content and human rationality to the creative utterances of the black slaves and Russian serfs who comprised the folk base of the national identity. Thus the origins of both Russian and African American cultural nationalism are entangled in a "dialogical" encounter with forms of literacy that have historically erased Russian and black folk from substantial existence. In such an environment it has not been accidental that Russian and African American literary discourse has devoted itself so intensely to philosophical definitions and artistic manifestations of a hitherto invisible national "soul."

There has been, in fact, a lengthy historic subtext linking these two diverse peoples in a similar confrontation with European cultural literacy. Long before educated American blacks became consciously aware of Russian culture, both Africans and Slavs had been made painfully aware of their collective expulsion from modern Europe's philosophy of history. It is well known, for instance, that the European Age of Enlightenment constructed a universal model of rationality predicated on a hierarchy of "natural" classifications—a chain of biological and climatological species—that left black Africans permanently immersed in subhuman lethargy and savage insensitivity.[4] It is perhaps less well known that the encyclopedic scientific research of the Sorbonne, as epitomized in the great Buffon's vast catalogues of flora, fauna, and humans, had launched lesser lights into remotest Russia, where another dark continent was discovered.

In 1761 a certain Chappe d'Auteroche received a royal commission to make observations on the transit of the planet Venus in the night skies over Tobolsk. He took advantage of the occasion to publish in 1768 a two-volume measurement of the cultural as well as the astronomical prospect he had viewed with his scientific eye. In *Journey into Siberia*, the philosopher-astronomer proved to his satisfaction that the frigid marshy expanse of the Russian continent would place an insurmountable obstacle in the path of Russia's cultural growth:

We may readily conclude from what has been said, that the nervous juice in the Russians is inspissated and sluggish, more adapted to form strong constitutions than men of genius; their internal organs have lost their elasticity and vibratory powers; the flogging they constantly undergo in the baths, and the heat they experience there, blunts the sensibility of the external organs. The nerves, being no longer capable of receiving impressions, cannot transmit them to the internal organs; and indeed M. de Montesquieu observes that, to make a Russian feel, one must flay him. The want of genius therefore among the Russians, appears to be an effect of the soil and the climate.[5]

For Russians as for Africans, cultural retardation was correlated with biological defects that had supposedly been induced by a climate wholly inhospitable to mental agility and civilized conduct. Thus began the insidious Western conception of the inherent inferiority of the Negro and Slavic races, initiating that harmful conflation of race with ethnicity, of biology with culture, that led the victims of such genetic and climatological theories to adopt similarly racialist and essentialist thinking in their own defense.

The great minds of German Idealist philosophy were no kinder to the world-historical position of Africans or Slavs, even though they did detect a teleological thrust directing the advance of human culture over time. In the magisterial progress of civilizations outlined in Hegel's masterplot of historical development, the Negro people had no dynamic role assigned to them: "The Africans, however, have not yet reached *recognition of the General*. . . . Thus we find nothing other than man in his immediacy. . . . The Negro represents the Natural Man in all his *wildness and indocility*; if we wish to grasp him, then we must drop all European conceptions. What we actually understand by 'Africa' is that which is without history and resolution."[6] In the grandly evolving upward spiral of the Hegelian World-Spirit, the Negro race was lacking all momentum—it figured as the very antitype of progress. The Russians fared only slightly better in nineteenth-century German historicism's sketch of the human story. Even at its most cosmopolitan and nonchauvinist, as in the thought of Herder, the Slavic race was still being defined as genially inert, and the Russians in particular were seen as a servile and passive race: "The figure made by the Slavian nations in history is far from proportionate to the extent of country they occupied. . . . They were liberal, hospitable to excess, lovers of pastoral freedom, but submissive and obedient. . . . Is it to be wondered that, after this nation had borne the yoke for centuries . . . its gentle character should have sunk into the artful, cruel indolence of the slave?"[7] Looked at from Europe's towers of learning, the Russians and the Negroes lacked full human stature. Whether regarded as primitive or bucolic, they were inferior races that displayed little aptitude for joining the grand procession of human civilization.[8]

Out of this exclusion from the advance of the world-historical "Spirit" the counterclaim of an ethnic essence was born. The concept of an innate collective or racial soul emerged to signify the veiled humanity of Europe's outcasts, those nonhistoric peoples shunted aside in the march of Man toward Reason. The dominant nationalist discourse about Russian "soul" (*russkaia dusha*) displaced a previous Hegelian phraseology of national "spirit" (*dukh*) soon after the publication of Gogol's *Dead Souls* in 1842.[9] This shift in terminology moved the focal point of the nation's character away from its historic institutions of governance onto the latent genius of its collective people. That is, "soul" became the term of choice to evoke the as yet unrealized cultural potential organically present in the body of the people; *dusha*, unlike the more abstract and impersonal entity of "spirit," denoted "that which gives life to flesh," or embodied spirit.[10] For the Russians as, later, for African Americans, the discourse of "soul" provided a means to enter cultural history behind the back of Western philosophy.

The literatures of Russian and African American "soul" represent an active quest to invent an idiom, an expressive medium, that can effectively convey "the uncreated conscience of the race." In a series of remarkably inventive philosophical and literary texts we can observe the unfolding of a culturally constructed and dialogically shaped experiment in scripting a historic presence that Western eyes had simply failed to see. In the book that follows, I emphasize the similar strivings of Russians and African Americans to give visibility and voice to a native culture that had been hidden from view and held in bondage to narrow Western standards of civility and literacy.

Each chapter juxtaposes significant careers and texts in the evolving theory and literary practice of Russian and black American cultural nationalism. Although differences are noted and, indeed, increase in importance in contemporary nationalist trends, I have not hesitated to underline the extraordinary degree of comparability that can be observed in the distinct phases of Russian and African American cultural self-consciousness. As the separate chapters unfold, a larger symmetry gradually becomes evident. Suffering the infliction (and internalization) of a harsh judgment of cultural inferiority, Russian and black American intellectuals battled the injury of racial denigration in a similarly constructed sequence of philosophical replies and artistic refutations. For these two groups of Westernized elites, the release from bondage to European standards and measurements was laborious and circuitous. Their paths toward cultural emancipation followed many of the same twists and turns.

The first stage of nationalist theorizing, as embodied in the exemplary figures of Peter Chaadaev and Alexander Crummell, was similarly Eurocentric and "civilizationist." The earliest claims for an exceptional Russian and African American manifest destiny gave new content to the scriptural promise that the last would be the first in the kingdom of heaven. Read allegorically as a reference to the belated and unredeemed peoples who had not yet been gathered into the providential history of Christendom, it became possible for religious minds to conceive of Russians and African Americans as most favorably positioned to complete the missionary advance of the one universal civilization. Belief in the privilege of such a history-making belatedness was purchased at a price, however. The journey up from slavery and up from Slavdom was thought to require a radical reconstruction of racial traits and heathen custom. (Indeed, the word "slave" derives from the Latin *sclavus* for "Slav.") Converts to "civilizationism" had to deny the existence of any previous indigenous culture of significance or value. It was that denial of ethnic "soul" that led directly to the second major phase in Russian and African American nationalist thinking.

In the reply of Ivan Kireevsky to his friend Chaadaev and in the response of DuBois to his mentor Crummell one can locate the beginnings of what may truly be described as cultural nationalism. DuBois's early essay, "The Conservation of Races," no less than the first writings of the Russian Slavophiles, represented an attempt to retain a privileged role for one's own racial group in the march of civilization while also proclaiming its inherent claim to an exceptional world-historical cultural identity. This excavation of a previously buried and devalued cultural ethnicity received its most mature and sophisticated literary expression in two comparable texts—Dostoevsky's *Notes from the House of the Dead* and DuBois's *The Souls of Black Folk*. In these two seminal works a literate intellectual undergoes an immersion in the lower depths of a degraded peasant culture and emerges with an appreciation for its unique spiritual contribution to a sense of collective nationhood. Yet this newly discovered folk "soul" is also imagined to animate a higher national destiny as it gradually fuses its distinctive qualities into an as yet unrealized amalgam of European and non-Western elements. The cultural nationalisms of Dostoevsky and DuBois envisaged the dynamic emergence of a Russian and American civilization predicated on a higher synthesis of previously segregated cultural communities within the borders of the nation.

To be fully apprehended, however, claims of cultural particularity must somehow be inscribed within the legible and accepted genres of literate discourse. In their experimental narratives of cross-cultural encounters, Ivan Turgenev and Charles W. Chesnutt devised similar literary strategies to signal the deliberate evasiveness of an oral peasant culture confronting the blindness and insights of Western literacy. With great subtlety and indirection, these two authors reproduced the semantic gaps and contested meanings present in numerous dramatized exchanges between a literate master and an illiterate peasantry. Turgenev's *Notes of a Hunter* and Chesnutt's *The Conjure Woman* cunningly exposed the limitations of an educated narrator (and of the enlightened reader) in presuming to decipher the meanings insinuated within the richly oblique utterances of wily Russian and black folk. Somewhat later, Zora Neale Hurston in her semi-fictional ethnographic travel narrative, *Mules and Men*, expanded on this tradition of textual subversion of the dominant literacy. Hurston compiled a deceptively "scientific" transcript of Southern black speech genres and voodoo rituals that in all its parts, including her own anthropological commentary, performs the mystifications practiced by someone natively schooled in the alternative literacy of the folk's lore. In its most sophisticated forms, the literature of Russian and African American "soul" effectively invents adequate means to confront the literate reader with an unfettered and unlettered native voice that is linguistically separate from but artistically equivalent to the discursive skills of the educated elite.

In both literary traditions, however, there exists a second competing form of cultural particularity, one that challenges the existence of a single authentic source of racial "soul" in the surviving vernacular of the folk. This alternative to the alternative literacy of the folk expressed itself in the innovative form of an "underground" confessional monologue—a dramatic representation of the internally conflicted voice of a culturally hyphenated speaker. Dostoevsky's *Notes from Underground* and James Weldon Johnson's *Autobiography of an Ex-Coloured Man* brilliantly reproduce the quite different yet remarkably comparable "double-voiced" discourses of self-divided bicultural characters who represent the paradoxical mentality of Westernized Russians and hyphenated African-Americans. It is their unhappy inability to acknowledge the ineradicable cultural duality within their embattled minds that makes antiheroes of Dostoevsky's and Johnson's prototypes of educated ethnic souls. Contrary to what may commonly be thought, cultural nationalism among Russians and American blacks has not only been expressed by ideologies that attempt to recuperate an authentic folk "soul." Dostoevsky and Johnson were instrumental in depicting the first embodied types of a Russian and African American "soul" that was natively hybrid; both confessional narrators were precociously modern in articulating their "double-voicedness" and anxiety-ridden eclecticism.

The literary genius of Russian and African American cultural nationalism has expressed itself in two distinct modes. One literary embodiment of "soul" articulates the presence of culturally distinct ancestral traits that symbolize the inherited "bloodknot" of ethnic identity. The other embodiment of "soul" dramatizes the historic contingency of a psychic "double-mindedness" that is understood to be the complex fate of bicultural Russians and African Americans who find themselves involuntarily at the forefront of a newly emerging nationality. Despite their different orientations—one toward essentialism, the other toward cultural pluralism—this internal bifurcation of "souls" illustrates the common dilemma of two literary nationalisms that have of necessity depended on an educated elite to redeem in full the debased value of the racial stock. It matters that the cultural construction of Russian and black "soul" has not been an enterprise of the folk masses but of a self-consciously literate class obligated by racial ties to identify with a vast population of illiterate and enslaved bondsmen. The literature actually written by the small number of educated black slaves and Russian serfs (who were even fewer in a peasant culture whose religion was rooted in Orthodox liturgy rather than scriptural warrant) was devoted to the abolition of cultural inequality and not to the preservation of cultural difference. It has been, for understandable reasons, the deracinated or socially advantaged brothers and sisters of the folk who have most felt the imperative to define the irreducible particularity of a nationality that had been denied any historic significance of its own.

The domination of intellectual life by European standards of cultural literacy has given rise, especially among those nationalities historically identified with slave cultures, to resistant strains of ethnocentrism that carry the potential curse of self-segregation and cultural marginalization. An awareness of this danger was forcefully expressed by two major writers whose upbringing was shaped by the living legacy of Russian serfdom and black slavery—Maxim Gorky and Richard Wright. Cultural separatism had little appeal for these two native sons who felt the desperate importance of transcending the limits of a birth culture that had imposed punishing restrictions on their right to open self-expression. Gorky's struggle with Dostoevsky's sanctification of Russian suffering, like Wright's polemics with Hurston's celebration of oblique black speech, testifies to the outspoken courage of the rebel who feels compelled to resist a disabling loyalty to what is seen in retrospect as an abject home culture. In their remarkably parallel lives and autobiographies, Gorky and Wright addressed the hidden (and not so hidden) injuries of a self-limiting culture of oppression, and they each adopted a militant humanism that demonstrated little patience with "identity politics" or the exaltation of a national or racial "soul." Yet each of them also understood the lacerated psyches of the insulted and injured in such depth that they could not refuse to enlist their writing in defense of the rage that was an inescapable consequence of the historic racism directed at the Russian peasantry and black folk. In the name of the materially dispossessed and culturally disinherited masses, these influential sons of the soil rejected populism and nationalism and sought instead to attach their people to a new secular universalism—the missionary cause of international socialism.

Despite some signs of internal resistance to cultural nationalism, the literatures of Russian and African American "soul" flourished in the twentieth century. Indeed, they underwent some remarkably similar mutations. In a fascinatingly parallel development, Russian and African American nationalists became more "cosmopolitan" in the 1920s. An innovative type of "multicultural" nationalism took shape in two manifestos published within a few years of each other: *Exodus to the East* (1921) proclaimed the "Eurasian" roots of Russian civilization; *The New Negro* (1925) announced the emergence of a transnational black culture that was as much African as American. Large historic forces and events had brought into being a newly awakened diasporic consciousness among Russian and black intellectuals. Russian émigré thinkers were forced to come to terms with an ancient homeland that had apparently embraced both a socialist revolution and modernism in the arts. At approximately the same time, Harlem writers and artists were coming to the realization that black folk were undergoing a cultural transformation of massive proportions as a result of their migration toward modern urban centers that were, in effect, laboratories of "race-welding." A notable feature of these revised versions of cultural nationalism was a sense of racial destiny based on the realization of a long-deferred dream of achieving a synthesis of civilizations.

The Russian "Eurasianists," like their counterparts in the "New Negro" movement, sought to redefine the ethnic "soul" as essentially multicultural and syncretic. It seemed apparent that Russians and Negroes were destined to express a distinctive and historic culture that would establish the modern foundations for a third world civilization located between Europe and Asia, between the Americas and Africa. A closer look at the careers of two major theorists of these "cosmopolitan" nationalisms, N. S. Trubetzkoy and Alain Locke, reveals major differences of emphasis, however. In seeking to persuade themselves that Soviet Russia was the historic instrument to reinstitute a long-suppressed authentic civilization shared in common by all the peoples of the vast Eurasian plain, the Eurasianists betrayed their nostalgic utopianism and cultural imperialism. By contrast, the Harlem Renaissance was led and inspired by progressive pluralists who envisaged the dynamic evolution of a multicultural Negro diaspora that would bring into expression a transatlantic civilization that was still in formation. Even with such differences duly noted, these newer strains of cosmopolitan cultural nationalism displayed a residual ethnocentrism—namely, the idea that Russians or African Americans were inherently more synthetic or more comprehensively multicultural than other modern nationalities.

Attempts among Russian and African American writers to reconstruct a more stable or purified version of collective ethnic identity have hardly ceased, however. Even in the latter part of the twentieth century, in a supposedly postmodern world of permeable borders, crumbling canons, and disintegrating empires, there have been strenuous efforts to reassert fundamentalist notions of race and ethnicity. Although the very concept of ethnicity has come under "interrogation" in some quarters, ethnic cleansing has resulted in wholesale purges of "impure" populations in other parts of the globe. The turn of the century has produced a surge of reactionary forms of cultural nationalism among post-Soviet Russians and American blacks, too. Theories advanced by some self-proclaimed "Afrocentrists" and "Russites" have veered toward rather xenophobic extremes, but there have also been more nuanced literary versions of this resurgent essentialism.

Two novels in particular, one Russian and one African American, stage a similar mythic action in which the conflict between a surviving ethnic enclave and the intruding modern world is sharply and memorably drawn. Both Valentin Rasputin's *Farewell to Matyora* (1976) and Gloria Naylor's *Mama Day* (1988) literally construct an island refuge of ethnic "soul" and relate its dramatic encounter with a "mainstream" culture that threatens to inundate it. Although the symbolic structure of these two texts is uncannily similar, these novels also illustrate some important differences between contemporary styles of cultural resistance to the erosion of ethnic particularism. In Rasputin's endangered Siberian heartland, the threat to the preservation of Russian "soul" and cultural authenticity is so dire that it provokes a direct analogy to the near extinction of Mother Russia by the Mongol horde. But in Naylor's novel, the sturdy African American matriarchal culture that knows how to "work roots" is able to achieve continuity across generations by constantly renewing its ancestral genius for improvisation and conjury. It would seem, then, that Russian ethnocentrism under duress places its trust in the reclamation of an imagined community of organic wholeness and consensual unity, whether that is understood as the Slavophile notion of an inherent Russian communalism or as Dostoevsky's concept of a peculiarly Russian "panhuman susceptibility" and gift for cultural synthesis. It would also seem that black nationalism in the American context has always had somehow to come to terms with the historic reality of miscegenation and cultural hybridity along with the indisputable facts of slavery and racism. Perhaps that is why African American cultural nationalism has tended to garb black pride in a many-colored literary coat that splendidly reflects the multiple "souls" and "double consciousness" of DuBois's black folk.

The keen attention devoted to Mikhail Bakhtin's "dialogic" and "polyphonic" analysis of cultural processes by contemporary theorists of "African American expressivity" is only the latest addition to a distinguished history of mutual awareness between Russian and black American literary intellectuals. It bodes well for a wider appreciation of the deep sources of kinship between these two innovative literatures situated by racism at the outer boundaries of European civilization. The creative response of African American specialists to Bakhtin's sociolinguistic analysis of "double-voiced" utterances might well become a call to Russian specialists to reconsider the complex cultural poetics of that nation's literary classics. Such an epilogue to the expanding dialogue and increased contact between Russian and African American writers and academics would indeed provide a happy ending to the story this book tells.

The Russian and African American experiments in developing a supple literary articulation of "soul" and in imprinting cultural "otherness" within the forms legitimated by Western letters and philosophy offer valuable precedents for our increasingly decentered and diversified world of disunited nationalities. Can there be forms of ethnic expression that allow for the assertion of cultural difference and yet be legible to outsiders? Is it possible to invent a medium of modern literacy that can accommodate the competing realities of ethnic identity and diasporic multiculturalism? The self-conscious literatures of Russian and African American "soul" have historically addressed, if not resolved, such inescapable cultural conundrums. The complicated politics of a postcolonial, multicultural, and borderless world have not and will not result in one global culture. Careful and respectful comparisons of the expressive features of particular cultural nationalisms are required in a world of proliferating diversity. This book examines two major modern precedents for constructing arguments and texts in which the denigrated cultures of Europe's bondmen finally assert and express their place in world civilization. The literatures of Russian and black "soul" have truly justified the margin, constructing an unanticipated richness of sound and sense in vast unmapped spaces that were once assumed to be blank and without significance.

1 CIVILIZING THE RACE

The Missionary Nationalism of Chaadaev

and Crummell

From the vantage point of the late twentieth century, two provocative thinkers seem to have induced, almost single-handedly, the long labor of ethnic self-consciousness among Europe's cultural stepchildren, the Russian Slavs and the African Americans: Peter Yakovlevich Chaadaev (c.1794–1856) and the Reverend Alexander Crummell (1819–1898). A notable peculiarity connects these acknowledged forefathers of modern Russian and pan-African nationalist discourse. Paradoxically, the abrasive personalities who directly stimulated their own people's historic quest for a special racial destiny were themselves thoroughly Eurocentric intellectuals.

Chaadaev, the impeccably fashionable francophone scourge of aristocratic Moscow salons, the hard-skulled, acid-tongued former Imperial guardsman become hermit-philosopher, was memorably characterized by his young admirer, the future philosopher of Russian socialism, Alexander Herzen, as "an embodied veto, a living protest" whose single scandalous publication was universally regarded as "a merciless cry of pain and reproach against Petrine Russia." [1] Crummell, the tall, angular ramrod of black Anglican rectitude, the unbending scold of Southern lassitude and plantation religion whose methodical sermons epitomized the severe discipline of "Negro improvement," was accurately placed by Frederick Douglass in the front rank of "the colonizationist class of theologians." [2] Although Chaadaev has long been seen as initiating a distinctively Russian philosophy of history and Crummell's writings have now been acknowledged as having "effectively inaugurated the discourse of pan-Africanism," it is equally true that these two thinkers were, in effect, native missionaries in the vanguard of a Western Christendom that enlisted its adherents in a global cultural crusade. [3]

The careers of Chaadaev and Crummell strangely coincide in their theorizing about the distinctive historic privilege available to their kin-folk. Both perceived the manifest destiny of their people to depend on a collective experience of penitence and conversion; only by virtue of an admission of cultural emptiness could Russians or Africans be ele-vated to a place of pride in the company of nations. The salvation of the racial cohort was analogous to the salvation of the individual soul—the innate substance required exposure to redemptive truth and a work of the will to perfect it. Oddly enough the first phase of modern Russian and African-American nationalism was thus characterized by a denial of specific cultural worth and a provocative rejection of ethnic "soul." Chaadaev and Crummell demonstrated a remarkable capacity to offend ethnic pride while enunciating their prophetic vision of a grand national destiny.

Perhaps two quotations can illustrate, at least initially, this odd con-juction of cultural denigration and missionary nationalism. One much-cited paragraph from Chaadaev's debut as a public philosopher in 1836 closely resembles the tone and content of one of Crummell's last public proclamations in 1897. Imagine the shock to patriotic Russian sensibili-ties administered by Chaadaev's *First Philosophical Letter* as printed in the *Moscow Telescope*:

> The experience of the centuries has no existence for us. One might think, considering our situation, that the general law of humanity did not exist for us. Outcasts in the world, we have given it nothing and taken nothing from it; have not added a single idea to the total ideas of mankind; have in no way contributed to the progress of human understanding and have distorted everything that has been conveyed to us by that progress. In the course of our entire social existence we have done nothing for the general welfare of man; not a single useful thought has sprung from our sterile soil; not a single great truth has arisen among us. . . . I wonder whether there is something in our blood that is repellent and inimical to progress. I only insist we have lived and are living as a great lesson to remote genera-tions that will surely make good use of it; at the present time, no matter what anyone says, we constitute a void in the order of reason.[4]

It has rightly been observed that no one before or since Chaadaev ever proclaimed with such force of expression "the essential, inevitable, and apparently irremediable inferiority of the Russian nation."[5]

Consider next a similar litany of racial deficiencies in Crummell's con-
vocation address to the American Negro Academy:

> And here, let me say, that the special race problem of the Negro in the
> United States is his civilization. . . . it seems manifest to me that, as a race,
> in this land, we have no art; we have no science; we have no philosophy; we
> have no scholarship. . . . And until we attain the role of civilization, we can-
> not stand up or hold our place in the world of culture and enlightenment.
> And the forfeiture of such a place means, despite, inferiority, repulsion,
> drudgery, poverty, and ultimate death![6]

It would be difficult to imagine two more drastic statements of an entire
people's cultural emptiness than these unsparing criticisms of the spiritual condition of Russians and African Americans. But it is important to
notice as well the rhetorical underlining in each passage of a *marked* absence, a historic exception so notable as to suggest some veiled meaning or prophetic significance. As we shall see, Chaadaev and Crummell
each affirmed a providential reading of history that managed to convert
deprivation to divine sense in the fullness of time.

The careers of Chaadaev and Crummell document the curious connection each made between Christian universalism and messianic nationhood. Western Christendom had propagated the idea of an apostolic
global civilization that could be embraced by all who freely subscribed
to the one saving faith graciously present within an irresistible history
of human redemption. Divine Providence had forecast the gathering of
all humankind into the Church Universal, thereby bringing a climactic end to cultural dissonance. This meant that the hurt of ethnic and
racial exclusion from organized Christendom would be alleviated when
the unconverted multitudes of the earth's refractory tribes finally shouldered the burden of Christian civilization. Indeed, a delay in the advent
of a truly catholic Christianity was only to be expected; each people, by
special grace, would experience a distinct moment of conversion when
its brute existence would be transformed into historic nationhood. But
the adoption of such a missionary nationalism necessarily entailed a repudiation of the prior rites and customs of an unhistoric race. Native
"civilizationists" like Chaadaev and Crummell employed the rhetorical
techniques of a culturally alien literacy to persuade their compatriots
that they could enjoy a privileged position in the providential script of
Christian history.[7] Ethnic pride would thus be best served by encourag-

ing a collective crusade at the leading edge of an advancing civilization. Precisely because it so little resembles contemporary styles of ethnic self-assertion, one needs to appreciate the curiously exhilarating denial of native worth that gave missionary nationalism its historic logic and spiritual pride.

Sometime between 1828 and 1830 Peter Chaadaev composed, in French, a series of eight *Lettres philosophiques* in which he exfoliated a theory of universal history predicated on a Christian metaphysic, ostensibly in response to a request for spiritual guidance by a gentlewoman, Ekaterina Panova, who was experiencing "remorses for inclining toward the Catholic faith." [8] Madame Panova herself never received even a portion of this extensive correspondence, but we do know that Chaadaev freely circulated manuscript copies of selected letters among his well-placed male friends, eliciting commentary from the likes of Aleksandr Pushkin and the pietistic brothers, Aleksandr and Nikolai Turgenev, who were strong opponents of serfdom. Beginning in 1831, Chaadaev undertook several unsuccessful initiatives to publish in Russian at least the historical aspect of his total argument; when these efforts were rebuffed by unsympathetic editors in Petersburg and the religious censorship in Moscow, he even attempted in 1835 to find a Parisian venue for his ideas. [9] This persistence was finally rewarded by a cruelly ironic succès de scandale when an enterprising young editor, Nikolai Nadezhdin, took advantage of a more relaxed Moscow censorship in 1836 to boost his readership with the printing in Russian of Chaadaev's "First Philosophical Letter to Madame ***," the most polemical of the entire sequence.

In a now famous contretemps, the minister of education, Count Sergei Uvarov, brought the text to the personal attention of Tsar Nicholas I. The tsar and his chief ideologist were just then busily concocting the doctrine known as "Official Nationality," with its sacrosanct trinity of "Orthodoxy, Autocracy, and National Identity," and the monarch was in no mood to tolerate public objections to his aggressive policy of Russian cultural imperialism. In one sour French note, the tsar sealed Chaadaev's fate: "After reading the article I find it to be a stream of insolent nonsense worthy of a madman." [10] By imperial edict, the author was declared insane and placed under medical and police supervision; in addition, all his papers were confiscated and he was placed under a lifetime prohibition from publishing any further writing. Chaadaev thus enjoyed the dubious distinction of becoming the first example in modern Russian history of a dissident officially reduced to a "nonperson." Indeed, his full rehabilitation has been painfully slow in arriving. Only in 1987, a century and a half after the original tsarist prohibition, was a complete Russian version of all eight letters finally published. Prior to that epoch-making side effect of perestroika, there had been a partial publication of Chaadaev's letters on history (letters 1, 6, 7) in 1914 and a scholarly printing of the remaining five letters in 1935. The completely reconstituted French text of *Lettres philosophiques adressées à une dame* finally made its much delayed public appearance in a handsome Moscow edition of 1991. Given this dismal history of repression and neglect, how is it that Chaadaev's name has, nonetheless, figured so prominently in the evolution of Russian nationalist discourse?

Not enough attention has been given, even by intellectual historians, to the social and ideological power exerted by the *genre* in which Chaadaev chose to express his controversial meditations on Russia's cultural marginality. Long before unofficial public opinion in Soviet Russia had perfected the subversive techniques of "desk drawer poetry" and "self-publication" (samizdat), eighteenth-century Russian intellectuals had firmly established the convention of exchanging hand-copied manuscripts producing, in effect, an epistolary tradition of dissent. In fact, independent aristocratic opposition to Russian autocratic rule had been formed by means of the privately circulated polite letter, often in a foreign tongue and shielded by a disguised addressee.[11] Chaadaev's relatives were themselves participants in this oppositionist tradition, keeping safe custody of Prince M. M. Shcherbatov's unpublishable essay, "On the Corruption of Morals in Russia," in a Moscow cellar until the close of Nicholas's reign.[12] By the turn of the nineteenth century, as William Mills Todd II has demonstrated, the "familiar letter" had become the literary genre of the aristocracy par excellence, being "the genre most suited to the rejection of official panegyric literature on one hand and immediate commercial success on the other."[13] The decorous custom of exchanging polished epistolary gems promoted standards of civility and literacy that could be imitated by polite society, and it allowed for the illusion of eavesdropping on intimate and/or sensitive themes proscribed in public genres. In the right hands, like Chaadaev's, the improving, educative letter could circulate among the cultural elite, become the focus of organized salon causerie, and in due time be translated for posterity into public print. Despite the many attempts to remove Chaadaev's name and writing from public awareness, there is abundant evidence that the missionary burden of his civilizing letters was communicated across many generations of Russian intellectuals.[14]

Although there has been much scholarship devoted to the philosophical context that informs Chaadaev's learned letters, the specific genre in which he chose to address his contemporaries has been ignored. Perhaps because it was perfectly conventional in Russian educated society of the time to address women, government officials, and abstract argument in French, it has largely slipped notice that Chaadaev's title for his eight epistles boldly alludes to a powerful literary precedent: Voltaire's *Lettres philosophiques* of 1734.[15] Voltaire's famous text emanated from a three-year refuge in England (1726–29) during which he became convinced that his home culture needed to appreciate and embrace the institutions and attitudes of British empiricism. Similarly, Chaadaev's letters directly followed his return from a three-year voluntary exile on the European continent (1823–26) during which, as we shall see, he became convinced that Russia had suffered greatly from not embracing the institutions and traditions of the Catholic West. Voltaire's letters were very much an *oeuvre de combat*, opening with a sharp seven-letter attack on religious "enthusiasm" and concluding with a sustained "defense of humanity" against the "sublime misanthrope," Pascal, who was for Voltaire the supreme antiphilosophe, the epitome of reactionary metaphysical resistance to the well-ordered world of Enlightened reason.[16] Just as Voltaire's true ambition was to inject Lockean liberalism into a resistant French culture that would then become integrated into the civilization of the worldwide Enlightenment, so Chaadaev hoped his epistles would promote the thought of a resurgent French Catholicism within an insular Russian culture that might belatedly unite with the traditional civilization of Christian Europe. In philosophical terms the two collections of letters could not be more opposed: Voltaire referred to his work, for short, as "Anti-Pascal"; Chaadaev might well have labeled his "anti-Locke." The argument advanced in Chaadaev's letters counters, point by point, Voltaire's notorious enmity toward organized religion, received ideas, and providential readings of history. This clearly was no coincidence. Chaadaev's deliberate Russian revision of the *Lettres philosophiques* was surely an *oeuvre de combat* intended to countermand in Russia the cultural appeal of the dangerous French original.

In the best known and deliberately provocative "First Philosophical Letter," Chaadaev appears in the persona of a self-appointed abbé, an anti-Voltaire, who writes as both a spiritual adviser and a disturber of the peace in the capital of Orthodox Russia, which he names "Necropolis," the city of the dead. He acknowledges that he has agitated the conscience of his devout female Russian correspondent, but refuses to be apologetic about "the intellectual disturbance" (ce trouble dans vos idées) he has set in motion: "If I had not been convinced that the distress which even an incompletely developed religious sentiment can arouse is preferable to complete indifference, I would repent of my zeal. . . . [But] the effect which my few words have produced on you assures me that your own intelligence will lead you to a mature result" (PS, 1:643). Scholars eavesdropping on this opening might well hear in it a buried allusion to one of the major sources of Chaadaev's pro-Catholic spirituality, Lamennais's Essai sur l'indifférence en matière de religion, which was a center of controversy during Chaadaev's sojourn in Paris in 1823.[17] The ordinary reader, however, might rightly guess that this sincere address to a troubled gentlewoman masks a larger reference to the Russian population as a whole. In any case, the religious ideas to which the addressee is asked to "yield fearlessly" quickly lead to a clear rejection of Russia's historic separation from the Church Universal.

Significantly, Chaadaev characterizes Russia collectively as an outcast nation (otshel'niki v mire), abandoned and separated from the rest of the world. This figure of speech had profound biographical as well as textual implications. Orphaned at an early age and adopted by maternal relatives who were lineally connected to Prince Mikhail Shcherbatov, the leader of the birth-gentry opposition to Empress Catherine's enlightened "despotism," Chaadaev was intimate with the outcast state. In his person and in his discourse, Chaadaev carefully cultivated the image of the noble persona non grata, the unappreciated honnête homme.[18] With fine dramatic instinct, he variously posed himself and his nation as the orphan of time. By class and temperament, Chaadaev was permanently attached to the neoclassical decorum and conservative virtues of a legitimist aristocracy that was increasingly marginal in an autocracy administered by status-seeking functionaries.

Chaadaev's argument rapidly connects the distressed woman's spiritual state with a national cultural condition of lamentable impoverishment: "Isolated by a strange fate from the universal history of mankind, we have derived nothing from those ideas which have transmitted continuity to the human species (*des idées traditives du genre humain*). . . . if we wish to compare ourselves to other civilized peoples, we shall have to begin anew for ourselves the education of the race" (PS, 1:651). Even worse, Russia appears to offer no domestic basis on which to nurture a civilized existence: "Look around you. Everything is on the move. We all might as well be nomads. We have no defined sphere of social existence, there is no good order anywhere, not only are there no rules for living, there isn't even a family rubric" (648). As a society Russia has been subject historically to the disruptive whims of arbitrary despots, living an utterly discontinuous existence: "We have to have beaten into our heads by hammerblows that which others achieve by custom and instinct. . . . This is all the consequence of a culture that is entirely imposed and imitative. . . . our minds are not implanted with the indelible traces of a progressive movement of ideas, which gives them their strength, because we borrow ready-made ideas. We grow, but we do not mature" (653). Given this dilemma of disconnectedness, what could possibly lessen the gravity of Russia's historic isolation?

Chaadaev's blunt answer to Russia's painful exclusion from world civilization was to advocate patient submission to the body of doctrine that had sustained the triumphant march of Christendom. "People understand nothing about Christianity, if they do not realize that there is a purely historical aspect which . . . includes all of Christian philosophy" (663–64). Borrowing from Chateaubriand's theological and teleological macrohistory in which the "genius of Christianity" was ineluctably converting "l'homme physique en l'homme moral" and from M. François Guizot's magisterial *Histoire générale de la civilization en Europe* with its confident prophecy of the Western world's gradual global inclusion of "isolated" cultural margins like Spain, Chaadaev could foresee a providential future, even for Russia.[19] But Orthodox Russia would be required to reject its attachment to "miserable Byzantium," an unfortunate bond that had fatally removed a vast Christian nation from the "vivifying principle" of unity and from universal fraternity through its toleration of slavery.

Chaadaev's letter, for all its cultural pessimism, is animated by an evangelical confidence that *formal* submission to "the teaching founded upon the supreme principle of unity and the direct transmission of truth in an uninterrupted succession of its ministers" will induce in time the great work of *social* redemption that Christendom is destined to achieve

(PS, 1:643). Toward the end of his published letter of spiritual counsel, a prophetic Chaadaev emerges: "If up to now the weakness of our beliefs or the insufficiency of our dogma has placed us outside the universal movement in which the social idea of Christianity was developed . . . isn't it clear that there must be a revival of that impetus to faith in us?" (667–68). The one thing necessary for Russia to claim its rightful place in the Christian dispensation of history was a humble disposition toward the "traditive ideas" and the holy sacraments of medieval Europe's unified faith. For Chaadaev, the history of civilization was not, as Voltaire thought, a linear progression of material improvements and scientific rationality. Rather, it was a redemptive gathering of orphaned races into a restored Age of Faith made perfect by a global solidarity of thought. Although thoroughly Eurocentric in its orientation, Chaadaev's inclination to perceive a visionary universal wholeness *(tsel'nost')* is also a very Russian cultural phenomenon. In this respect, his notoriously unpatriotic "First Philosophical Letter" anticipates later ethnocentric Orthodox versions of a restored world order emanating from a revived Russian spirituality.[20]

The belated publication of the "First Philosophical Letter" in 1836 had the effect of obscuring the actual evolution of Chaadaev's thinking toward a messianic nationalism. Disappointed by political events in France, especially the deposition of Charles X in 1830, and stimulated by Pushkin's extensive research on the reign of Peter the Great, Chaadaev had begun to develop chiliastic hopes for a Russian state that would be capable of leading a renewed advance of European civilization. There is indisputable evidence in letters written to A. I. Turgenev from 1833 to 1835 that Chaadaev had already sketched out the providential logic by which Russia's historic isolation could become a prophetic advantage. We know that he avidly read influential post-Napoleonic commentaries by Philarète Chasles and Alexis de Tocqueville predicting that an exhausted Europe would be succeeded by the rising cultures of "young" America and Russia. And by 1832, Chaadaev had come into direct acquaintance with Schelling, taking particular interest in the German philosopher's utopian historicism and religious vision of a spiritual *Weltgeist*.

As early as 1833, Chaadaev was confiding to Aleksandr Turgenev: "A short time will pass and, I am sure, the leading ideas, once they have reached us, will find in us a more receptive soil for their realization and embodiment than anywhere else, since they will not encounter among us rooted prejudices, or old customs, or stubborn routines to impede them" (PS, 2:79). Considering the presence in Chaadaev's thought of a nearly Emersonian euphoria over his nation's cultural potential, it is difficult to explain his motive for publishing in 1836 the anachronistic "First Philosophical Letter" with its rude deflation of any national aspiration to greatness. Indeed, Chaadaev felt compelled, in 1837, to circulate a second notorious, equally odd document with the rather ironic title, *Apologie d'un fou.*

Often misread as a recantation before the authorities and outraged public opinion, Chaadaev's "Apology" is more properly understood as an addendum to the first letter that summarizes the ultimate historical argument of the unexpurgated *Lettres philosophiques.* In a letter to Aleksandr Turgenev of May 1, 1835, there is an interesting clue to what may have motivated Chaadaev to make public his opening letter with its extreme statement concerning Russia's empty cultural coffers:

> Just at present a strange process is occurring in our intellectual world. A theory of nationality is being worked out which, for lack of any solid grounding since it decidedly lacks any material basis whatsoever, will end up being . . . a wholly artificial creation. . . . we ought to be seeking a foundation for our future in an elevated and profound evaluation of our actual situation in this century and not in some past which is nothing other than a phantasm (PS, 2:91–2).

In other words, the "First Philosophical Letter" might well have served the purpose of administering a strong antidote to the chauvinistic pabulum being dished out by the Imperial ideologists who were promoting an official nationalism that vaunted both Orthodoxy and autocracy. In the same letter to Turgenev it becomes clear that Chaadaev entertained his own version of a Russia designated for future greatness: "Russia is called to an immense intellectual labor: its task is to resolve all the issues now arousing debate in Europe. . . . able to consider calmly and perfectly impartially all that agitates minds and arouses passions there, Russia, in my view, has been delegated to solve the human enigma" (PS, 92). Thus at the very moment his infamous rebuke to Russia appeared in print, Chaadaev was already contemplating what is arguably the central thesis of modern Russian nationalism: the precious advantage of backwardness in leaping to the forefront of historical development.

The original epigraph to Chaadaev's "Apology" quoted Coleridge's English to indicate that no simple recantation was intended: "O my brothers! I have told / Most bitter truth, but without bitterness." Similarly, the French title, *Apologie d'un fou*, hardly indicated an unambiguous penitence, suggesting as it does not only the "apology of a madman," but also the "apologia of a fool." Was the text composed in excuse of madness or in praise of folly? To be sure, Chaadaev admits to "some exaggeration in the type of indictment hurled at a great people whose only crime, in the last analysis, was to have been relegated to the extremities of the civilized world" (PS, 1:302). Yet a careful reading also reveals that the "Apology" functions as a new manifesto that strategically revises Chaadaev's central thesis.[21] In fact, it might be said that Chaadaev had chosen to cloak his conservative Westernism in the royal robes of Peter the Great's revolutionary patriotism. When Chaadaev attacks the rising school of "fanatical Slavs" who exhume curios from the native earth "to fill up the emptiness in our souls" and, instead, declares that he loves his country "in the way that Peter the Great taught me to love it," he was, in effect, associating himself with a patriotism that suppressed vestiges of an archaic local culture in order to participate fully in "the grand sphere of humanity." The "Apology" enlists the modernizing Petrine state as both ally and precedent for a missionary nationalism that battles ethnocentrism in the name of an advancing universal civilization and Christian perfectionism: "I think that if we have come after the others, it is in order to do better than the others" (300).

The "Apology" boldly advances the paradoxical argument that Russia's unique destiny is to be situated, historically and geographically, so as to hasten the earthly realization of the dictates of universal Reason. Specifically, Russia's national good fortune is to possess a tradition of "enlightened absolutism" that assists the unimpeded assimilation of the lessons taught over time by the march of Western civilization. By this reading, Peter the Great becomes the Prince of Russian princes, the avatar of Russia's national talent for cultural effacement and transcendent rationality: "When forsaking royal majesty and his land, he concealed himself among the lowest ranks of civilized people, did he not offer the universe the unique spectacle of a new effort of man's genius to emerge from the narrow sphere of the fatherland?" (292). Moreover, Tsar Peter's *deliberate* and *willed* adoption of external models of governance and conduct is connected, in Chaadaev's argument, to a Russian history of ahistoricity: "Whatever the genius of this man or the enormous force of his will, his work could not have been accomplished except in a nation whose antecedents did not dictate the path it had to follow, whose traditions did not have the power to create a future, whose memories could be expunged with impunity by an audacious legislator" (293). Chaadaev even reaches as far back as medieval Russia to invoke precedents for the nation's abdication of political and cultural will in deference to a unifying autocracy intent on regenerating the entire social order. In his immodest "Apology," Chaadaev comes close to claiming for Russians a national talent for Christian self-abnegation that permits them a historic privilege not extended to others: "It has been given to us to measure each step that we take, to reason with each idea that brushes our intellect, to aspire to a prosperity far grander than what the most ardent believers in mere progress have imagined" (301). The outcast, the orphan, the disowned among nations is free as none other to adopt impartially the wisdom of the ages, the "traditive ideas" that have sponsored the advance of a Christendom that is stateless and timeless.

Out of the ashes of Chaadaev's public humiliation in 1836 arose the first prophet of Russia's paradoxical mission to create, in Osip Mandel'shtam's words, a "synthetic nationality."[22] The pages of the "Apology" envisage for the first time a beneficent version of Russian belatedness that allows the nation to enter world history as both latecomer and forerunner, provided that Russians exercise their particular talent for divesting themselves of nationality while voluntarily adopting a civilizing regime. Chaadaev had managed to draw a wider circle around the vicious circle inside which Western cultural imperialism had placed the backward Russian nation. His ingenious argument for Russia's synthetic nationality and missionary nationalism provided a valuable first proof that a nation could be both marginal and central in the narrative of history that had been revealed to Western Christendom. Like Chaadaev himself, his Russia was both history's orphan and the legitimate heir of the West.

On December 1, 1863, an imposing Anglican missionary, the first black American to graduate from Cambridge University, addressed "the young gentlemen of Monrovia" on the occasion of the fortieth anniversary of

Liberia's first settlement. In his address, the Reverend Alexander Crummell articulated an inspiring myth of national origin that was, in effect, a writing of Africa as a rereading of America:

> On the 1st December, 1822, a few brave colonists were beset by hosts of infuriate savages, intent upon the complete destruction of the weak, sickly, and enfeebled settlement which was then encamped upon Fort Hill. . . . Just then occurred one of those events, as beautiful and poetic as it was decisive, which secured the fortune of the day. A female colonist, by the name of Mary Newport, seeing the perilous position of the settlers, snatches a match and applies it to a cannon now held by the enemy, and scatters death among hundreds of the native foe. That single touch of woman saved the colony! . . . they flee, broken and defeated, into the wilderness; and from that day supremacy and might have ever crowned the hill of Monrovia and sent their influence abroad along the whole line of our coast. . . . the permanent occupancy of the land, and the ultimate growth from it, of a civilized nationality, has excited your interest and made this a holiday.[23]

Were it not that the "planters" of this colony were African American emigrants and the "infuriate savages" were pagan Africans, this narrative could easily be mistaken, in its diction and rhetoric, for one of the innumerable accounts of the founding of the New England Puritan commonwealth ritually recited in Election Day sermons.

Later in the same speech, Crummell made even more explicit his reading of the African colonization movement as a providential extension of the American Puritans' "errand in the wilderness": "For I take it, that when the Almighty takes up a people in any of the great centers of civilization, and transplants them into a region of ignorance and benightedness, he gives such people a commission, and imposes an obligation upon them, to undertake the elevation of the degraded people who become subject to them, in all the respects of their mental and moral nature" (150). Following exactly the strictly patterned argument of a typical Election Day sermon, the clergyman next warned his auditors of the ever-present danger of declension from the holy mission: "In all colonies and new countries, the bonds of olden manners and ancient customs are wanting . . . hence, laxity prevails, freedom is exaggerated, control is loose and relaxed, and the young, for the most part, desire to do as they please" (153). Lest the younger children of the dream relapse into their natural state of barbarism, they must defer forthwith to the authority and polity of the elders: "Let me tell you that the theory which is getting in vogue in our country, *and in none other under the sun*, namely, that young men are the life, the soul, the main-stay, the real strength of a country, is all balderdash! *The real might of a country is centered in character*" (160). Fortunately, however, Divine Providence has proferred signs of a glorious destiny—nothing less than the civilizing of the last unredeemed continent—to incite the young gentlemen of Monrovia to shoulder the responsibilities demanded by Crummell's religious reading of the black man's burden in the larger history of the world.

The clergyman who delivered that stern admonition to Liberia's race leaders in 1863 was already a published author and an acknowledged leader of the New World emigrationist movement that was the harbinger of pan-Africanism. The year previous, Charles Scribner had issued in New York an influential volume of sermons and addresses titled *The Future of Africa*. In that collection, Alexander Crummell had forged a powerful ideological alliance that linked his Anglican faith to a popular African American belief in "Ethiopianism" and to the more intellectually respectable doctrine of progress outlined in Guizot's general history of European civilization. "Ethiopianism" denoted a particular Negro variant of the widely held theory of the cyclical nature of human history; it was inspired by an interpretation of Psalm 68:31 ("Ethiopia shall soon stretch out her hands unto God") that appeared frequently in antebellum black publications.[24] The Bible verse was presumed to offer scriptural warrant for believing that the African peoples would be the last "also chosen" race to join the universal Christian redemption, thus ushering in the final conversion of the entire world. In his first book of public pronouncements, Crummell skillfully connected this popular article of faith to a sophisticated metahistorical argument he derived from Guizot.[25]

Much like Chaadaev, Crummell interpreted holy scripture and human history as evidence of a special providence reserved for those peoples who were latecomers to the evangelical progress of Christian civilization. Crummell did not deny that Africans appeared to be "the withered arm of the human species," weakened and degraded by a history of spiritual neglect and physical brutalization. But the pattern of racial experience painfully inflicted on Negroes by a history of paganism, slavery, exile, and diaspora strongly suggested that they were, in the aggregate, the world's latter-day Israelites. In short, Crummell discovered theological and secular signs of a compensatory grace that promised to justify the previous exclusion of Africans from historic significance.

Employing the logic of a Puritan "typological" reading of events, it was evident that Africans were the modern "antitypes" of the hardy tribe of ancient Jews, similarly destined to usher in a worldwide age of revelation. Even by the logic of a secular reading of the march of civilization, it was evident to Crummell that the nineteenth century was slowly advancing, under the aegis of English law and language, the irresistible tide of Negro emancipation and African evangelization. Thus a dire and desperate racial past could be seen, assuming a benevolent providence, as a necessary preparatory exercise.

Crummell, again like Chaadaev, had persuaded himself that belatedness was, in its way, beatific. Although the race had been "spoiled and degraded for centuries" and hence despised, history had all along been testing its "soul" power: "We belong to a race possessed of the qualities of hope and endurance, equal at least, to any class of men in the world. . . . Not merely the life of the *body*, but the moral being, the SOUL of this poor race, has stood the shock of mental pain, and anguish, and sorest desolation, and yet come forth at last triumphant!" (167–68). Moreover, history had been keeping the scattered African people in reserve, learning through its endless migrations and colonial existence to appreciate the interdependence of all nations in the rising culture of universal Christendom. As early as 1855, Crummell was entertaining some very large aspirations for the very small company of Liberian settlers: "The world *needs* a higher type of true nationality than it now has: why should we not furnish it? . . . Why not seize upon . . . cautious, prudent eclecticism, now, in our masculine youth, instead of going the round of stale, perhaps a foul, experience? Why not make OURSELVES a precedent?" [26] The rhetoric here is characteristically American; it soars aloft on the wings provided by an Emersonian confidence in national self-reliance. Crummell's vision of cultural belatedness as enabling the rational creation of a "synthetic nationality" also resembles Chaadaev's fondest hopes for modern Russia. But what is heard most distinctly in Crummell's missionary language is the ancient music of a militant Anglo-American Puritanism.

The speeches and sermons of Alexander Crummell reveal a master practitioner of a discursive form that was central in the formation of an emerging sense of American nationality. As with Chaadaev, not enough attention has been devoted to the specific genre in which Crummell chose to express his ruminations on a national mission. Crummell's discourses represent a rather strict reiteration, albeit with an Anglo-African bias, of the old-time New England jeremiads. His sermons preach the necessity of planting "cities on the hill" amid Negro heathens who are destined to be collectively regenerated by a "saving remnant," a Christian elect. A large proportion of Crummell's published writing takes on the formal method and argumentative shape of the classic "American jeremiad" memorably defined by Sacvan Bercovitch as "the political sermon- what might be called the state-of-the-covenant address, tendered at every public occasion . . . warning of the special perils of high enterprise for those pilgrims pledged to God's 'special appointment.' " [27] Crummell's books are, in fact, gatherings of exhortatory sermons and recruitment speeches, often delivered to mark special religious or political anniversaries and events. And, precisely in accord with the characteristic emphasis of an *American* jeremiad, these formal admonitions advance an argument that manages to invert the doctrine of divine vengeance into a promise of ultimate success, converting the Lord's chastisements into gracious signs of a collective "errand." The errand is, by definition, unfulfilled, so the prophetic speaker, or "Jeremiah," is empowered to intensify feelings of individual insecurity and communal probation in order to incite greater efforts to realize cherished millennial hopes. In the American jeremiad, events no matter how dire had both literal and eschatological meaning. Harsh and depressing facts were acknowledged frankly, yet they also had a progressive significance. They were emblematic of the larger history of Christian redemption, which was itself a prophesied global reenactment of the rescue of the ancient Hebrews from sin and captivity.

Crummell's missionary nationalism expressed itself in two phases during his long public career. He first emerged as a proselytizer for African colonization schemes and then, after 1873 and his return from Liberia to the United States, he became an early spokesman for a domestic brand of black nationalism that was called "race progress" but that might more accurately be labeled Black Reconstructionism. Despite the impression commonly shared by his contemporaries that Crummell underwent a dramatic shift in ideology, a profound consistency underlies his thinking about race matters. In both phases, we can see that he adhered faithfully to a strict and formal Protestant fundamentalism that expressed itself in his devotion to the Anglican liturgy, the King's English, and Puritan homiletics.

The centrality of the American jeremiad in Crummell's intellectual formation can perhaps best be demonstrated by focusing on two representative addresses. A recruitment speech, "The Regeneration of Africa," delivered in Philadelphia in October 1865, contains a classic statement of Crummell's colonizationist nationalism. The discourse begins by lamenting the melancholy facts of racial exclusion and apparent incapacity. In two thousand years, the religion of Jesus has visited with saving power all the continents, and yet Africa's hundreds of millions of Negro souls are still heathen. Moreover, "you cannot find one single instance where a rude, heathen people, have raised themselves by their own spontaneous energy from a state of paganism to one of spiritual superiority"; men are morally elevated only by the missionary activity of those who are superior in "either letters or grace" (434–35). Yet, ultimately, as the history of evangelization has demonstrated, "Christianity never secures *thorough* entrance and complete authority in any land, save by the use of men and minds somewhat native to the soil" (437). The regeneration of Africa would thus appear to be a hopeless case. But, in an argument that invokes both biblical analogies and citations from Guizot, Crummell musters evidence of the marvelous and mysterious agency of providential history. Millions of African Negroes have been stolen away and enserfed for centuries, but through "contact with Anglo-Saxon culture and religion, they have, themselves, been somewhat permeated and vitalized by the civilization and the Christian principles of their superiors" (439–40). And now, black Christian emigrants who are "indigenous in blood, constitution, and adaptability" are returning as colonists to the African homeland. Is not this a special providence? Is not history witness to a grand completion of that winnowing of Europe that had inseminated the new world with a saving remnant of select souls? Crummell implores his auditors, the fortunate few who are Anglophone Protestant African Americans, to accept the exalted duty of evangelizing their less fortunate race brethren. For Alexander Crummell has had a vision: "I see it here, in this dark and dreadful history of my race—that history which has frenzied many a soul, and made many a man an infidel, because they could not see 'God's hand' upon the black man; at *first* retributive—and *now* restorative; but *by and by* honoring and glorifying!" (446–47). By Crummell's reckoning, the African colonization movement appeared, in 1865, as the heavenly sign of a special mission in Christendom reserved for the much-chastised but also chosen American Negro people.

Twenty years and many disappointments later, we find Alexander Crummell at Harper's Ferry addressing the graduating class of men and women at Storer College. Emancipation from slavery had arrived sooner than the regeneration of Africa, and the future of race progress, always beclouded, seemed once again dimly possible on America's shores. Crummell had come to the realization that his Anglican respectability and Puritan righteousness were less well adapted to Liberia's Africans than to the advancement of America's Negroes. In this address of 1885, "The Need of New Ideas and New Aims for a New Era," Crummell made his bid for prominence as a race leader in Reconstruction America. In the process, as he boasted in the preface to *Africa and America*, he elicited from Frederick Douglass, who was in attendance, an "emphatic and most earnest protest" (iv). Earlier, Douglass had stood forth as a respectful opponent to Crummell's advocacy of colonization, seeing it as an unfortunate separation of American blacks from the battle to claim their due as equal citizens. Understandably, he now felt equally compelled to take exception to Crummell's advocacy of a different form of African American separatism. Although easily misunderstood as a declaration of changed convictions, Crummell's address was only a variant of his usual American jeremiad to a congregated black elite, albeit in a secularized form. Much like Chaadaev in his misunderstood "Apology," Crummell surely intended no recantation of former principles; he was reaffirming his claim that civility was a "primal need" of the race.

Crummell's powerful words, spoken at the site of John Brown's tragic raid, call for a rejection of mental bondage to a grievous past: "It seems to me that there is an irresistible tendency in the Negro mind in this land to dwell morbidly and absorbingly upon the servile past" (14). Crummell takes to task those in pulpits and Congress who continue to fashion life "too much after the conduct of the children of Israel" by turning back in memory and longings toward the land of captivity long after their safe exodus from bondage and the destruction of Pharaoh. Although this may seem like a rejection of a favorite Old Testament prototype, nothing could be further from the truth. Crummell goes on to assert an analogy between the foolish nurture of grievances harbored by the Israelites in the promised land of Canaan and the constant harping on

political wrongs and personal sorrows that obsesses the Negro leadership: "For 200 years the misfortune of the black race has been the confinement of its mind in the pent-up prison of human bondage" (16).

An authentic jeremiad must warn the present generation of an impending peril, and that is what Crummell accomplishes in his address.
Although natural memory is a valuable storehouse of useful facts and
ideas, he fears that the mind of the young Negro generation may be
seduced and harmed by a cultivated pride in victimhood: "As slavery was
a degrading thing, the constant recalling of it to the mind serves, by the
law of association, to degradation" (19). In what may well have been a
studied offense to Douglass, the famous ex-slave and champion of violated rights, Crummell argues that the cultural and psychic imperative
for an emancipated people should be to escape from both the word and
the thought of slavery: "As a people, we have had an exodus from it"
(ibid.).

Crummell does not deny the grievous hurt of slavery, but he does reject what he sees as futile attempts to find political or aesthetic com-
pensations for the harms actually wrought by a condition of servitude.
We cannot live healthily, he claims, in the yesterdays of existence. The
age in which African Americans now find themselves is not inappropri-
ately called Reconstruction, and it is nothing less than "the duty of the
moral and material restoration of our race" that Crummell places on
the shoulders of the new generation of black leaders. In a passage reminiscent of his call to a small party of emigrants to regenerate heathen
Africa, Crummell appeals to the newly educated black elite to lift up a
degraded people to a "grand civility." To be sure, the burden is stagger-
ing, requiring nothing less than the moral reconstruction of a humble
people whose families have been shattered, labor debased, and character spoiled. But Crummell relies on the proud literacy of the graduates
of Storer College to sustain them in their task; he reaches back to enlist
Tacitus in his modern campaign to invigorate the spirit of race progress.
The chronicler of Rome's decline spoke of the primitive virtues of the
Germanic tribes, "pagan though they were," and his words "are lessons
to us, by which we may be taught that the true grandeur of a people is not
to be found in their civil status, in their political franchises . . . not even
in letters and culture" (33). Crummell reminds his young audience that
history is the long march of survivors, and what keeps communities alive
"in the race for manly moral superiority" is a "soul power" well within

the reach of rude populations who rely on no philanthropy other than their own capacity to discipline themselves in "the qualities of thrift, order, acquisitiveness, virtue, and manliness" (34–35). Ultimately, this is a vigorous call for the moral separation of black America from the corrupting influence of a degrading past and a degenerate present. Crummell's "new ideas for a new era" are meant to update the evangelical project of antebellum African colonization, transforming it into a muscular Protestant campaign for a postbellum Black Reconstruction. In both cases, the emergent new Negro is a reborn Negro culturally shaped in the image of an established apostolic Christian civilization.

In his long, stormy career as a black Anglican leader, Alexander Crummell managed to advocate, often simultaneously, emigration to the African homeland and edification of the American Negro at home. Although contemporaries were often bewildered by his apparent vacillation between opposing and embracing colonization, and even scholars continue to have difficulty deciding whether he was a pan-African nationalist or a "Black Yankee," a separatist or an assimilationist, Crummell's thought, like Chaadaev's, displayed the integrity of a consistent paradoxicality.[28] The son of a freeborn New York black woman and a formerly indentured servant of African princely blood, Crummell was raised Episcopalian at a double remove from the Southern slave culture and its plantation religion. Like the aristocratic Chaadaev, he was a child of privilege in his own ethnic cohort, and he inherited a similar dual allegiance to a noble native ancestry and classical Western civilization. A member of a select literate elite, he was educated at the prestigious African Free School in Manhattan. In fact, the first African American newspaper, *Freedom's Journal*, was founded in the Crummell living room in 1827. It was in this paper during Crummell's youth that a furious debate raged between early black militants who agitated for full American citizenship or, alternatively, for a reclaimed African nationhood. In the cruel and disenchanting antebellum years, Crummell was understandably torn between his father's fierce dedication to American civic equality and his friends' romantic identification with a welcoming African homeland. Although the young Crummell's first writings attacked the American Colonization Society, his later Liberian mission and Civil War advocacy of African American emigration were not as contradictory as might be supposed. Crummell allied himself with the African Civilization Society led by his friend, Henry Highland Garnet, in its fight for the abolition

of slavery and voluntary migration to English West Africa. Yet in his recruitment speeches, Crummell conceded that three centuries of residence in a country gave a people the right to undisturbed citizenship;
his was an appeal for *selective* emigration by educated and enterprising
Christians eager to display the active, saving power of the race amid
their benighted brethren.[29] Even after his permanent return to American
parish work in 1873, Crummell's two volumes of writings, *The Greatness of
Christ* (1882) and *Africa and America* (1891), significantly included admoni-
tory discourses directed at the advancement of African evangelization
alongside the campaign for Negro self-improvement in Reconstruction
America.

A single important address of 1877, "The Destined Superiority of the
Negro," helps explain how Crummell reconciled his two agendas, how
he managed to combine a sense of racial exceptionalism with cultural
Westernization in a missionary nationalism not unlike the paradoxes of
Chaadaev. Crummell's speech elaborates a philosophy of history under
the appropriate guise of a Thanksgiving Day sermon. A cryptic epigraph
from Isaiah 41 ("For your shame ye shall have double, and for confusion they shall rejoice in their portion") is employed to initiate "an investigation of God's disciplinary and retributive economy in races and
nations."[30] Appealing to the historic record, both ancient and modern, of aboriginal peoples, Crummell concludes that most nations in
rapid succession come into prominence and then rapidly vanish; for evidence, he cites the uninhabited remains of Pompeii and Nineveh and
the unreadable Bibles in extinct Amerindian and South Pacific tongues.
Providence is largely a history of national destructions, but there are
peoples like the ancient Hebrews, singled out for chastisement and preservation, who undergo a corrective ordeal of temporal probation: "The
Almightly seizes upon superior nations and, by mingled chastisements
and blessings, gradually leads them on to greatness" (196). These superior nations share conditions of character and society "to which the
divine purposes of grace and civilization are more especially fitted" — in
other words, certain select peoples are resilient and educable. In the five
hundred years in which Christianity has overspread the heathen world
outside Europe only the Negro race, Crummell notes, has retained its ancestral kingdoms and also flourished in exile.

This undeniable collective vitality is taken to be the seal of divine favor
on a race whose punishing history is plainly disciplinary and prepara-

tive. "Although often formulated into a slur," it is precisely the flexibility, the plasticity, the *imitativeness* of the Negro character that conveys, historically speaking, the promise of a progressive nationality. "In the Negro character resides, though crudely, the same eclectic quality which characterized those two great, classic nations" of Greece and Rome that gained superiority by becoming "cosmopolitan thieves" (202). Despite the infliction of slavery and the affliction of ignorance, the gradual emancipation of Negro manhood and evangelization of the African continent are current, partial manifestations of a *covenant* in history between the subjugated black race and the unfolding triumph of a universal Christian civilization. Thus Crummell, like Chaadaev, was able to read Holy Scripture and the script of history with growing pride in an assured providential role for his still-unformed people. Indeed, even as early as 1846, Crummell had announced his fundamental faith in Negro exceptionalism: "History reverses its mandates in our behalf—our dotage is in the past. 'Time writes not its wrinkles on our brow'; our juvenescence is in the future." [31]

It is important to recognize that Crummell's racialism is as peculiar an example of ethnocentrism as Chaadaev's Russian nationalism. Whereas most modern concepts of ethnic or racial identity presuppose the persistence over time of a cultural particularity, the missionary nationalisms of Chaadaev and Crummell actively battle static or "essentialist" notions of national identity. Just as Chaadaev felt compelled to rise in public opposition to the emerging ideology of a changeless Russian essence, Crummell clearly felt embattled by the prevailing racist stereotypes widely accepted by whites and blacks that consigned the Negro to an "aesthetic" level of development. In his address to the graduates of Storer College, one feels strongly Crummell's struggle to overcome a reductionist definition of blacks as a rhythmic "soul folk":

After two hundred years' residence in the higher latitudes, we are still a tropical race; and the warmth of the central regions constantly discovers itself in voice and love of harmonies, both those which appeal to the eye by color, and those which affect the sensibilities through the ear. Such an aboriginal quality is not to be disregarded, and I do not disregard it. All I desire to say is that there is something higher in life than inclination, however indigeneous it may be. . . . There are circumstances constantly occurring wherein we are bound to ignore the strongest bent of nature and yield to the manifest currents of Providence. . . . Art and culture must yield to these needs. (22–23)

As we have seen, both Chaadaev and Crummell had reason to fear that an increasingly defensive group pride among Russians and African Americans would focus on a cultural ethnocentrism that threatened to exclude their people from true historicity, from universal civilization. Both of them argued strenuously for a vision of nationality that was providential rather than essentialist. Hence they argued somewhat paradoxically that the special identifying feature, the constitutional gift of the Russian and Negro character, was its capacity to imitate and synthesize the civilization of a universal Christendom. By definition, missionary nationalism crusades against the inertia of merely indigenous and inherited values; it seeks to regulate ethnic pride by a universal standard measurement of civilized being.

Although the phenomenon of missionary nationalism does not meet the current expectation that successful nationalist movements must be populist and ethnocentric in their ideology, it would be a mistake to dismiss figures like Peter Chaadaev and Alexander Crummell as antiquated "civilizationists." As Liah Greenfeld has recently pointed out, modern nationalism need not necessarily be a collective assertion of ethnocentric cultural particularism; it can be the expression of an authoritarian political or religious ideology that attaches the population of a country to a "super-societal system" of belief or model of governance.[32] Both the rising tide of pan-Islamic fundamentalism and the broken wave of Soviet internationalism illustrate that a form of nation-centered universalism is possible among modern states. It may be naive not to attend carefully to the early theorists of "civilizationist" Russian and black nationalism. It certainly is naive to imagine that ethnic pride cannot be well served by a community's imagined attachment to the global ambitions of a dynamic universal cultural model.

Missionary nationalism is, finally, a nationalism. But it is one that locates ethnic fulfillment at a climactic moment in world history when a chosen people's capacity to sacrifice its native culture and renovate itself ushers in the victory of a global order. Missionary nationalism is particularly attractive, for obvious reasons, among ethnic groups that feel themselves positioned on the margins of an expanding cultural system. It is no accident that modern Russian and African American nationalism first arose in the guise of a missionary nationalism advanced by conservative Christian Westernizers determined to reconstruct a "backward" native culture. At least one observer of the strange career of Chaadaev has noticed an uncomfortable similarity in the mentalities that first shaped Russian and black nationalism: "Like native African-American writers in the early period of the black movement in America, Chaadaev was filled with a feeling of self-hatred. . . . the western European imposed this feeling upon the Slav. . . . Idea number two in his mind was similar to the development in the most recent period of the black movement: namely, there could be a virtue in this so-called 'cultural backwardness.' " [33] The two thinkers at the forefront of modern Russian and African American ethnic self-consciousness were Eurocentric intellectuals who successfully converted their people's historic disadvantage into a national opportunity to advance world civilization by a great leap forward. It was, however, a redemption of the nation's honor that required a purification of its soul.

2 CONSERVING THE RACE

The Emergence of Cultural Nationalism

It was, to be sure, only a matter of time before the evangelical call of racial "civilizationists" like Chaadaev and Crummell was met by a conscientious refusal to sacrifice the native culture at the altar of an idolized Western faith. Even so, it is hard to ignore the rapidity with which that initial message of a national Christian mission was transformed into a new gospel of messianic cultural nationalism. Remarkably, the two theorists most responsible for this rapid ideological shift were themselves younger protégés of the elder missionary nationalists. This intimacy suggests that the notion of a stark opposition between "civilizationist" and cultural varieties of modern Russian and black nationalism may disguise more than it reveals. Although there can be no doubt that Chaadaev's pronouncements quickly stimulated the formation of a "Slavophile" reply or that Crummell's sermonizing invited a strong response in defense of a more homespun black spirituality, it is not clear that the leading voices in the emergence of a more culturally based nationalism were fundamentally antagonistic toward their missionary forefathers.

Ivan Kireevsky (1806–1856) is, by all accounts, the primary formulator of the ideology of Moscow Slavophilism, the distillation of which is presented in his long essay, "On the Nature of European Culture and Its Relations to the Culture of Russia" (1852). W. E. B. DuBois (1868–1963) is generally acknowledged to be the moving intellectual force behind African American racial and cultural self-consciousness, the classic expression of which remains *The Souls of Black Folk* (1903). Yet Kireevsky was closely associated socially and intellectually with Peter Chaadaev during the crucial years of the composition and distribution of the *Lettres philosophiques*. And DuBois revered as his mentor the aged Alexander Crummell, the founder of the American Negro Academy at which, in 1897, the young scholar presented his first extended analysis of the concept of race. Early in their careers Kireevsky and DuBois displayed close ties of affiliation with the famous "civilizationists," yet very soon after Chaadaev's public disgrace in 1836 and Crummell's death in 1898, they each began writing articles that represent departures from, or corrections of, their predecessors. A closer look at Kireevsky's transition from "European" to "Muscovite" between 1828 and 1838 and DuBois's complex racial and cultural theorizing between 1897 and 1903 provides a useful means to measure the different ways that cultural nationalism first came into being among Russians and African Americans who had already had an intoxicating foretaste of missionary nationalism.

Younger than Chaadaev by a decade, Ivan Kireevsky was born into the heady atmosphere of philosophical speculation and national expectation that accompanied Russia's historic victory over French imperialism in 1812. The question of the specific character of Russia's national destiny took on particular urgency in the aftermath of its defeat of the Napoleonic system. With Russian troops in occupation of Paris in 1814, there could be no doubt that a new power had arisen in the East. The young Kireevsky found himself poised, like his nation, between the contending demands of an ancient and a new culture. On his father's side Kireevsky, like all the future "Slavophiles," was embedded in the provincial patriarchal world of Orthodox Russia's "quiet gentry nests"—a world stolidly opposed to "Voltaireanism" and the assertion of individual rights.[1] On his mother's side Kireevsky was connected to the highest, most cultivated circles of Imperial Russia's "literary aristocracy," the elite and cosmopolitan group that jealously preserved the independent vocation of the writer and constituted itself as a "noblesse de race."[2] After the death of his father and his mother's remarriage, the family moved to Moscow in 1821, and Kireevsky became even more closely associated with Russia's "new age" literati. His stepfather became an avid student and translator of Schelling's philosophy; his elegant and highly educated mother, Madame Elagina, conducted a famous salon that became the focal point of Moscow literary life. And the young Kireevsky joined the hothouse atmosphere of several Moscow University study groups, including the *Liubomudry*, or "Lovers of Wisdom," who initiated each other into the higher mysteries of German metaphysics and indulged themselves in fashionable prophecies of a dawning age of universal knowledge.[3] Kireevsky's (and Russia's) intellectual coming of age coincided with a moment of spiritual fatigue in a Europe that felt its cultural momentum had been lost in the post-Napoleonic balance of power. By the second and third decades of the nineteenth century, more and more observers began to sense that "Old Europe" had devolved into a political and cultural vacuum waiting to be filled. Russia had once believed that it was moving along the path of universal Enlightenment, but that idea of the progress of European civilization had collapsed, and the task of becoming enlightened was replaced for Russia with the more complicated task of becoming original.[4] Kireevsky, along with Chaadaev, was one of the first Russians to think large thoughts about the odd opportunity history had apparently thrust on his unprepared nation on the periphery of European civilization.

There was, in fact, a remarkable intersection of views in the first writings of Chaadaev and Kireevsky, even though they are not known to have encountered one another until after Chaadaev emerged from his "house arrest" late in 1831. Judging by chronology alone, Chaadaev could have read Kireevsky before the younger man could have scanned private copies of the *Lettres philosophiques*. The two men were part of the same intimate Moscow society, and it is plausible that the notorious opinions of the senior philosopher were sufficiently bruited about for his influence to be felt.[5] In any event, both men participated in a wider environment of European speculation about the phases of national emergence that invited comparative measurements of cultural vitality. It was not uncommon for their contemporaries to lament the still-unevolved, highly derivative state of Russia's national literature even as they anticipated grand developments in the near future. There was, too, a widespread consciousness of theories about the origins and completed evolution of European civilization, often accompanied by nervous reference to the rising power of the American republic on the Western horizon. As early as 1827, the Moscow historian Nikolai Pogodin had borrowed Thierry's influential theory about the founding of the European state on coercion and class conflict to argue, for the first time, that the Russian polity was founded on a different principle of "voluntary invitation to rule." [6] It was not unusual, then, that Kireevsky and Chaadaev simultaneously began to address the vexing problem of Russia's placement on the map of "world-historical" cultures.

It is surprising, however, that the future Slavophile first appeared before the public as a Russian "occidentalist" virtually in agreement with Chaadaev's private writings of the same period. Ivan Kireevsky made his debut as a cultural commentator in 1828, the same year that he announced his intention to "read all of Herder." [7] Not so surprisingly, his debut article, "Something about the Character of Pushkin's Poetry," makes the suggestion that Pushkin's mature work entitles him to be considered as Russia's Herderian national poet. Kireevsky boldly proclaims that Pushkin's most recent works, especially *Boris Godunov*, have that *quelquechose* ("too manysided, too 'objective' to be merely lyrical") to qualify as the dramatic expression of the unconscious life of the Russian people (2:13). Amusingly, he admits to having to borrow the foreignism, "ob"jektiven," to express that quintessentially Russian quality. But this is consonant with the article's generally cosmopolitan tone in celebrating what is "new" about Pushkinian Russia: "The age of the Childe-Harolds, thank God, has not yet arrived for our fatherland: young Russia has not participated in the life of the Western nations, and a people, like an individual, cannot grow old vicariously. A brilliant career is still open to Russian activity; all the modes of art, all the branches of learning have yet to be incorporated into our national life; to us it is given to still be hopeful" (10). Here is that note of promising absence, that energetically embraced task of recapitulating and outdoing Western culture so characteristic of Chaadaev.

Kireevsky's second appearance in print, the lengthy "Survey of Russian Literature in 1829," continues in the same vein, both acknowledging Russia's national underdevelopment and announcing its impending emergence: "The laurels of European civilization have served as the cradle of our culture; it has come into existence as other nations are already completing the course of their intellectual development, and where they are coming to rest we are just beginning" (38). But a startling new emphasis is added that anticipates by five years Tocqueville's famous comparison of the two giants on Europe's doorstep: "Out of the whole enlightened world two peoples are not taking part in the universal drowse; two peoples, young and fresh, are flourishing with hope: the United States of America and our fatherland. But the geographic and political remove, and above all the one-sided nature [*odnostoronnost'*] of English culture in the United States, shift all Europe's hope onto Russia" (39). Europe was no longer Russia's future so much as Russia was the true fulfillment of Europe's future. Again, there is an uncanny resemblance to Chaadaev's type of Russian patriot, the Eurocentric missionary nationalist. But Kireevsky's cryptic and invidious remark about Anglo-

American "one-sidedness," as we shall see, is the embryo out of which a quite different type of Russianness will eventually grow.

First, though, Kireevsky brought forth a major statement in his capacity as the founder and editor of a newly launched journal of the literary aristocracy, *The European*. In January 1832, he published a lead article in all senses of that term, an immodest survey of the general condition of Western culture titled "The Nineteenth Century." It was the type of bold gesture one associates with Chaadaev's ill-fated career and, ironically, Kireevsky suffered in advance of his mentor the serious consequences of Tsar Nicholas's displeasure. Kireevsky was officially reprimanded for speaking about politics under the guise of literature, and his journal was closed down. The offending essay was, indeed, what we would now refer to as an act of "cultural intervention," and it has been cited as evidence of a "reciprocal influence" that came into being after Chaadaev reentered Moscow salon life in late 1831.[8] The main argument of the essay aligns Kireevsky solidly with the defenders of Petrine Westernization, which is remarkable given his own brother's outspoken enmity toward Chaadaev as a barbaric wrecker of Russia's national memory.[9] But while Kireevsky deplores that "a kind of Chinese wall stands between Russia and Europe, only allowing us the air of Western enlightenment through a few gaps" (1:95), it is also true that he offers a dialectical scheme of the development of European culture that characterizes the contemporary West as spiritually exhausted and thirsting for a renewed age of faith in which there can be a "popular consensus" rooted in shared customs and "embodied in unitary and unanimous rituals" (93–94). This sounds quite in accord with the religiously motivated missionary "civilizationism" toward which Chaadaev's thought had evolved.

Kireevsky also initiates in this same essay, however, a very influential manner of thinking about Russia's distinctiveness. He borrows from the then fashionable French historian Guizot a triadic formula to account for the essence of Western civilization: Christianity; the character and spirit of the barbarians who vanquished Rome; the heritage of classical culture. But then he thinks to apply this formula contrastively to his own Eastern Christian world, and he concludes that Russia crucially lacked one element—the heritage of Roman law and civil society. It was that heritage that the Roman Church incorporated into itself as it established a pan-European feudal order of crusading Christianity. "In Russia," by contrast, "the Christian religion was purer and more holy.

But the lack of the Classical tradition was the reason that the influence of our Church in the Dark ages was neither as decisive nor as powerful as the Roman Church" (100). When Russia did become a unified state, it was not through a spiritual integration or a moral force but by virtue of material might and physical subjugation. This historic record was painful for Russians to contemplate, and Kireevsky's summation rivals the gloom of Chaadaev: "By this means Renaissance Europe realized the full inheritance of prior human civilization. . . . [but in Russia] the place of thought yielded to personality, random accident, and usurpers of authority" (101–2). Kireevsky's final verdict in "The Nineteenth Century" is indistinguishable from Chaadaev's position: civilization in the true sense of the word could not come to Russia otherwise than by Peter the Great's revolution from above. Kireevsky, too, could be brutally blunt: "For us to seek what is truly national means to seek ignorance" (106). In 1832, Kireevsky appeared to have been securely enlisted in the ranks of the Russian Westernizers.

By 1838, however, Kireevsky delivered on one winter night in his mother's Moscow salon an initial sketch of what one commentator has named "the great Russian myth of the nineteenth century"—the Slavophile idyll of the patriarchal pre-Petrine national family.[10] It is generally agreed that Kireevsky's widely distributed speech "In Reply to A. S. Khomiakov" became the ideological fount of Slavophile nationalism. In it, he repeats Guizot's triadic explanation of European culture, but with one crucial difference—now the legacy of classical civilization is understood to have imposed on the West a culture of "one-sided" rationalism that has subordinated everything to its abstract formalism, its syllogistic logic, its "soulless calculation" and "morbid insatiability" (111–13). Everything from the scholastic theology of Catholicism to the legal codes of constitutionalism can be attributed to a common Western imperative to secure individual consent to what is deemed reasonable. And the result is a social order that is nothing but the systematic manipulation of disorder and self-interest:

All private and public existence in the West is based on the concept of separate, individual independence presupposing individual isolation. From this follows the sacredness of external, formal relations, the sacredness of property and of contractual regulations considered more important than personhood. . . . The first step of each person in society is to surround himself with a fortress, from the core of which he enters into negotiations with other independent powers. . . . The *social contract* is not the invention of the *Encyclopédistes*, but the operative ideal toward which all Western society has been gravitating unconsciously and now consciously. (113–16)

Fortunately, however, an alternative to the West's soulless contractual civilization already exists: "Landed private property, the source of personal rights in the West, was among us replaced by affiliation to society. . . . A countless multiplicity of small communes [*miry*] comprising Russia was envelopped in a network of churches, monasteries, and hermitages from which emanated everywhere a single understanding about social and personal relations" (115). In this passage, Kireevsky points prophetically to the still beating heart of an Old Russia that had apparently preserved all the conditions for a future indigenous culture rooted in consensus and holy communion. Any analysis of what became Russian Slavophilism would surely place the idea of the agrarian commune, the *mir*, along with a doctrinaire opposition of Orthodox holism (*tsel'nost'*) to Western rationalism (*razumnost'*) at the core of the newborn ideology. Ivan Kireevsky had provided the staples to nourish a newborn Russian cultural exclusivism.

What, though, accounts for the transformation of the former "European" into a full-fledged "Muscovite"? Most accounts of the six years between the suppression of Kireevsky's journal and his emergence as a new-style Russian nationalist emphasize the interaction of several factors: his depression, his marriage, and a closer association with both his younger brother and an old friend, Ivan Khomiakov. Clearly, Kireevsky was crushed by the rude curtailment of his self-appointed career as an "enlightener" of the realm. He nursed his wounds in the quiet of his country estate, Dolbino, where he rediscovered the consolations of kinship and finally achieved the support of his family in wedding his second cousin, Natal'ia Petrovna Arbeneva. That marriage undoubtedly played a major role in the "conversion" of Ivan Kireevsky, for his young wife was a devout and well-connected Orthodox intellectual who took a hand in redirecting her husband's education.[11] It is also highly likely that Kireevsky in these years turned a receptive ear to his brother's extensive research and reading about Russian folksongs and folkmoots, and Khomiakov surely was engaging him in provocative conversations about the spiritual superiority of Orthodox Slavdom.[12] By 1838, these future Slavophiles were jointly involved in an agitated reaction to the well-known opinions and scandalous fate of Peter Chaadaev. The resulting "conversation" between the Slavophile philosopher, Kireevsky, and the pro-Petrine Westernizer, Chaadaev, has never ceased to preoccupy Russian nationalist discourse. It is, therefore, well worth asking what separates and what binds together these two formative voices of a newly self-conscious "Russianness."

The most complete summation of Kireevsky's mature thought is unquestionably to be found in his lengthy essay of 1852, "On the Nature of European Culture and Its Relations to the Culture of Russia," subtitled "Letter to Count E. E. Komarovsky." The genre of a formal public epistle that ostensibly expands on a private conversation makes this text, in effect, Kireevsky's version of a "First Philosophical Letter," his direct (if much delayed) response to Chaadaev's prototype. Indeed, the opening paragraph already indicates a fundamental disagreement with Chaadaev. It asserts that Russia is in possession of a distinctive national culture, "traces of which are not only observable to this day in the customs, manners, and ways of thinking of the common people, but which permeate the entire soul, the whole cast of mind, the inner fibre, if one may say so, of any Russian person still not transformed by a Western education" (1:174). Whereas thirty years earlier no thinking person could possibly have imagined Russia's culture to be anything other than an imitation and extension of European culture, a massive change has taken place both in Western civilization and among Westernized Russians. In the second half of the nineteenth century, "the very triumph of the European mind has revealed the limit of its basic aspirations" (176); the Western culture of abstract rationality has devoured itself in self-reflexive analysis, turning unsparingly critical of reason itself. Kireevsky cleverly employs post-Kantian epistemology and Hegelian historical dialectics to present an elaborately philosophical version of the familiar "Decline of the West" argument. Whereas Europe "may be said to have completed the course of development it began in the ninth century," (181), Russians need no longer be beguiled by the prestige of Western progress; even those who have closely followed European thought are now well advised to turn their attention "to those particular cultural principles, underestimated by the European mind, by which Russia existed and which still can be noticed despite European influence" (180). There is, in short, an ethnic *quelquechose* "totally different from the component elements comprising the culture of European peoples" that is, moreover, still capable of further development. And, Kireevsky adds, "after the recent interpenetration of Russia and Europe, it is inconceivable that any development in the intellectual life of Russia would not affect Europe" (181).

What, then, constitutes Russia's unique cultural contribution to the unfolding dialectic of civilization, and what is the source of this distinctive national gift? As Kireevsky interprets the dusted-off archives of the national past, a providential history had enabled the Russian people to preserve its racial and societal predisposition toward "microcosms of accord blending into other, larger accords" (207); untouched by Roman law or the Roman Church, the Russian folk had continued to live its ancient, nonconflictual communal existence underneath the sovereignty of its Mongol overlords. Kireevsky does not hesitate to ascribe to the very nature of his ancestors a self-abnegating spirituality denied to the contentious European mentality that promoted the advance of Western civilization. Not only are we reminded that the early Russians peaceably invited Norman princes to rule over them, eschewing the burden of worldly power, but we are also told that "even the ethnic traits [*plemennye osobennosti*] of the Slavic mode of life promoted the full assimilation of Christian principles" (185). Tapping the purest sources of early Greek Christianity and holding true to customary Orthodox rites, the Russian religious mind, in Kireevsky's view, thinks and worships differently from the Romanized Christians. Schooled by the Eastern Church Fathers and reinforced by popular tradition, "the very meaning of social relations and private morality" (210) is wholly different among Russians. Western man fragments his life into separate strivings and exercises his various faculties to realize a coherent self; the "striking peculiarity of the Russian character," however, is that "no individual, in his lived relations with others, would ever seek to assert his uniqueness as worthy of merit" (214). Nothing could be clearer than the difference between Western European and ancient Russian culture; it is, for Kireevsky, the difference between *divisiveness* and *wholeness*, between analytic *rationality* and intuitive *reason* (218).[13] There remained, however, one unsolved problem: how to bring into being an authentic Russian Renaissance, the new birth of Russia's indigenous civilization.

Unlike Chaadaev, whose missionary nationalism anticipated a holy alliance between European Christian civilization and the power of the

Russian autocratic state, Kireevsky's cultural revivalism relied on a wide-spread unofficial conversion of the hearts and minds of the educated Russian gentry, a change of class consciousness that would usher in a renewed age of "the great Russian commune" and, incidentally, rescue the declining West from the curse of its spiritually exhausted formalism and rationality. If Chaadaev's Eurocentric nationalism presupposed a malleable Russia emptied of any cultural content, Kireevsky's Slavophile utopianism predicted the withering away of a decaying West devoid of spiritual substance. Kireevsky did, indeed, transform himself from a "European" into a "Muscovite" in six brief years, and in that process he formulated an ideology of Russian cultural nationalism that is self-consciously the systematic opposite of Chaadaev's civilizationism. Yet both thinkers share an underlying premonition of Russia's messianic status among history's nations. At the conclusion of his "philosophical letter," Kireevsky fervently expresses his one wish that "those principles of life which are preserved in the teaching of the Holy Orthodox Church . . . those lofty principles, in dominating European culture, should not oust it but rather enfold it in their fullness, giving it higher meaning and its ultimate development" (222). For Russia is reserved the concluding unscientific postscript to the story of Western civilization.

When William Edward Burghardt DuBois strode to the platform on the evening of March 5, 1897, to deliver one of the three inaugural addresses at the founding session in the nation's capital of the American Negro Academy, he was already, at twenty-nine, the wunderkind of the "Negro Saxon" race leadership. He was also quite obviously the favorite son and heir apparent of Alexander Crummell, the founding father of America's first major black learned society. The young DuBois must have seemed the very embodiment of Crummell's lifetime message to his people, re-iterated that very morning: "Civilization the Primal Need of the Race." Like his distinguished elder, DuBois was the proud exception that proved the capability of his race for rule and self-mastery. Raised a Congregationalist in the Berkshire hills of Massachusetts, it was his privilege to be poor and gifted at a moment when his New England neighbors had good reason to invest in a sterling proof that abolitionism was justified and Negro uplift was possible. The young DuBois more than justified the hopes of black advancement placed on his willing shoulders, and the rapidity of his intellectual progress was nothing short of astonishing. Admitted with advanced standing at Fisk University, he enrolled for a second bachelor's degree at Harvard, from which he graduated cum laude in philosophy in 1890; within one more year he completed a master's thesis on the Atlantic slave trade that earned him the distinction of becoming the first Negro scholar to make a presentation before the American Historical Association. Having become the recipient of a much-coveted Slater Fellowship, he enrolled for graduate studies at the University of Berlin and completed a dissertation in economics there after three semesters; indignant at not being approved for early graduation, he returned to Harvard and wrote a second doctoral dissertation in history, "The Suppression of the African Slave Trade," which received the honor of appearing as the first volume in Harvard's Historical Studies series.[14] It was while DuBois was finishing that dissertation and teaching (in the Classics Department) at Wilberforce University that "Father" Crummell entered into his life as a welcome black mentor before whom he could, as he put it, instinctively bow. The commencement sermon that Crummell delivered that spring of 1895 thrillingly reiterated his call for race leadership by a devoted and tireless "aristocracy of talent," the very message that DuBois would later promote in his famous article of 1903, "The Talented Tenth." By 1897, when DuBois's evening lecture, "The Conservation of Races," was by acclamation voted to be published as the second occasional paper of the American Negro Academy, it appeared that the young New Englander had, indeed, been anointed as Crummell's legitimate successor, the one most likely to continue the mission of reforming the race upward to glory.

There was much in DuBois's background to suggest that he was, by intellect and temperament, sympathetic to Crummell's particular combination of racialism, civilizationism, and elitism. But there was also in DuBois a deep-rooted indeterminacy of identity and tentativeness of mind, characteristics that Crummell in his rigid black rectitude often dismissed as "mulatto" traits. If we examine certain crucial moments of self-presentation in DuBois's young life, both in his private correspondence and public speeches, we find him thinking always in terms of racial types, but with some rather interesting fluctuations in his own sense of attachment. At Fisk he writes home to his Great Barrington pastor that he "can hardly realize that they are all my people," that great assembly gathered there of a race that was in bondage twenty years ago (1:5). Very early on, DuBois seems genuinely puzzled by the spectrum of possibility represented by "his people." Within his own family, he feels the tug of relationship to the rustic "black Burghardts" and to the worldly "Huguenot" clan of his absent "too white" father. During the years of his education in the American South, DuBois learns more about what it means to be a Negro. He touches there "the very shadow of slavery" among the black peasantry, and he has a first brush with the seductive gentility of "mulattoes with money." As a Harvard graduate making application for a European fellowship, DuBois stresses his own, as it were, native cosmopolitanism: "I omitted stating that I am, in blood, about one half or more Negro, and the rest French and Dutch" (13). But when he is giddy with success (and wine) as a student prince in Berlin, he sees himself on his twenty-fifth birthday as quite literally the hand of Ethiopia majestically outstretched: "Is it egotism—is it assurance—or is it the silent call of the world spirit that makes me feel that I am royal. . . . The hot dark blood of that black forefather—born king of men—is beating at my heart. . . . These are my plans: to make a name in science, to make a name in literature and thus to raise my race." [15] By the time that DuBois finishes his German dissertation, he is confiding to his notebook a self-image of truly Bismarckian proportions: "I have finally proved to my entire satisfaction that my race forms but a slight impediment between me and kindred souls . . . Therefore, I have gained for my life work new hope and zeal—the Negro people shall yet stand among the honored of the world." [16] The phrasing of this heroic aspiration is tellingly ambiguous, however. Is the would-be Atlas who carries his people's dignity on his shoulders transcending racial impediments to a universal culture, or is he embodying what Negroness is destined to achieve? The rapidly developing nationalism of the young DuBois is a richly complicated and volatile phenomenon.

It certainly looks as if DuBois yearned to cast himself in the mold of the nation-building hero, the disciplining agent of an entire people's collective will. In retrospect, the many commencement speeches it was DuBois's honor to deliver seem to display a distinctly Crummellian (or Teutonic) cult of the culture-bearing hero. But we should remember that the New England air he breathed as a child was inebriate with an Emersonian confidence in Representative Men. An energetic faith in heroic vitalism flares up on all those occasions when DuBois was singled out as a commencement speaker. The young black scholar somehow found inspiration in an increasingly odd series of great white men: Wendell

Phillips (Great Barrington High School, 1884), Bismarck (Fisk University, 1888), and Jefferson Davis (Harvard College, 1890). For too long this sequence has been adduced as damning evidence of DuBois's incorrigible elitism and authoritarianism. Praise for Wendell Phillips, the incorruptible tribune of racial and economic justice in a lapsed land of freedom, surely requires no explanation. But DuBois's words in praise of the German chancellor and the Confederate leader are taken to require an apology, or at least a clever apologist.

To be sure, the aspiring young race leader was powerfully attracted to any words or music that celebrated the force of a unifying will. Like other males of his generation, he was highly susceptible to the red-blooded appeal of Carlyle's prose and Wagner's operas; he was surrounded by a contemporary Anglo-Saxon and Germanic cult of muscular Teuton vitality.[17] Yet DuBois's own words in public acknowledgment of these conquering white heroes were carefully qualified and sometimes even laced with cutting irony. Bismarck is lauded as the nation-building "Man of One Idea" who is unquestionably "the most distinguished and autocratic statesman of modern times." His aristocratic disdain for caution and compromise well illustrates "the power of purpose," but his career also carries a warning "lest we raise a nation and forget the people, become a Bismarck and not a Moses." Bismarck's commanding will has made Germany a nation, but one that "knows not the first principle of self-government."[18] At his Harvard commencement, DuBois was even more skilled in making a backhanded compliment to a great white racial type.

Only recently have careful readers noticed the unmistakable ironies that were lost on the condescending and self-congratulating auditors of the slender black orator who spoke in Harvard's Memorial Hall on "Jefferson Davis as a Representative of Civilization." The topic and the setting dangled the promise of a reassuringly Reunionist speech that would graciously honor the courage and civility of the vanquished Southern planter aristocracy. But what DuBois actually delivered was a bold reading of Jefferson Davis as nothing less than "a typical Teutonic hero," the very embodiment of the Anglo-Saxon "idea of the Strong Man."[19] The bold, indomitable guardian of his people's slave-holding privilege was, in DuBois's second paragraph, insidiously connected to the Indian-murdering, Mexico-bashing advance of an American civilization based on one dominant idea—"Individualism coupled with the rule of might"

—an idea supported by "the cool logic of the Club" (811). In one deft clause, Jefferson Davis had become the perfect representation of the Harvard clubman.[20] Ultimately, the type of Teutonic civilization Davis so nobly embodied was "a system of human culture whose principle is the rise of one race on the ruins of another," but "such a type is incomplete . . . until checked by its complementary idea" (812). Fortunately, a complementary idea of civilization is arising in the Southern hemisphere, where the Negro race is making its "singularly unromantic" advance toward nationhood. The Negro race arrives on the scene of world history not as the muscular warrior "but as the cringing slave"—the victim of civilization. It offers, however, a forceful correction to European one-sidedness similar to the redemptive virtues of Kireevsky's pacific and communal Russians: "In the history of this people, we seek in vain the elements of Teutonic deification of Self, and Roman brute force, but we do find an idea of submission apart from cowardice, laziness or stupidity, such as the world never saw before" (813). Collectively, the Negro race represents the idea of the Submissive Man, and it adds to the future development of civilization the essential notion that "not only the assertion of the I, but also . . . submission to the Thou is the highest Individualism." The world-historical process ultimately requires "the submission of the strength of the Strong to the advance of all," since "civilization cannot afford to lose the contribution of the very least of nations for its full development." Is not this a way of suggesting that the Negro race is the advance embodiment of a dawning civilization that extends itself by absorbing rather than vanquishing what other nations offer? The remarkable turn of thought taken by DuBois's commencement speech of 1890 already anticipates the grand theorizing about race that so enthralled the first gathering of the American Negro Academy in 1897.

"The Conservation of Races" remains one of the most controversial (and elusive) statements of DuBois's position as an emerging black nationalist. It marks that moment in DuBois's career when he openly acknowledges that prejudice and discrimination require the American Negro seriously to consider "the real meaning of Race" (815). But the slipperiness of the concept is made patently obvious as DuBois grapples with the many competing implications of the division of humanity into racial types. The speech is unsettling precisely because it affirms the need for Negro solidarity and self-consciousness even as it unsettles the basic criteria for making racial discriminations. Not surprisingly, there are many different explanations and interpretations for what DuBois was "really" proving in his inaugural address to the American Negro Academy. It has been read as a specific endorsement of Crummell's racial collectivism and elitist black separatism at the expense of the assimilationism advocated by Frederick Douglass; but it has also been read as the first indication of a higher-order Hegelian assimilationism in which DuBois integrates the Negro into the dialectical process by which each world-historical people contributes its *Volksgeist* to the next evolutionary stage of human civilization.[21] In either case, what is struggling into view is a precocious attempt to understand the existence of a black racial identity as *primarily*, one might even say "essentially," *a historically determined sociocultural construct*. In this bellwether essay, DuBois is leading his people toward a cultural rather than a biological or theological definition of the racial nation.

Although DuBois concedes that "the final word of science" would seem to indicate at least two, and perhaps three, "great families of human beings" as judged by external physical criteria, he is not impressed that one can come to any definite conclusion regarding the "essential difference of races" (815–16). The trouble is that in the actual line of descent, the specific physical criteria of race become "exasperatingly intermingled"; beyond that, the perceived physical unlikenesses are not greater than the biological likeness of the human species. "Yet there are differences—subtle, delicate and elusive though they may be—which," DuBois avers, "while they perhaps transcend scientific definition, nevertheless, are clearly defined to the eye of the Historian and Sociologist" (817). DuBois wishes Negroes not to ignore the reality that racial groups exist, as does "the race idea in human history," but such concepts cannot rest securely on physical distinctions. What, then, is the operative distinction that makes a racial group cohere? For DuBois, "It is a vast family of human beings, generally of common blood and language, always of common history, traditions and impulses, who are both voluntarily and involuntarily striving together for the accomplishment of certain more or less vividly conceived ideals of life" (817). It is important to notice what is invariable in DuBois's formulation of racial identity. To belong to a race group is to participate in a collective kinship *always* shaped by the perception over time of shared narrative and ritual forms, but not necessarily united by a common lineage or language. There is, however, a further indicator necessary for a historically operative racial identity to exist: a sense, both conscious and unconscious, of impelled yearning toward a collective realization of common ideational goals. It is, of course, the intrusion of the language of physiology ("impulses") that has led philosophically minded critics to point out that DuBois has by no means managed to transcend or evade the taint of a biological mystique in his theory of racial cohesion.[22] But what motivates DuBois's peculiarly complex, notably confused definition of race is visible in the next sentence of his discussion: "Turning to real history, there can be no doubt, first, as to the wide-spread, nay, universal, prevalence of the race idea, the race spirit, the race ideal, and as to its efficiency as the vastest and most ingenious invention for human progress." *Real* history demonstrates to the eye of the "Historian and Sociologist" that the efficient engine of group emergence from an unhistoric existence is the construction of a racial idea.

DuBois quickly leaves behind the three "scientific" racial categories and moves on to his elaboration of the "distinctly differentiated races" he finds "upon the world's stage today." Eight in number, they include the Slavs and Negroes, whose "strivings" have just begun, whose "spiritual message" has not yet been given to the world. Is not this evidence enough that DuBois's primary concern in "The Conservation of Races" is to behave responsibly as a race leader by promoting an awareness of the necessity of an affirmative discourse of differentiation for Negroes, who are chiefly visible only as different bodies or as cultural inferiors? DuBois consistently gives priority to the sociocultural over the physical indicators of racial types because he understands how Western civilization has historically elevated nationalities into prominence: "The whole process which has brought about these race differentiations has been a growth, and the great characteristic of this growth has been the differentiation of spiritual and mental differences between great races of mankind and the integration of physical differences" (818–19). His elusive and logically inconsistent definition of race is simultaneously pragmatic and metaphysical, both instrumentalist and Idealist, no doubt knowingly so. It is the ingenious invention of the brilliant young philosopher who studied with both William James and Josiah Royce.

The essay DuBois offered in tribute to Alexander Crummell is also, along with the simultaneously published *Atlantic Monthly* article, "Strivings of the Negro People," the beginning of his swerve toward cultural nationalism. He makes it clear that world-historical race groups need not be of pure lineage: "We are apt to think in our American impatience, that while it may have been true in the past that closed race groups made history, that here in conglomerate America *nous avons changer tout cela* . . . and have no need of this ancient instrument of progress" (817). Major contributions to civilization are, in fact, made by conglomerated peoples who develop a cultural heterogeneity that brings new spiritual and psychic gifts into the world. DuBois, like Crummell, identifies the eight million American Negroes as the race's "advance guard," having a "just place in the van of Pan-Negroism," as long as their destiny is *not* absorption by white America (820). But what DuBois strives toward is not Crummell's version of black separatism: "Their destiny is not a servile imitation of Anglo-Saxon culture, but a stalwart originality which shall unswervingly follow Negro ideals." American Negroes need not reject the commonly shared laws, language, and religion that make them American in order to develop as "the first fruits of this new nation, the harbinger of that black tomorrow which is yet destined to soften the whiteness of the Teutonic today" (822). Although it is not yet very specific, DuBois is issuing a clear call for an earnest, organized effort to develop the cultural self-consciousness of American Negroes as a peculiar people of destiny who must conserve their race spirit in order to supplement and advance the growth of human civilization. African Americans possess an as yet unarticulated cultural mission that their common history, traditions, and impulses tell them is theirs alone to achieve.

In the years immediately preceding the publication of *The Souls of Black Folk*, DuBois was engaged in a scrupulous and intellectually courageous effort to make better known the multiplicity as well as the common features that actually obtained in the historic circumstances of American Negro life. In *The Philadelphia Negro* (1899) and in an ensuing series of Atlanta University Conference reports, he took professional pride in amassing careful statistical, historical, and physical evidence of the undeniable social diversity and genetic hybridity that had to be recognized in any proper study of the African American condition. At the same time, however, he distinguished the true object of sociological investigation as having a different aim: "to study those finer manifestations of social life which history can but mention and which statistics can not count, such as the expression of Negro life . . . that manifest the existence of a distinct social mind." [23] In the period between 1897 and 1903, DuBois's

publications are notable for their rare tolerance for two mutually antagonistic schools of historical inquiry—the empirical, social-scientific approach with its respect for specific, contextualized facts and the idealist,
philosophical approach with its high regard for symbolic constructs and
generalized verities.

As early as his brief tenure at Wilberforce, DuBois was encouraging his
students to think in the plural and in the singular at the same time. He
instructed them not to think of themselves as the Negro but as "Afro-
Americans," and they were to understand a fundamental peculiarity
about any social science problem: "That the thing studied as well as the
student, is a living, breathing soul, all of whose numberless thoughts
and actions must be ascertained and allowed for in the final answer." [24]
Yet they were also to cultivate a collective pride in themselves as a literate aristocracy called forth to guide "the undeveloped and plastic condition of [their] people." The empirical scientist in DuBois deconstructs
social stereotypes only to replace them with the culture-building constructs deemed necessary by the philosophical historian. This constant
striving to be unimpeachably factual and credibly inspirational is visible
in the heroic labors of the emerging cultural nationalist.

Striving is, of course, one of DuBois's recurring terms. Both a noun and
a gerund, it captures the very essence of his people's collective being.
Interestingly, the word has both spiritual and competitive connotations;
it names any purposive, situationally transcendent activity born from
strife. The term, especially as it is stitched into the argument of his 1897
Atlantic Monthly essay, becomes associated with two equally firm threads
of meaning:

> an American, a Negro; two souls, two thoughts, two unreconciled striv-
> ings; two warring ideals in one dark body, whose dogged strength alone
> keeps it from being torn asunder. The history of the American Negro is
> the history of this strife, —this longing to attain self-conscious manhood,
> to merge his double self into a better and truer self. . . . This is the end of
> his striving: to be a co-worker in the kingdom of culture." (194–95)

This famous passage fully evokes the combined strivings so central to
DuBois's vision of his race's destiny. Here he glimpses as nearly within
reach an integrated African American self that will be recognized as both
assimilated and other, having been uplifted to civil equality yet also remaining immersed in cultural distinctness. One striving is toward full

citizenship in a shared democratic body politic; the other striving labors to articulate the message of a "world-race."

It is clear that DuBois shouldered the "Negro Saxon" burden of secular uplift for his people, but he was not a culture-blind missionary "civilizationist." Indeed, to some he appears as early as 1897 to be the bearer of a cultural messianism devoted to redeeming the "self-obliteration" of black people.[25] From whence, however, did DuBois expect help to come in conserving the cultural gifts of the historic Negro race? The perhaps surprising answer is that DuBois conceived of the racially specific genius of his people as primarily spiritual and aesthetic. As a historian of slavery, DuBois early and often acknowledged that the sole precious vestige of traditional African social life not destroyed by the slave ship was the voluntarily organized Negro church: "The Negro church came before the Negro home . . . and in every respect it stands to-day as the fullest, broadest expression of organized Negro life." [26] David Levering Lewis has recently pointed out that as a young man DuBois filed regular newspaper reports on the active social life of Great Barrington's AME Zion Church and even served as secretary of its Sewing Society.[27] Though DuBois is thought of, sometimes rightly, as a proper late Victorian gentleman, it is becoming clear that he felt a guarded emotional dependency on the more rapturous and communal aspects of Negro religion and that he appreciated its central role in perpetuating a coherent link with ancestral custom. By 1903, when DuBois edited (and largely wrote) the Atlanta University study, *The Negro Church*, he was frankly acknowledging that the "real units of [African] race life" had survived slavery and had been embedded in the hierarchical yet communitarian worship conducted within the Negro evangelical assemblies organized in the plantation South.

The rituals and rhythms of a complex racial past had survived the Middle Passage. And the American slave culture, against all odds, had nurtured and developed the authentic expressive powers and social remnants of the nearly extinguished African spirit. In a 1903 speech, "The Possibilities of the Negro: The Advance Guard of the Race," DuBois concluded an enumeration of exemplary African Americans with a remarkable prophecy: "Thus we have striven in the world of work. But the Negro, as the world has yet to learn, is a child of the spirit, tropical in birth and imagination, and deeply sensitive to all the joy and sorrow and beauty of life. His message to the world, when it comes in fullness of speech and conscious power, will be the message of the artist, not that of the politician or shop-keeper" (1:166). Unlike Crummell, DuBois awaited the dawning of a Negro cultural renaissance as the sign and seal of the race's civilization.

The first stirrings of cultural nationalism among Russians and African Americans displayed a similarly curious admixture of particularism and universalism. Unlike their "civilizationist" predecessors, Kireevsky and DuBois attached the collective destiny of their people to the conservation and proliferation of a culturally specific mentality and spirituality that differed in essence from "Roman" or "Teutonic" models of religion and society. Yet the ethnic or racial specificity that these two thinkers descried in their people's historic culture was also interpreted as being historic in a second, prophetic sense. Culturally distinct Russians and Negroes were understood to be the bearers of a "message to the world" and, thus, their national differentness was embedded in an evolutionary history that privileged certain peoples as messianic nationalities. Kireevsky and DuBois stand at the beginning of a tradition of Russian and African American cultural nationalism that is simultaneously conservationist and expansionist. Each theorist initiates an intellectual tradition that strives to enunciate a persuasively non-Western national culture that is also seen as evolving toward a higher stage of more universal universalism than European civilization has yet attained. This phenomenon should probably be understood more as a consequence of the West's exclusion of black people and Orthodox Christians from "world-historical" status than as the individual legacy of Kireevsky's Schellingism or DuBois's Hegelianism. There is a long history behind the proclivity of Russian and African American nationalism to announce its differentness in messianic tones.

Although Kireevsky and DuBois stand together in the sense that they each first formulate a fully theorized cultural nationalism for their ethnic brethren, their differences are far more significant than their similarities. Unlike DuBois, Kireevsky believes that he can look back on a deep-rooted and continuous native culture. For Slavophiles, conserving the race appeared to be a matter of persuading the Russian ruling class to preserve and promote the extant, timeless traditions of folk communalism and Orthodox worship. With a raised consciousness of Russia's historic spirituality and ancient collectivism, the entire nation could lend its charismatic Christian talent for harmony and humility to the corrupt and exhausted culture of Western Christendom. Kireevsky's Slavophile nationalism imagines the Russian people as a vast cultural and religious whole shaped by a providential history to offer a redemptive model of spiritual solidarity, a living choir of social accord and self-abnegating consensus. However idyllic or utopian the picture, it provides a firm ideological support for a militant opposition to Western rationalism and legalism that continues to appeal to Russians, whose customary lives have been so frequently disrupted by a modernizing and despotic state. Kireevsky establishes the precedent for a Russian cultural nationalism that identifies the Russian soul as profoundly non-Western and authentically Christian, securely rooted in its own ancient and Orthodox civilization of communalism.

By contrast, DuBois realized full well that the Negro race could not be reliably measured or unified except as a commonly sensed historic experience of dislocation and tribulation. African Americans did not have the luxury of imagining a single uninterrupted ancestry of blood or tradition on which to rest their collective sense of identity. Slavery and the diaspora had made the Negro race a "nation without grandfathers," yet there existed a shared identification of themselves as a vast family of human beings involuntarily and voluntarily participating in "the development of a people," striving and surviving together in a laborious historic process (1:203–15). DuBois's thought actively constructs a historically determined sociocultural mentality and spirituality that constitutes his version of an elusive racial essence. This construct at times strikingly resembles Kireevsky's non-Western typology of Russianness, especially when DuBois posits the Negro race as a collective embodiment of healthy submissiveness and absorptiveness that advances civilization beyond Roman and Teutonic assertiveness and ethnocentricity. But if DuBois's cultural nationalism, at least in its early stages, is to be criticized for not overcoming a metaphysical racial essentialism, it is also useful to note how it differs from the precedent set for Russian nationalism by Kireevsky's Slavophilism. Unlike Kireevsky's organic and holistic insistence on a homogeneous, continuous Russian cultural essence, DuBois's thought strives valiantly to acknowledge biological heterogeneity and cultural syncretism as the very essence of Negro nationhood. What David Levering Lewis accurately describes as a prevalent "subtext of proud hybridization"[28] in DuBois's complex sense of his African American self is a strength, rather than a weakness, in his intellectual struggle to define the unrecognized soul of black culture. At the dawn of the twentieth century DuBois had already made a prophetic connection between Negro identity and multiculturalism.

3 NOTES FROM THE UNDERWORLD

Dostoevsky, DuBois, and the Unveiling of

Ethnic "Soul"

A genuinely innovative and remarkably similar literary experiment was boldly undertaken in what have come to be recognized as the foundational documentary accounts of modern Russian and African American cultural nationalism: Fyodor Dostoevsky's *Notes from the House of the Dead* (1862) and W. E. B. DuBois's *The Souls of Black Folk* (1903). This deep affinity is no random coincidence. The intellectual and structural similarities that connect these two influential depictions of a discovered cultural particularism are the result of a long historical "subtext" that prepared the way for the emergence of two distinct but related literatures of ethnic "soul."

Well before the end of the eighteenth century, individual Russian and African American intellectuals had displayed an unquestioned capacity to assimilate the highest standards of European cultural and scientific literacy. But the nineteenth century had raised the question of their races' collective contribution to the advancement of civilization and the growth of a world-historical consciousness. This was the sensitive issue that had irritated into being the first theoretical statements of a manifest destiny for the Russian and the Negro people in the larger evolution of human culture. By the mid–nineteenth century, however, the claim to some specific virtue inherent in the development of the race had become complicated by the long-delayed emancipation of Russian serfs and American slaves. The heightened visibility of an ethnic majority that existed as a benighted feudal underclass, the illiterate Russian *narod* and the black folk of the American South, offered a spectacle and a challenge that their educated brethren could no longer politely ignore. Suddenly a numerically insignificant literate elite of Russians and African Americans was confronted with the vast sociocultural reality of huddled and ignorant masses who were their unlettered brethren. Those who hoped to advocate for their race's privileged destiny now had an immense task before them. They needed to account for the undeniable yet unrecognized cultural particularity of an ancestral underworld that had long been hidden from public view. This daunting responsibility could only be taken up by the most observant and articulate of literary intermediaries and interlopers into that other world, the netherworld of the denigrated folk. Fortunately, both Dostoevsky and DuBois were biographically positioned and temperamentally suited to fulfill this new demand for bold acts of literary ethnography.

The task previously faced by abolitionist Russians and American exslaves had been to invent some adequate means to make credible the unacknowledged human equality of their racially excluded brothers and sisters. The solution to that challenge was a literature devoted to demonstrating the humanity and natural rights of an entire population that had been categorized as subhuman. But with emancipation achieved, a new and, frankly, more complex task of persuasion loomed. Any writing devoted to uncovering a previously veiled legacy of the illiterate folk would need to invent the means to recover this subliterate alternative culture in a readable narrative. This delicate business (and necessary enterprise) was bravely ventured by Dostoevsky and DuBois in their pioneering literary excursions. Both works famously enact what Robert B. Stepto has defined as a "cultural immersion ritual" in which a literate native son undergoes a "descent" into the rich subsoil of a slave culture.[1] Not surprisingly, modern interpretations of both narratives typically perceive in them a deliberate crossing of the boundaries of genre. What at first appears to be a nonfictional documentary examination of the lower depths of a debased subculture gradually takes on the narrative shape of a spiritual autobiography that climaxes with an unanticipated baptism in the submerged culture of an ethnic "soul."[2]

Although now securely canonized as national "classics," both texts are, in fact, rarely read with a careful eye on the integrity of the whole composition. All too often the works have been read and summarized in excerpts that buttress tendentious notions suggesting that each author embraces a single message or occupies a stable ideological position. Conventional wisdom still tends to assume that the cultural aspiration of The House of the Dead and The Souls of Black Folk is to promote an ethnic solidarity, a class-unconscious version of identity politics. Dostoevsky and DuBois are frequently hailed (or railed at) for promoting the

"homecoming" of an alienated intelligentsia to an authentic ethnic identity that was always already embodied in the cultural particularity of the
enslaved native folk. One good reason for conducting a simultaneous
and comparative reexamination of these Russian and African American
prototypes of the literature of ethnic "soul" is to restore a healthy respect
for the sheer complexity of the compositional experiments Dostoevsky
and DuBois were attempting. Neither in their time nor in ours can it be a
simple matter to construct a cultural continuity with a vast population of
kinfolk historically relegated to shadowy existence in an ignored underworld.

Dostoevsky's unprecedented book about the hidden world of a Siberian
convict population is a bewildering first exposure to that "broad Russian
nature" that so astonished Western readers of his later novels. Arrested
and convicted in 1849 for distributing and conspiring to print seditious
literature, it was Dostoevsky's singular fate to be spared execution only
to undergo hard labor and uncomfortable intimacy with a cross-section
of Imperial Russia's designated criminal types.[3] What Dostoevsky ultimately brought forth from his involuntary four-year ordeal in that oddly
representative national microcosm known as Omsk prison was a curiously oblique confessional narrative. *Notes from the House of the Dead* is
itself, in Winston Churchill's quotable phrase about things Russian, "a
riddle wrapped in a mystery inside an enigma." At first glance, the book
appears to be a thinly disguised autobiographical fiction. Yet it is a
weirdly distorted mask that the author has chosen to wear. Dostoevsky's
truthful narrative is cast in the form of a posthumous document left behind by an ex-prisoner who has not lived to publish his own unedited
tale. In several senses, then, these "notes of a nonsurvivor" amount to
a double-tongued account of life among the legally dead population of
Russia.

One initial riddle about the book is, perhaps, easily understood. Dostoevsky's fictionalization of his own thickly detailed memoirs of Omsk
prison was, from the beginning, an open secret. By adopting an inten-
tionally transparent disguise Dostoevsky was able to hint at his real authorship while also taking certain liberties with biographical and factual truths to protect himself against censorship.[4] Certainly no educated
reader in 1860, when the first installment appeared, failed to guess that
this authoritative insider's account of Siberian convict life had been

penned by the recently returned political prisoner and acclaimed writer, Fyodor Dostoevsky. But what is less easy to understand is the particular mystery in which the author wrapped the riddle of his disguise. Why had Dostoevsky chosen to cloak his actual identity as a political prisoner in the unseemly garb of the tormented criminal, Goryanchikov, a wife-murderer who completes his ten-year sentence yet remains a gloomy settler living on the outskirts of the prison town? Why burden the ethnographic record with the voice of a self-castigating social outcast?

Stranger yet, this mysterious Goryanchikov was himself wrapped inside a further enigma. Dostoevsky took the trouble to invent a frame narrator who serves to introduce the primary document. The reader first encounters an unnamed gentleman neighbor who has rescued Goryanchikov's notes on penal servitude but who also manages to question their reliability by referring to his own editorial deletions from them of "strange, terrible reminiscences, inserted irregularly and convulsively, as if under some compulsion."[5] Although Dostoevsky had the opportunity, in 1875, to revise and reprint his book, it is worth noting that he took no action to remove the editorial frame, nor did he "correct" the startling disruptions of logical coherence that are characteristic of Goryanchikov's often contradictory ruminations on the denizens of the Dead House. It must, therefore, be assumed that Dostoevsky intended *The House of the Dead* to obstruct the reader's easy access to available truths and expected it, indeed, to introduce "a completely new world, as yet unknown" in a series of highly problematic "remarks about a lost people" (394).

How, then, might one explain, despite all the textual interruptions and ruptures of logic, the long-standing tradition of reading *The House of the Dead* as if it were a transparent reflection of Dostoevsky's spiritual rebirth as a folk-identified Russian nationalist? It would be the height of presumption to dismiss generations of readers as "vulgar idealists" who have simply ignored or bracketed the unstable narrator who shoulders the heavy burden of the prison's distorted humanity. The hefty three-hundred-page transcript that Goryanchikov/Dostoevsky left for posterity poses a genuine interpretive challenge: at various moments, it takes on the appearance of quite different forms of encoded speech. One generic code that the narrative appears to observe is that of a Dantesque allegory of descent and resurrection from a purgatorial inferno. Both in its larger narrative structure and in several paradigmatic scenes, Goryanchikov's ostensibly mundane document seems deftly composed to reveal the hidden lineaments of a spiritual history.

The House of the Dead is divided into two unequal but complementary parts. The opening section describes in detail the first impressions of the locale and desperate characters encountered in Goryanchikov's initial year of imprisonment, a long December-to-December winter of discontent. The second portion collects reflective observations and recorded conversations from an entire decade of incarceration, with an emphasis on certain metaphorically and literally unfettered moments; it ends with a December exit from prison that appears to culminate a preceding series of ritual and symbolic resurrections. Each part builds from a nearly total immersion in hellish captivity toward religiously tinged moments of transcendence. The first year climaxes with a famous bathhouse scene that is both a Dantesque inferno of steaming bodies and a touching travesty of the biblical Christ's washing of feet, and it concludes with lengthy depictions of the Feast of Christmas and a liberating "stage show" that exhibits the genuine talent and traditional genius of Russian folk theatricals. The second section begins in the prison hospital's rank atmosphere of diseased and bruised bodies and moves outdoors to air some refreshing tales of attempted protest and escape. These gestures toward transcendence of confinement are preceded by a depiction of Eastertide hopes of rebirth and a famous scene in which a wounded eagle is released by an ecstatic community of prisoners. The book concludes with "the wondrous minute" of Goryanchikov's literal unfettering and his apparent emancipation into "new life and resurrection from the dead" (702). Mutual blessings are exchanged as the hardened convicts gruffly celebrate the gentleman prisoner's release, and the gentleman in turn releases his benediction on Russia's "lost folk": "It's necessary to tell the whole truth: this was a remarkable people. They were, perhaps, the most gifted and strong among our people" (701). It would appear, then, that Dostoevsky's sequence of prison notes is structured to convey the spiritual pilgrimage of a penitent nobleman who recovers his fullest humanity in the company of his ostracized and degraded Russian brethren.[6]

All this may be looked at another way, however. As a problematically framed confessional narrative, Dostoevsky's text resists such redemptive coherence. Just as Goryanchikov's official status as a wife-murderer or as a "political" criminal is left unresolved, his position within the prison population as a fellow convict or an "outcast" is in constant flux. The edited manuscript's veiled narrative of a pilgrim's progress is inconveniently shackled to a distressing introduction that subjects the book's final redemptive moment to the disedifying spectacle of a Goryanchikov who was freed only to die unfettered in guilt-stricken torment and spiritual isolation. Moreover, a close inspection of the prisoner's memoir reveals a pattern of radically unstable generalizations and patent contradictions that are acknowledged in occasional passages that despair of capturing the elusive nature of the fettered folk. Based on this evidence, Russian and Western critics have recently become much more sensitive to an aesthetics of disorder actively at work in Dostoevsky's text. In the words of V. A. Tunimanov, the narrator's extended monologue is "disconnected, adogmatic"; wholly unlike Tolstoyan discourse, all aphorisms and generalizations are nested in contingencies, so that "deductions and definitions are important but no less substantive are nuances, exceptions, and digressions."[7] What emerges from this discourse-centered reading of *The House of the Dead* is a rather surprising linkage between Dostoevsky's account of the underworld of the Russian folk and the chaotic, tormented irrationalism that would soon find its voice in *Notes from Underground*.

There is, then, a sharp dissonance between readings of the Dostoevsky/Goryanchikov memoir that choose to underline either moments of communion or moments of rupture between the outcast nobleman and the imprisoned folk. This interpretive gap is a direct result of the unmediated contradictions that distinguish (or mar) the prisoner's narrative. For example, an early and often quoted assertion from *The House of the Dead* holds that "Man is a creature who accustoms himself to everything and that, I think, is the best definition of him" (396). But within the space of six pages, a bewildered Goryanchikov is also observing that "often a man will endure several years patiently, resigning himself, will bear the cruellest punishments and then suddenly will erupt over some trifle, some nonsense, almost over nothing at all" (402). Between these two contradictory statements the reader encounters a long paragraph that begins with a remark about the "glaring commonality among this strange family" (399) and ends with the comment: "They all had been gathered here against their wills; they all were strangers to one another" (401). This notable narrative quirk of accumulating mutually exclusive assertions about the common features of the convict population con-

tinues throughout the text; eventually, the wary reader begins to anticipate the violation of all norms and the reversal of all expectations. Ironically, everything is volatile in this house of the dead. The communal joy
and shared reverence of the Christmas celebration gives way to reeling
drunkenness and depressed stupor; seemingly abject creatures suddenly
steal Bibles and flash daggers; the most monstrous criminals occasionally display surprising deference and decorum. Even when the narrator
claims to experience close communion with the assembled convicts during the Lenten prayers, his pronouns display a telling vacillation, an uncertainty of identification:

> Now it was my turn to stand in their place. . . . we were fettered and ex-
> posed to public disgrace; everybody drew aside from us, everyone even
> seemed to fear us, and each time they gave us alms I remember I found it
> somehow pleasant, even taking a subtle and peculiar strange satisfaction
> in it. "If that's how it is, so be it," I thought. The convicts prayed very fer-
> vently, and each time they came to church each one of them would bring
> his pittance for a votary candle or to contribute to the daily collection. "I
> also am a man," is perhaps what he thought or felt as he made his dona-
> tion, "everyone is equal before God." We took communion at early mass.
> (626)

This passage, like so much else in Goryanchikov's notes, nervously
hovers between a sense of ostensible belonging and inner dividedness.[8]
From this, it would appear that even the syntax of *The House of the Dead*
reiterates Russia's painful cultural separation between a literate, alienated elite and the folk underclass with which it desires communion. In a
rare moment of reflexive consciousness, Dostoevsky's narrator is forced
to abandon his passion for reliable generalizations: "Here I have been
trying to make our entire prison submit to categories, but is that really
possible? Reality is endlessly various when compared to the deductions
of abstract thought, even those that are the most clever, and it will not
tolerate sharp or grand distinctions. Reality strives toward fragmenta-
tion" (654). But if such be the case, how can Goryanchikov or his readers
possibly hope to derive a yearned-for sense of national identity from his
descent into the hidden and chaotic underworld of Russia in fetters?

   Each section of the prison memoir features one chapter in which Goryanchikov relates an unusual moment of relationship to the entire folk
collective acting in unison. It would appear, however, that these two ex-

emplary episodes cancel each other out, since one presents Goryanchikov's inclusion in the community of captives and the other dramatizes his exclusion. Taken together, these climactic scenes seem deliberately positioned as parallel and contradictory. But since they also prove to be mutually illuminating, it may be that Dostoevsky provides his readers a means to emerge from the dark labyrinth of his narrative with some flicker of revealed truth. First, though, it must be noted that each chapter begins with a signpost of irony and ambiguity. The chapter that recounts the integration of Goryanchikov into the collective prison culture is titled "Predstavlenie." This is usually translated as "The Stage Show," since the chapter does, indeed, focus on the folk theatricals that enliven the entire prison in the Christmas season. But the title might better be rendered as "The Presentation" to capture the double denotation in Russian of a theatrical performance and/or the delivery of a thesis. What the chapter actually stages is a representation of the artistic traditions of folk theater along with Goryanchikov's attempt to represent the Russian "soul." In a parallel manner, the chapter that features the ostracism of Goryanchikov from the prison collective is also headed by a word that carries a dual implication. It is titled "Pretenziia" and usually is translated as "The Complaint" to refer to its central event: the prison population's unexpected petition to the authorities for better treatment. But the chapter also might well be titled "The Grievance" to indicate the narrator's prominent protest against the insurmountable barrier the prisoners erect to exclude him from solidarity with their complaint. We see dramatized both a collective and an individual "pretense" for claiming the attention and regard of the outside world. Etymologically, there is an identity between the two complaints that are voiced. To put it perhaps too simply, both Goryanchikov and the folk are "grieved" parties who suffer from an arbitrary separation that cruelly constricts their lives.

The chapter known as "The Stage Show" is centrally positioned as the final chapter of the first section; with ten chapters preceding and following, it is literally at the core of Goryanchikov's memoir. It has also been suggested that this chapter is the ideological nucleus of the work, containing the moment when the "outer, superficial husk" is removed from the Russian people's essence as they perform, in time-honored fashion, ritual spectacles of excess and transfiguration.[9] Goryanchikov is, indeed, much taken with the special form of vitality released among the imprisoned folk when they are allowed to practice their traditional arts. It is in this portion of the prison notes that Goryanchikov first conceives an idea of what the crude folk instruments were capable of expressing: "I understood perfectly well for the first time that there really was something endlessly riotous and bold in the bravura of the Russian dance melodies" (552). It is here also where the deep-rooted conventions of the Russian folk theater come to the surface; Goryanchikov is exhilarated by the improvised miming and extravagant cross-dressing that accompany the playing out of the formulaic ancient dramas. In Goryanchikov's own "presentation," the theatricals provide the narrative occasion for displaying the yearning toward self-transcendence, the desire for a just assessment of performance that he deems characteristic of the common folk: "Imagine [*predstav'te*] the prison, its fetters and servitude, the long doleful years stretching ahead, its life monotonous as waterdrops on a dank autumn day—and then suddenly all these oppressed and confined men being allowed to unwind for a time . . . to construct a whole theater. . . . It is not a fantasy of my imagination. . . . each individual underwent a moral transformation, even if it only lasted for several minutes" (553; 561). What is presented is a brief glimpse of a collective imagination that resists social limits and crosses boundaries; a population of branded convicts constructs a realm of carnivalesque transcendence, even if only in stolen ephemeral moments within a harshly confined existence.

The chapter devoted to "The Complaint" would seem to revoke this redemptive vision of spiritual unanimity. The burden of the narrator's complaint is not only that the assembled convicts cannot imagine a commonality of being and purpose that would bind the Russian gentleman into their collective protest. Worse even than his personal ostracism is his grievous awareness that an "abyss" (*bezdna*) finally separates the educated class from the ungraspable folk: "Not even if you associate with the common people all your life, mingle with them for forty years every day . . . will you ever come to know their essence. Everything will be an optical illusion and nothing more" (656). The real, the substantial complaint in this chapter is, then, that even a fellow Russian who falls into the house of the dead from the outside cannot merge with the souls of the fettered folk. Yet this same chapter that apparently foreswears any reliable understanding of the Russian underclass also makes a credible pretense of accounting for the volatility of these Russian folk:

The endless restlessness that expressed itself silently but evidently, the strange fevered impatience of involuntarily expressed hopes that were at times so unfounded that they verged on delirium and that, most strikingly, seemed frequently to persist in the most sober intellect—all this lent an unusual aspect to the place, so much so in fact that these traits, perhaps, constituted its most characteristic feature. . . . Here everyone was a dreamer. (652)

This passage reveals, and not for the first time, Dostoevsky's great discovery in the previously inconceivable underworld to which he had been consigned—namely, that the irrepressible unpredictability and psychological "maximalism" of the shackled Russian folk was a culturally constructed consequence of the involuntary servitude imposed by the state on serfs and convicts alike.

With equal plausibility, both "resurrectionist" and "deconstructionist" readings appear to be invited by Dostoevsky's baffling prison memoir. Yet what emerges from the carefully structured tension between the two is one stable, if uncomfortable, leitmotif that is strung throughout the narrative. This note is struck early and late, and it allows for the possibility of a destabilizing generalization about the millions of confined Russian souls who inhabit the "house of the dead" and who constitute the majority culture of a hidden folk nation.

As early as the first three days of his confinement, at the time of his "first contact with the folk," Goryanchikov suspects that he is becoming "a convict just like them." Interestingly, the formal Russian term for serfdom, *krepost'noe pravo*, literally meant "fortress law." Dostoevsky's subtle conflation of the Russian *narod* in general with the category of a prisoner undergoing involuntary servitude (*katorzhnik*) makes a point that keeps expanding and gathering larger consequences: "Convicts are great dreamers. . . . The whole meaning of the word 'convict' [*arestant*] signifies a man deprived of his will, but . . . he already acts *willfully*" (472). During his confinement, Goryanchikov becomes amazed witness to sudden eruptions of personality that assert, if nothing else, a "phantom freedom": "All the while the probable cause of this sudden outburst in a man from whom one would least expect it is nothing more than an anguished, convulsive manifestation of personhood, an instinctive longing for selfhood, a desire to reclaim one's degraded self. . . . it is not a matter of reason, but of convulsions" (473). However unaccountable the abrupt shifts of behavior and however erratic the forms of self-transcendence encountered in the house of the dead, what remains in full view thoughout Dostoevsky's disruptive narrative is an allegorical figuration of Russia's apocalyptic, transgressive folk "soul." [10]

Nowhere is this recurrent assertion of utopian undercurrents within the unsightly, disfigured underworld of Russians in chains more evident than in the marvelous scene where the narrator and a motley crew of convicts stand in fused fascination before the spectacle of Isai Fomich's athletic Sabbath prayer:

> "Look, the spirit's seized him," the convicts used to say. I once asked Isai Fomich what the sobs and sudden solemn transitions to happiness and bliss meant. . . . He explained to me at once that the weeping and sobbing denoted the idea of the loss of Jerusalem . . . but that at the moment of the most intense sobbing, he, Isai Fomich, *must suddenly*, as if by chance, remember (this *suddenly* was also prescribed by the Law) that there exists a prophecy of the return of the Jews to Jerusalem. . . . Isai Fomich was extremely fond of this *sudden* transition and of its absolute obligatoriness. (513)

The point of this passage is not, for once, to underline the Jewish "otherness" of Isai Fomich but to insinuate the ethnic identification of the assembled Russian prisoners, despite racial prejudice, with the ecstatic Hebraic anticipation of a promised national restoration. In the midst of captivity and humiliation, true believers enact sudden, convulsive turns from lamentation to exultation; one is obliged not to let go a long-deferred dream of liberation. This scene, however momentary, indicates a much larger Russian phenomenon of cultural transference and ambivalent identification with the Jews not unlike the profound emotional attachment of the African American "sorrow songs" to the psalms of the children of Israel. [11] What is also signified here is the presence of a redemptionist hope that is ironically confined within a narrative that embodies an aesthetics of disorder. Dostoevsky's fettered folk of Russia, like the exiled Jews, feel compelled to envisage and enact an impossible, cataclysmic "change of fortune." *Notes from the House of the Dead* is a text that confirms the former prisoner's hard-won conviction that the Russian folk mentality resides in an apocalyptic history that is decidedly non-Hegelian. [12] It is precisely those who have been denied personal or historic agency, those who have been marked as last and least and lowest, who seem destined to express the widest extremes of an un-encompassable human nature. Dostoevsky's astonished and terrifying first encounter with the "broad Russian soul" was mythically embodied in the oblique confessional autobiography he stubbornly retrieved from his immersion in the vast underworld of an unemancipated people.

The remarkable complexity of the book W. E. B. DuBois assembled in 1903 when he was invited by a Chicago publisher to gather together some of his "fugitive essays" has only recently come into full view. Although long regarded as a seminal work in the construction of a modern African American cultural identity, the formal innovation and sophisticated argument of *The Souls of Black Folk* has been acknowledged only in the aftermath of many attempts to recruit it for narrower ideological ends than those it serves. Carefully composed as a strategically deployed sequence of documentary and autobiographical testimony written by an insider within America's "veiled" Negro population, DuBois's text exerts great demands on readers attuned to black-and-white editorials on the "race problem." We now know that DuBois selectively adapted eight of over three dozen previously printed journal articles, added five wholly new pieces of "subjective" writing, and proceeded to organize a fourteen-chapter excursion into the notably plural "souls" of black folk.[13] He visibly signaled that his book had been organized with both "Forethought" and an "Afterthought," and he also indicated in a unique system of double-noted epigraphs (one poetic, one musical) that his own writing had emerged from a dialogue between literate and oral sources. Incredible as it may seem, much of this strenuous compositional effort was love's labor lost. Generations of readers have nearly succeeded in contextualizing DuBois's text out of existence, either seizing on his prominent dispute with Booker T. Washington or dwelling on his "immersion" in the rural South to make an available ideology out of a brave expedition into the hitherto veiled underworld of a divided racial consciousness. No less than in Dostoevsky's case, DuBois's newfound intimacy with his suppressed brethren resulted in a double-tongued acknowledgment of a hidden ethnic "soul."

The belated and long overdue attention to the artistic organization of *The Souls of Black Folk* is the fortunate result of a stalemate between two rival readings of the cultural politics of DuBois's influential book.

For understandable reasons, there has been an unresolved tug-of-war between two deeply entrenched camps of opinion claiming DuBois as either a "civilizationist" or an "essentialist" in his racial thinking. The first party duly notes DuBois's unambiguous opposition to Booker T. Washington's Tuskegee platform of vocational education and political accommodation in Reconstruction America; it also points to the simultaneous publication in 1903 of "The Talented Tenth," DuBois's openly elitist call for an educated Negro vanguard to raise up a black citizenry to civil equality. The second group rightly notes DuBois's unprecedented proclamation of a distinctive African American identity founded on an extension into modern times of the expressive powers of a slave culture that had transformed and transcended all attempts to rob it of its native voice. Unquestionably, *The Souls of Black Folk* speaks of race progress in a dark hour, but it is less than clear whether its primary hope for collective salvation rests with the acculturated "Negro Saxon" elite or with a growing contingent of reracinated soul-brothers and soul-sisters. A book famous for its progressive appeals to civilization and uplift also undeniably urges the cultivation of a racial aesthetic rooted in an organic folkness.[14] On the horns of that dilemma has arisen a pitched battle to appropriate the legacy of DuBois's foundational narrative of African American ethnicity. Can this deliberately double-voiced text be read, as Robert Stepto suggests, as a paradigmatic and fertilizing "cultural immersion ritual," or might it be seen, as Paul Gilroy argues, as "a narrative of emergence from rather than immersion in racial particularity"?[15] Clearly, much is now at stake in venturing an answer to that question, yet for all its current urgency it should not strike us as a question DuBois himself failed to grasp.

Thirty years ago it was still possible to complain that only "an occasional appreciative glance" had been given to the *literary* aspect of *The Souls of Black Folk*.[16] That is no longer true, yet there is far less consensus about the aesthetic organization and discursive peculiarities of DuBois's book than about its thematic development. Virtually everyone agrees that the book is a three-part sequence of essays that exhibits the history of being black in America, the sociology of bondage in the New South, and the spirituality of the black folk. Small variations exist as to where the precise boundaries of each section are to be drawn, and different readers draw different implications from the increasingly poetic and tragic tonality of the concluding cluster of elegiac chapters. What should elicit particular attention, however, is rarely given thorough consideration—namely, the interpretive difference created by the new insertions and aesthetic reshapings in the 1903 sequence of DuBoisian materials. As in the case of *The House of the Dead*, the deliberately odd framing and fashioning of the text tells us more about the hidden world it strives to express than its separate parts by themselves reveal.

It matters that DuBois chose to address his readers first with the "Forethought." More precise than an introduction or preface, a "forethought" denotes thinking beforehand, careful anticipation, provident care—in short, a duly deliberate, even wary approach to an act of speaking. And what is it that we are told in advance of reading about the souls of black folk? "Herein lie buried many things which if read with patience may show the strange meaning of being black here in the dawning of the Twentieth Century. This meaning is not without interest to you, Gentle Reader; for the problem of the Twentieth Century is the problem of the color-line." [17] This is, as it were, an invitation to excavation; "we" are modestly but firmly urged by DuBois to devote ourselves to a labor of patient attention, "studying my words with me," for we are hardly disinterested parties in this process of examining the meaning of words uttered from behind a color-line. We are told that our patience "may show the strange meaning" we seek; there can be no guarantee, since, at best, the author can honestly offer us but a sketch "in vague, uncertain outline" of a still-cloaked spiritual world. "Leaving then the world of the white man, I have stepped within the Veil, raising it that you may view faintly its deeper recesses. . . . need I add that I who speak here am bone of the bone and flesh of the flesh of them that live within the Veil?" DuBois has, indeed, had the forethought to warn us that all speech about this subject, the inner reality of black American life, is necessarily "veiled" and partial speech. Even so, we cannot fail to be interested.

As if to confirm immediately the obscure and coded meanings that will require our patience, the first chapter (titled "Of Our Spiritual Strivings") is headed by the first of many juxtaposed citations from Western poetry and black spirituals. Arthur Symons's plangently voiced thirst of the heart for rest is a "call" met (for those who can read and recognize musical notation) by the "response" of black folk: "Nobody Knows the Trouble I've Seen." In each subsequent chapter these antiphonal responses must be read alertly; the "dialogue" between the poetic stanzas and musical fragments conveys mixed messages. In the troubled fourth chapter that interrogates "the Meaning of Progress," Schiller's tribute in German verse to "The Maid of Orleans" (which is obscure enough to most gentle readers) is answered by the opening bars of "My Way Is Cloudy." Even Eric Sundquist, who has done so much archival work to identify the musical texts evoked by DuBois's notations, somewhat underestimates the challenge thrown at the "cultivated" reader by these double epigraphs.[18] If ideally one should "hear" the song lyrics that are not printed on the page, it is not enough to be literate and a sight reader of music; the DuBoisian epigraphs task readers to be fully bicultural, proficient in two media of expression and able to identify the unnamed source of each poetic and musical citation. In addition, we are invited to be good eavesdroppers on the implied conversation across the color-line that separates the worlds of the two epigraphs. Very few readers, then or now, could possibly rise to such feats of multiliteracy, but that seems hardly the real point. The "device" of the double epigraphs is doing much more than subversively signifying the cultural equivalence of black spirituals and Western poetry; it is also indicating the inadequacy of standard literacy and pointing readers in the direction of a yet-to-be-attained goal of multicultural awareness. As early as the first chapter and the first epigraphs, *The Souls of Black Folk* is striving to tell us that the book we are trying to read is only partly about black-white equivalents or ethnic authenticity. Rather, it is directly presenting us with a challenge to acknowledge the presence and pressure of an "other" deep within any formulation about "the meaning of being black in America." If we can intuit the implicit dialogue between the epigraphs, we can begin to comprehend what it means to be African and American, to be someone who inhabits a single space in which two cultures are separately voiced.

DuBois surely intended his opening chapter as a "keynote" address or, in his words, as a brief sketch in large outline of what he will "tell again in many ways . . . that men may listen to the striving in the souls of black folk" (44). The chapter announces itself as an experiment in responding to the seldom-answered "real question" posed to every Negro: "How does it feel to be a problem?" (37). Appropriately, it is this chapter that famously enunciates DuBois's concept of history's mixed blessing to the Negro race and to African Americans in particular: "double consciousness." DuBois deliberately revises Hegel's naming of six successive "world-historical" peoples, adding the Negro as a "sort of seventh son, born with a veil, and gifted with second sight in this American world" (38).[19] To be born a modern Negro is, then, to inherit an unsolicited prophetic destiny, much like infants with cauls veiling them from the outside world were believed to possess visionary power. Historic circumstances had thrust on American blacks an inner doubleness, a self-consciousness experienced both within and underneath a veiled identity, a culturally mediated "twoness" of self-perception that could not help but strive to express a higher synthesis of its divided consciousness.

But this veiled existence is not so easily surmounted, nor can it simply be unveiled by a black artist: "The beauty revealed to him was the soul-beauty of a race which his larger audience despised, and he could not articulate the message of another people" (39). In America's racist climate, the expressive power of a dark race had been effectively obscured; its speaking voice had been muted by the oppressive weight of a Western standard of literacy outspoken in its denigrating words about black inferiority. In this peculiar context, African American words were forced to do double duty, seeking to be comprehensible within a standard national discourse even as they begged to differ from it. The souls of black folk, DuBois would thus have us believe, strive to express themselves in two distinct tongues: "there are to-day no truer exponents of the pure human spirit of the Declaration of Independence than the American Negroes; there is no true American music but the wild sweet melodies of the Negro slave" (43). However obscurely, the agenda of DuBois's notes from the black underworld had been set forth. African Americans could be identified as a people shaped by history to speak to the world in a double discourse of human rights and spiritual rites. But this complexity of expression gives rise to a contested group identity as difficult to read as Dostoyevsky's apparently unresolved tension between an anarchic and a redemptive reading of the folk soul of Russia.

It is useful to remember that DuBois entered the Southern homes of black folk as a schoolteacher. He spoke, without apology, the emancipating language of literacy and social uplift that had been brought to former slaves from his native New England by the Freedmen's Bureau. He saw himself as an agent of human advancement among his brutalized and ignorant brethren, the illiterate black "serfs" of the not-so-new South. He was destined, however, to learn that "character" and refinement also existed in the residue of a Southern slave culture that exerted an unaccountable attraction, considering that he had never been directly exposed to it and regarded it as undeniably regressive in a modern world. Little wonder, then, that "the meaning of progress" came under special interrogation as DuBois contemplated the impact of education on the world of black folk. Puzzling over progress becomes a preoccupation midway through DuBois's textual journey. He inserted one "new" chapter, "On the Wings of Atalanta," at a strategic point, mediating between a painful review of his own educational career in the South and his anti-Tuskegee manifesto, "Of the Training of Black Men." Irony and ambivalence are strongly present as DuBois measures his own performance as an agent of "progress" and then takes the measure of Atlanta as the epicenter of Southern Progressivism. The fourth chapter, "Of the Meaning of Progress," focuses on his favorite pupil, Josie, whose devotion to DuBois's disinterested pursuit of learning is only surpassed by her selfless female devotion to patriarchal family values. She dies young and unfulfilled, exhausted in her pursuit of higher learning and worn down by the struggle to alleviate her family's constant debts and woes. Leaving behind the mixed record of his schoolhouse career, DuBois utters a stream of uncertainties: "How shall man measure Progress there where the dark-faced Josie lies? . . . —is it the twilight of nightfall or the flush of some faintly-dawning day? Thus sadly musing, I rode to Nashville in the Jim Crow car" (81). The last sentence is laden with characteristic verbal mischief: DuBois the classicist "muses" as he rides the rails of a segregated engine of progress away from his erstwhile pupils.

The Atlanta/Atalanta chapter, which immediately follows, appears to continue this uncertainty about the location of cultural progress: "South of the North, yet north of the South, lies the City of a Hundred Hills, peering out from the shadows of the past into the promise of the future" (82). The classical scholar reappears here to shape an allegory that bedecks the capital of the New South in the mythic garb of the fleet-footed maiden who stooped to the temptation of a mortal's golden apple and lost the favor of the gods. Eager to race into the future, the city is a new Atalanta poised to leap ahead; this time, she may once again lower herself to acquire material gain, or she may choose to stand tall, occupying the educational high ground of Atlanta University in its speculative quest for timeless universals. DuBois's choice is, of course, all too clear. Black men, he informs us in the following chapter, must be trained to rise to the heights of a manly disinterestedness. Venal self-interest may bring wealth, but it cannot gain the respect that educational equality alone can achieve for blacks who strive for full citizenship.

DuBois hears echoing from slave times forward the plea of disregarded black voices, "the confused, half-conscious mutter of men who are black and whitened, crying "Liberty, Freedom, Opportunity—vouchsafe to us, O boastful World, the chance of living men!" (91). Trapped by history between two worlds (black and whitened), the Negroes of the diaspora must insist they, too, are entitled to the universal rights of Man as defined by Western humanism. It would appear, then, that a black soul can hope to "dwell above the Veil" only if winged with the rhetoric of a classical education. Or so it might seem if the reader chooses to hear nothing but DuBois's famous polemic against the "Atlanta Compromise" and Booker T. Washington's degrading vocationalism. But the reader who has studied patiently "the Meaning of Progress" and observed the self-irony and humility reflected in the Northern teacher's account of life among the lowly will not think it likely that DuBois wishes us to believe that the souls of black folk must be "whitened" to achieve visible dignity.

Indeed, even if individual Negroes learn to speak in the tongue of Cicero, the "sons of Master and Man" are no longer able to acknowledge one another's features beneath the descending veil of segregation: "There is almost no community of intellectual life or point of transference where the thoughts and feelings of one race can come into direct contact and sympathy with thoughts and feelings of the other" (144). Most of the "new" material added to DuBois's sequence of essays in 1903 expresses despair in face of the frustrated promise of race leaders, of the "talented tenth," and instead strives to give literate expression to the eloquence of the oddly encouraging "sorrow songs" that moved weary hearts and enabled generations of black folk to transcend despair. DuBois's text culminates with three powerful threnodies to lost heroes of black advancement: the autobiographical lament for his prematurely dead "first-born son"; the eulogy to the race leader, Alexander Crummell; and the fictional requiem to overeducated John, a secular "baptist" whose coming is ahead of time and who is spurned by blacks and lynched by whites for his zealous pursuit of uplift.[20] Significantly, these painful black losses are framed between the two chapters that introduce and conclude DuBois's discussion of the Negro genius for religious expression ("Of the Faith of the Fathers" and "The Sorrow Songs"). At first ambivalently and then more confidently, DuBois's book moves toward its climactic discovery of a soulful medium of expression.

No less so than Dostoevsky in the presence of the excesses of the unfettered "broad Russian soul," DuBois is at first awestruck when exposed to the frenzy of a Southern black revival: "A sort of suppressed terror hung in the air and seemed to seize us, — a pythian madness, a demoniac possession, that lent terrible reality to song and word" (148). One can note with amusement the presence of the cautious classicist in this sentence, making learned allusions to the ancient world even as he is swept into a shared seizure. But what is truly distinctive about DuBois's baptism in the convulsive spirit of the folk religion is his immediate perception that this survival of slavery is "the one expression of [the Negro's] higher life" (149). The rhythmic singing of the slave culture is deemed nothing less than a transcendent articulation of the aspirations of a devoiced people: "Sprung from the African forests . . . it was adapted, changed, and intensified by the tragic soul-life of the slave, until, under the stress of law and whip, it became the one true expression of a people's sorrow, despair, and hope" (149). To his credit, DuBois was among the very first African American intellectuals to have an ear for what black spirituals were signifying. Even that, however, does not tell the whole story.

W. E. B. DuBois was the first American writer to seek to reach the literate public's ear with an unapologetic representation of the double-tongued speech of African American people. He understood that no one tongue, neither the elevated language of formal equivalence nor the denigrated and obscure black vernacular, could convey fully the "veiled" reality of the meaning of being black in America. Only a discourse that experimented with uttering in print simultaneously the several *souls* of black America could do justice to the cultural breadth and human reality of modern Negro life. Unlike Dostoevsky, who strove to depict a transgressive Russian "soul" within an apocalyptic metahistorical canvas, DuBois devoted himself to a conscientious effort to transcribe the several "strivings" variously expressed in the souls of black folk.

In the memorable first words of his final chapter, DuBois associates his own writing with the illiterate eloquence of a fettered folk's tongue:

They that walked in darkness sang songs in the olden days — Sorrow Songs — for they were weary at heart. And so before each thought that I have written in this book I have set a phrase, a haunting echo of these weird old songs in which the soul of the black slave spoke to men. Ever since I was a child these songs have stirred me strangely. They came out of the South unknown to me, one by one, and yet at once I knew them as of me and of mine. (204)

The deracinated Northern leader of the Negro vanguard movingly reads his own text's expressive performance as an act of solidarity with his Southern spiritual predecessors. Here, the author of *The Souls of Black Folk* announces himself as a fellow "sorrow singer," joined flesh to flesh with all the previous generations of "children of disappointment" who rose in song above their defeats. Paradoxically, those who can sing of sorrow possess a power of transcendent expression even as they speak in eulogy and elegy. It would appear, then, that DuBois is both uncovering and recovering a racial gift, reclaiming the ethnic privilege of a soulful discourse that black folk alone command and comprehend.

Yet DuBois also acknowledges that any truly transcendent form of expression surmounts conditions and circumstance; it must necessarily cross over and go beyond the cultural and linguistic restrictions that gave rise to its articulation. The black spirituals that sing of death and suffering and express a deferred, transfigured hope are "naturally veiled and half articulate," but they have carried the slave's message to the world. DuBois proudly tells of how "the glory of the Jubilee songs passed into the soul of George L. White," the white man "whose life-work was to let those Negroes sing to the world" (186). Ever the teacher, DuBois establishes in his last chapter a musical syllabus for his readers; "ten master songs, more or less" are elevated to canonical status as expressions of the collective speech of the Negro slave. DuBois's taste would later be criticized for its highly selective emphasis on "sorrow songs" and its reliance on inauthentic transcriptions and performances by concert singers, but that criticism fails to appreciate DuBois's commitment to create a recognition of African American culture within a developing and authentically syncretic American civilization. The song-texts made popular by the Fisk singers embodied a commodified black music that through multiple reprintings and performances expanded the cultural power and reach of the original spirituals; these "Europeanized" rewritings and re-voicings of the folk vernacular helped promote an awareness of the true hybridity of a black-inflected American culture.[21] In the chapter devoted to the black sorrow songs, music is allowed to voice strivings that pass beyond the high barriers of language and culture. DuBois "knows the meaning of the music" his grandmother sang in an unknown African tongue, and he claims to hear in "Poor Rosy, poor gal" the same voice that sings in a German folk song (191). The signs are abundant that DuBois contemplates the existence of a universal song discourse that is the vocal writing of a folk's emergent sense of its meaning in the world. With patience, blacks and whites alike may come to perceive the many things buried in the hieroglyphic notations of music's coded speech.

This subliminal song language, no less than the literate discourse of human rights, strives to express the souls of black folk. Both tongues are, as it were, equally "native" to Negroes in America, who speak in two languages simultaneously to those who exist outside the veil imposed by racism. One can only continue to pray, as does DuBois in his "Afterthought," that in time "may infinite reason turn the tangle straight, and these crooked marks on a fragile leaf be not indeed THE END" (217).

The idiosyncratic form and discourse of DuBois's double-tongued narrative implies the dawning of a cultural consciousness as complex and destabilized as Dostoevsky's tragically affirmative encounter with his brethren in the Russian "house of the dead." In their passionately honest transcriptions of notes from the "underworld" of a denigrated Russian and black folk, Dostoevsky and DuBois were making visible in literate form, in "belles lettres," the previously devalued and veiled expressive culture of an ethnic majority still in bondage to the sovereign contempt of modern Western civilization. We would be well advised to pay close attention to the unveiling of ethnic "soul" scripted in these early experimental attempts to construct a modern Russian and African American cultural identity. Neither "essentialist" nor "civilizationist" in ideology, these seminal books are difficult and tellingly impure accounts of a quest for an elusive cultural nationality. If read with patience, these texts may show that the classics of the literature of "soul" are deeply immersed in a bicultural dialogue that speaks to the essence of what it still means to be Russian or black in the contemporary world.

4 RECOVERING THE NATIVE TONGUE

Turgenev, Chesnutt, and Hurston

It is one thing to assert the existence of an alleged cultural particularism in the propositional language of philosophical abstraction or ethnographic commentary. But it is quite another thing to *inscribe* the drama of actual cultural confrontation. Ultimately, there can be no persuasive representation of a distinctive "native" mode of expressivity without creative experiments that replicate an unbridged cultural gap—those linguistic lacunae and cognitive lapses that emanate from exchanges between literate outsiders and indigenous insiders. It is precisely this unresolved and unresolvable interpretive conflict that is embodied and exposed to view in three innovative literary ethnographies penned by Ivan Turgenev (1818–1883), Charles W. Chesnutt (1858–1932), and Zora Neale Hurston (1901–1960). Unlike the exemplary narratives of an emerging national cultural identity unveiled by Dostoevsky and DuBois, each of these regional anthologies of intercultural episodes cunningly undermines the reader's trust in the authority of the literate narrator's guiding voice.

Struggling in 1904 to restrain the didactic tone that was threatening to overwhelm a projected novel about the American South, the accomplished African American writer Charles W. Chesnutt announced to his editor: "If I can handle some of these things in a broad and suggestive way, without disgusting detail—if I could follow even afar off the Russian novelists of the past generation, who made so clear the condition of a debased peasantry in their own land, I might write a great book."[1] Ironically, Chesnutt had already written at the start of his literary career a great if modest book, *The Conjure Woman* (1899), which resembled more closely than he could have realized the remarkable album of rural sketches, *Notes of a Hunter* (1852) with which Ivan Turgenev had established his reputation as an acclaimed master of delicate cultural and environmental observation. Chesnutt's early "conjure tales" have only recently come to be appreciated as important precursors of the creative ethnography so cunningly practiced by Zora Neale Hurston in her unique anthology of African American "lies" and "hoodoo," *Mules and Men* (1935). An ambitious student of the literary marketplace in the heyday of American "local color" regionalism, the young Chesnutt had made a well-calculated decision to exploit (in several senses) the folk idiom spoken by a wise black elder. The wildly imaginative tales spun by Chesnutt's Uncle Julius were quite obviously written in pointed response to the contemporary popularity of Joel Chandler Harris's genial black storyteller, the thoroughly domesticated Uncle Remus. Less obviously, Chesnutt's clever staging of an educated Northerner's encounters with a shrewd "native speaker" from slave times served to transplant on American soil the ingenious master-serf dialogues of Turgenev's famous literary excursion into the unenlightened (and unemancipated) Russian countryside.

In all three works similar structural and biographical peculiarities are in evidence. Composed as quasi-documentary explorations of local cultures, the blurring of the boundary between the imaginary and the verifiable is made thematic by virtue of recurring crises of credibility that punctuate each narrative as a whole. Typographically, each text takes the form of an "intertext" that adjoins the separate orthographies and mentalities of standard and dialect speech communities without integrating them. The three works share another striking oddity as well. These narratives that grant such remarkable autonomy to uneducated "native" speakers were produced by highly educated, professionally trained writers. Turgenev aspired to an academic career in philosophy and had pursued two years of graduate education at the University of Berlin during the high tide of Hegelianism. Hurston was a doctoral candidate in anthropology at Columbia University whose mentor was the eminent Dr. Franz Boas. Charles Chesnutt was a well-schooled pupil of the segregated classical academy of Fayetteville, North Carolina, who kept a private journal throughout the 1880s that has been cited as "a great document of American culture-hunger."[2] In organizing narrative journeys that gave uncustomary attention and deference to illiterate souls among the lowly folk, these three gifted writers were revealing a doubled (and possibly troubled) cultural consciousness.

The cultural anthropologist James Clifford has made the controversial suggestion that all ethnographic writing is necessarily allegorical and redemptive; that is, any narrative that purports to bring an "exotic" culture into textual representation is simultaneously traducing it and saving it, appropriating its treasures and rescuing it for posthumous existence as a literary object lesson.[3] This allegation is especially disturbing because of its implication that the very activity of writing ethnographic narrative promotes the demise of the vital resources and true alterity of another cultural system. But this critique shows little sympathy for the socio-political dilemma faced by writers who are immersed in and supported by the institutional privileges of a literacy that denies positive substance and worth to an undifferentiated "primitive" mass of ignorant peasants and peons. Such writers, if they happen to dissent from the complacencies of the educated, must feel an imperative need to dramatize the not-fully-comprehensible experience of confronting a distinctive vernacular culture. That, as I understand it, is the fundamental activity undertaken by those Russian and African American writers who strove to compose a literature that would convey the unmastered tongue, the *speaking* "soul," of an unlettered folk culture.

A wholly original genre of Russian writing was initiated with the publication in 1852 of Ivan Turgenev's carefully compiled album of twenty-two rural sketches. Titled *Zapiski okhotnika* (*Notes of a Hunter*), the work signaled the beginning of many such narrative expeditions into the environment and ecology of the Russian hinterland. The immense appeal of this genre of the "journey to the interior" obviously derived from the widespread anxiety of an urban-dwelling landholding aristocracy and literate intelligentsia that sought, out of guilt and self-interest, more intimate knowledge of the masses and the vastness over which it claimed custodial rights. Turgenev's particular choice of a huntsman narrator had even wider implications, however. In Russian, *okhota* signifies both the hunt and any passionate desire, so Turgenev's narrative persona, his rural rambler, is both a hunter and a lover who stalks the Russian countryside hoping to capture by stealth natural creatures who elude him. It matters, too, that this narrative hunt had firm biographical grounding in an author who was both an avid sportsman and a disillusioned philosopher. Turgenev's remark in 1842 upon qualifying for a master's degree already portended his defection from Idealism and abstraction: "I have passed my philosophy examination in brilliant fashion—that is to say I babbled on about various generalities—and pleased my professors no end, although I am certain that all specialized scholars (historians, mathematicians, etc.) could not but inwardly despise both philosophy and me; and indeed I would despise them if they did not despise me."[4] From the very beginning of Turgenev's composition of his hunter's notes we can detect an individual hunting for a manner of narrating; each sketch is an occasion for testing the limits of literacy and its conventions.[5]

The first episode in Turgenev's album, "Khor and Kalinych," was also the first written. Embedded in the complete itinerary of the hunter's travelogue (which concludes with a similar conjoining of paired types, "Forest and Steppe"), it functions as a keynote to the narrative, setting forth the thematic orchestration of the whole excursion. Here, as elsewhere, the narrator's quest for game causes him quite literally to stumble across unanticipated characters and scenes from the Russian interior whose puzzling features he tries to comprehend. Turgenev provides a carefully structured sequence of significant juxtapositions within and among his sketches, and it is this compositional feature that truly defines the narrative syntax of his book.[6] Moreover, the narrator's authority is frequently subject to structural ironies suggesting that the reader is invited to question the adequacy of the text's resident guide. Turgenev has, in short, gone to great lengths to compile a deliberately problematic manual for reading the lay of the Russian land and the mind of its people. Because of the circumstances surrounding the initial publication of the first sketch, however, it has been possible to misread both "Khor and Kalinych" and the work as a whole.

Assuming that one can be known by the company one keeps, a particular political motivation has been ascribed to the composition of *Notes of a Hunter*. The first sketch appeared in 1847 to help initiate the revival of the progressive journal, *The Contemporary*, and it is well known that the editors urged Turgenev to continue with a series of similar hunter's notes. Given this circumstantial evidence, it has long been tempting to view "Khor and Kalynich" as Turgenev's first contribution to a campaign by liberal Westernizers to advance the cause of emancipation and agrarian reform—in particular, to promote anticollectivist notions about the inalienable "personhood" of each peasant and the higher productivity and worth of the yeoman agriculturalist.[7] Somewhat inconveniently, prominent Slavophiles extended a warm reception to Turgenev's initial sketch, and it has not gone without notice that the "Westernizer" author filled his book's pages with touching evocations of peasant superstitions, fatalisms, and spiritual ecstasies.[8] The contents and implications of Turgenev's microcosm of rural Russia are simply wider than the grasp of the narrator's mind and the ideologies of his time.

"Khor and Kalynich" appears to have not one but two beginnings. The reader encounters two imposing block paragraphs that have been set beside each other without the mortise necessary to secure their connection. The first sentence of the sketch has the semantic "markers" of one familiar contemporary genre: "Whoever has happened to cross over from the Bolkhov district to the Zhizdra region surely will have remarked the sharp differences between the types of people in Orlov province and in Kaluga."[9] Here, the entry into a new territory is accompanied by the impersonal, assured syntax of the writer of a "physiological sketch"; we meet the confident cataloguing of closely observed local phenomena into generalized types or species (*porody*).[10] The rest of the paragraph proceeds to elaborate in a strictly contrastive syntax the neat oppositions of landscape and populace to be found on either side of the county border being crossed. But then comes the lead sentence of the second paragraph: "While out hunting in the fields of the Zhizdra district, I came across and acquainted myself with a local Kaluga landowner, Polutykin, an avid huntsman and, consequently, an excellent fellow" (8). Here intrudes the personal voice and rather erratic verbal mannerisms of a recognizably unreliable narrator; we encounter in the subsequent paragraph the odd logic and chatty familiarity of a local informant who lives comfortably with his grotesque aristocratic neighbor.[11] The narrator's sense of what makes an "excellent fellow" is itself a concoction not terribly unlike the obligatory French cuisine of Polutykin's cook, which "consisted in a complete alteration of the natural taste of each dish." The juxtaposition of these two opening paragraphs has in effect begun *Notes of a Hunter* with an unmediated generic shift. Turgenev's initial narrative gesture has been to dramatize a clash of conventional codes or literary protocols for addressing the enigma of rural Russia.

After the opening cacophony between the voices of the ethnographic typologist and the loose-tongued Gogolian tale-teller, Turgenev's narration wends its gradual way, in an episodic reportorial prose, toward its title encounter with Khor and Kalinych. Clearly, our leisurely stalker of the countryside has a tale of two peasants to deliver, but what is the nature of the conjunction that links them? We have been prepared by the opening paragraph to read the narrative for definitive oppositions that contrast this and that; but the second paragraph has playfully confused qualitative distinctions and indiscriminately linked this and that. We might well wonder what, indeed, is the semantic value of the title's conjunction of Khor *and* Kalinych. Careful readers will not find that basic question easily answered.

Our visit to the prosperous and remarkably roach-free family enterprise that runs on the quitrent system and is manned by Khor's robust "young giants" would seem to fulfill the promise of an announced ethnographic type: the pioneering Kaluga peasant, or *muzhik*. It is the introduction of Kalinych, though, that complicates any conventional expectation of what the Kaluga interior holds. Kalinych shambles into the narrative like a walking contradiction of all categories. This instantly likeable old scout is both master of the local environs and abject bondman to the foolish lord, Polutykin, whom he so amiably suffers. Kalynich's twice-emphasized "meek" (*krotkii*) nature imports into the ethnography of Kaluga province traces of the opposed Orlov type of the unpaid serf laborer, down to and including the cheap bast *lapti* on his feet and his residence in a hovel. The hunter's opening sketch has clearly strayed beyond the strict boundaries it began to delineate in its literary mapping of rural Russia's peasant demography.

Long before we observe the actual conjunction between Khor and Kalinych, the narrator's separate encounters with them accumulate quite a weighty load of contrastive remarks—even "binary oppositions." The reputation of Turgenev's first sketch as a programmatic anti-Slavophile statement derives from one often-quoted passage in which the hunter explicitly summarizes the cultural oppositions he reads into the physiology and behavior of the two peasant types he has come to observe. The rural peasantry of Russia is proclaimed to have generated its very own symmetrical contrast between the "rationalist" and the "romantic" sensibility—Khor was Goethe to Kalinych's Schiller in the initial version of the sketch (394). The hunter is clearly more engaged by the bald-pated argument-loving Khor, whose features remind him of Socrates and whose curiosity about foreigners and transformation of a marshland into a thriving enterprise evokes the primary Russian model of enlightened despotism. In the narrator's considered opinion, the shrewd cleverness of a type like Khor may be taken as proof positive that "the simple intelligent speech of the Russian *muzhik*" confirms the idea that "Peter the Great was predominantly a Russian type of man, Russian especially in his reforms" (18). But by this reading, the hunter's portrait of the Russian interior is primarily the story of Khor, not Kalinych. The sketch reads quite differently, however, when the narrator's editorializing is recontextualized into the narrative structure Turgenev himself composed.

The hunter's extended typology of the two Kaluga peasants as allegorical embodiments of cultural dichotomies is immediately preceded by a scene that takes the gentleman observer by surprise. Kalinych suddenly enters Khor's cabin bearing wild strawberries as a token of his affection and friendship. The narrator looks on "with astonishment" and confesses he hadn't expected such "courtesies" from a peasant (14). One also suspects that the hunter's intellectual discourse had made no allowance for the conjunctive coexistence, the natural symbiosis, of "types" like Khor and Kalinych. Previously he had seen various types of Russian peasants as unlinked opposites; now he is impelled to regard them as linked but unequal opposites led forward by an emerging enterprising "Petrine" vanguard. It is surely significant, however, that Turgenev's sketch does not conclude with the hunter's ringing peroration about the "Russianness" of Khor.

Before concluding that Khor's speech epitomizes the sane common sense and progressive mentality of the Russian man of the land, the narrator experiences some difficulties in communicating with him: "He seemed to agree with me about everything, only after a while I began to feel a twinge of conscience. . . . Khor sometimes expressed himself in puzzles, no doubt out of caution" (12). In their conversational exchange, Khor is asked why he doesn't buy his freedom from Polutykin. The answer given is neither logical nor comprehensible to the educated narrator: "If Khor fell in with free people, whoever lived without a beard would be one size bigger than Khor." The wily peasant obviously understands that freedom is likely to have additional costs. Under Peter the Great shaving the beard was a symbol of enlistment in Russia's enlightenment; but Khor is either not willing or not able to shave off his patriarchal beard.

After the hunter delivers his pronouncements on what he has learned from his physiological account of Kaluga province, the narrative resumes its episodic reportage of daily life and conversation. The sketch, like the others to follow, ends with a modest plainness that speaks volumes. Among the many things the reader learns is information that reverses the learned conclusions of our official guide. Surprisingly, it is

Kalinych, not Khor, who is literate. And it is Kalinych who is truly in harmony with the local environment, dispensing medicinal and musical cures to the local population. Meanwhile, Khor is content to live in ignorance, spouting the misogynistic prejudices of proverbial peasant wisdom. Yet in the last vignette of the two Kaluga peasants together, we glimpse a curious blending of the patriarchal and the passive strands in traditional rural life. At evening, the lordly Khor sits idly by, softly communing with the plangent melodies of a folk lament performed by the servile and selfless Kalinych. The categories and roles established by the initial typologies have worn very thin. Turgenev's narrative structure poses at its end the quiet collusion of complementary opposites. As the hunter departs, the two peasants (and Ivan Turgenev) imply that the rural environment of Russian serfdom is subtle enough to elude capture by educated gentleman hunters.

"Khor and Kalinych," along with the concluding ecological companion piece, "Forest and Steppe," provides the basic frame for a vast gallery of sketches that introduce Turgenev's aristocratic hunter (and the literate public) to some remarkable sets of paired opposites that are naturally accommodated by the Russian countryside. In addition, *Notes of a Hunter* includes a number of sketches that suddenly inject the solitary outsider inside the normally impenetrable circle of collective folk life. Two closely linked prototypes of this dramatic Turgenevan variant on the pastoral interlude are "Bezhin Meadow" and "The Singers." [12] These sketches, too, perform subtle structural ironies at the expense of Turgenev's sympathetic but culturally removed intruder. "Bezhin Meadow" centers on a wonderfully individualized band of young peasant lads who are obliged to stay awake on summer nights keeping watch on the village horses. These campfire boys frighten and entertain one other with a rich anthology of authentic peasant ghost tales (or "hants" in African American parlance). The natural setting allows Turgenev to retell traditional peasant superstitions about "wood demons" and "water sprites" on location and in lively dialect. But the sketch accomplishes even more. Its dramatic organization exposes the limits of standard reasonableness at the same time that it "naturalizes" superstition.

The core encounter of "Bezhin Meadow" is preceded by a prolonged descriptive prelude that recounts a perfect July day when the well-satisfied sportsman is tempted to overstay his welcome in a familiar hunting ground. As night slowly descends, the familiar contours of the land vanish, and soon the hunter is blundering and wondering, "What's this riddle? Where am I?" (94). Before long, the hunter and his hound are both disoriented in the dark woodland. Stumbling forward desperately, the hunter panics, with serious consequences. First, he finds himself in a strange place that stirs up eerie feelings: "The gully looked exactly like a cauldron with sloped sides; on its bottom there jutted up several large white stones—it seemed as if they had crawled down to that place for a secret consultation" (95). In full flight, the hunter draws back his leg just before stepping over "a fearful abyss." After this nearly lethal misstep, he looks below and sees the campfire in the meadow. Turgenev's leisurely prelude is a discreetly ironic commentary on the remove of the educated mind from the "childishness" of superstition.

Turgenev's plotting of the hunter's one-night stand with the gullible peasant boys is also laced with irony. The narrator is especially drawn to one lad, Pavlusha, for reasons that resemble his similarly high regard for Khor. Among the variegated cast of boys Pavlusha is the one who consistently has a "natural" explanation for the frightening sounds and shapes evoked in the haunting tales and that invade the atmosphere around the flickering campfire. He is also the only lad brave or brazen enough to chase down on horseback the terrifying noises of the night. And he is alone in telling a comic story that demystifies credulous village legends about "Trishka," the large-headed stranger whose coming will precede the end of the known world. The hunter clearly admires the inquiring spirit and the practical rationality of the enterprising Pavlusha. Meanwhile, it is worth noticing that Turgenev accompanies the children's tales of village superstitions with references to the lived reality of sudden deaths and vanishings in the treacherous physical and human environment of the Russian forest. Even Pavlusha can be unnerved; he's had the sensation of hearing a drowned boy's voice calling his name from the water of a pool. Finally, there can be no mistaking the implication of the story's clipped ending that announces Pavlusha's death: "He didn't drown; he died falling from a horse. A pity, for he was such a fine lad!" (113). Confident rationality does not have as much survival value as traditional superstition in the Russian countryside, probably with good reason.

"Singers," too, begins by offering what looks like surefooted guidance into one of Russia's dark interiors: "Very likely, not many of my readers have had the chance to drop in on a country tavern, but we hunters get to go everywhere!" (230). In this famous sketch, Turgenev's hunter takes refuge in a local pothouse on a beastly hot July day and is lucky enough to eavesdrop on a remarkable peasant singing contest. The writing of this episode is an occasion for Turgenev to display his own extraordinary skill at expressing the performance styles and artistry of authentic Russian folk singing. For the first time in Russian literature the written word actively conveys the untranscribable throat warblings, halftone glissandi, and syllabic elaborations that made the Russian folk song the means by which serfdom articulated its message to the world. Indeed, the climactic moment in the contest offers a "peak experience" that anticipates later scenes in Dostoevsky and DuBois when the soul of a culture seems instantly audible. Turgenev's hunter ecstatically coalesces with a motley assembly of provincial types in shared awe of Yashka the Turk's rendition of the traditional Russian song— "More than one path through the field wound its way":

> I confess that I had rarely heard such a voice: it was slightly broken and rang as if cracked; to start with it even had a suggestion of sickliness about it; but it also contained unfeigned depth of passion, and youthfulness, and strength, and sweetness, and a kind of attractively careless, plaintive sorrow. The true, fiery soul of Russia resounded and breathed through it and quite simply seized you by the heart, plucked directly at your Russian heartstrings. . . . He sang, and in every sound his voice made there wafted something native and vastly spacious, just as if the familiar steppe were spreading out before us, stretching off into the endless distance. (241)

The hunter's syntax noticeably stretches itself to accommodate in one long phrase ungraspable shifts of emotion and nuance. The prose labors mightily to deliver an inconceivable blend of tender woe and furious yearning as the singer's voice soars above the stifling heat and suffocating environment of the miserable serf village in which the tavern is situated. Yashka's unique performance in the distinctive rhythms and style of a folk *protiazhnaia*, or "melismatic" song, like one of DuBois's sorrow songs, is a music of "misty wanderings and hidden ways" that somehow becomes the collective possession of all the "soul" brothers who listen to it.[13] Like the prison population mesmerized by Isay Fomich's uncannily familiar chant for redemption, Turgenev's parched company of local drinkers is elevated to a shared national sentiment by a half-breed's improvisation on a common folk lyric. In both of these epiphanies of

Russianness, a momentary fusion of auditors in a classless aesthetic response heals inner divisions and suggests the existence of a vast, unrealized horizon of cultural possibility for all Russians.

In the descriptive prelude to "Singers" we learn that the local tavern is perched precariously, with one window "keeping a watchful eye" on a fearsome ravine that runs through the very center of Kolotovka village. Originally titled "The Hide-away Tavern," Turgenev's sketch makes painfully clear that the watering hole is the one place of refuge in a mercilessly exposed landscape stripped bare by its absentee owners. Significantly, the only vitality seen on the approach to the tavern is a company of sparrows who alone "kept their spirits up and, fluffing their feathers, chirped away and squabbled on the fences more fiercely than ever" (228). Like the human counterparts they anticipate, these singers are alternately lyrical and savage in an unforgiving land. After the epiphanic moment in which the hunter celebrates the transcendent and soaring "soul" of Russia he beats a suspiciously rapid retreat from the scene of Yashka's victorious chirp. By evening's fall another music dominates the atmosphere of the tavern as ugly carousing replaces beautiful caroling. The last sound heard fills the night air with a shrill cry calling "Antropka-a-a-a" home to receive his father's beating. At the tale's end, the narrator has been exposed to the painful coexistence of beatitude and brutality in the heartland of peasant Russia. Once again, there is a conjunction of gaping dissimilarities for which the literate hunter has no adequate words.

Notes of a Hunter is no nostalgic pastoral depicting a vanishing breed of picturesque countryfolk.[14] Nor is Turgenev's anthology of rural sketches a confident ethnography of a hidden Russia fully unveiled. The complex cultural ecology of the unemancipated Russian interior seems to elicit both a deglamorization of pastoral conventions and a poetization of intellectual typologies. As if to emphasize the cacophonous reality of the historic peasant culture bordering on the Russian forest and steppe, Turgenev uncharacteristically tampered with his established text and inserted two penultimate sketches into the final authorized edition of 1874.[15] Read together, these two additional episodes provide a particularly dramatic double climax just before the concluding lyrical farewell to the two abutting landscapes of the narrator's hunting ground. Two extremes of rural Russian culture are deliberately juxtaposed in the revised 1874 version of the hunter's expedition into the remote parts of the interior. The pairing of "Living Relics" and "The Knocking" stands as Turgenev's reminder, long after emancipation, that the territory occupied by folk Russia continued to shelter both a sanctified passivity and an unholy rowdiness.

Traditionally, readings of "Living Relics" have painted it as a restored icon, a modern hagiography dedicated to a saintly image of Christian meekness. To do so is, however, to ignore the hunter's evident discomfort before the spectacle of his mummified former nursemaid, Lukeria. On the very periphery of one of his mother's country estates the narrator "turns rigid with amazement" as he encounters the prematurely wizened and paralyzed body of a once buxom beauty who quite literally fell to her destruction while in a state of romantic rapture. In a tense interview the hunter watches as Lukeria struggles heroically to present herself as a radiant martyr of patient suffering. It is as if the secular intelligence of the hunter is in danger of being captive to his former serf's spirituality: "The cruel, stony immobility of the lively, unhappy creature lying before me was transferred to me: I also was literally fettered" (359). At first horrified by this capacity to celebrate paralysis as an avenue to piety, the hunter finally empathizes with the half-dead creature's hymn to life: "No longer was it terror I felt: an inexpressible pity wrenched my heart" (360). Yet Lukeria's undemanding quietude remains a disturbing model of sanctity, even to her fellow villagers. And the vivid visions of redemptive suffering she so ecstatically relates are, it is suggested, aided and abetted by a potent mixture of folk Christianity and a soporific dose of opium. With much delicacy Turgenev's sketch depicts the spectacle of the peasantry's capacity for "patient endurance" (*dolgoterpenie*) as an ambivalent phenomenon, partly a feat of collective strength and partly the opiate of the people.

Ambivalence and mystery also confront the narrator in Turgenev's second climactic supplement to his hunter's notebook. "The Knocking" is titled in Russian with an exclamatory verb, "*Stuchit!*" which can refer either to the noise of an external hammering or the internal pounding of the heart. Either way, the suspenseful approach of a dramatic uncertainty is signaled, and the sketch does not fail to deliver on its promise. Having mysteriously run out of ammunition and not knowing whether to trust his peasant guide to return sober with a new supply, the hunter is persuaded to engage a local "simpleton" and his shaggy nags to take him on a long night's journey across the landscape of central Russia. What follows is a relentless sequence of reversed expectations, both for the narrator and Turgenev's readers. Distrust of rustic stupidity gives way to a grateful trust in the sixth sense of the peasant coachman as the party is able to ford a "bad place" in the tricky current of a local river. As in "Bezhin Meadow," deference for what the educated dismiss as superstition seems the path of reason when traveling in a treacherous environment. When night closes in, the shifting moonlit landscape evokes in the hunter literary associations with ancient Russian warriors and with ballads about highwaymen. Suddenly the peasant driver hears the "knocking" of a large cart behind them, and his intuition tells him that "bad folk" and certain doom are approaching. The road to Tula is notorious for attacks by marauding robbers, and the hunter is told to prepare to die. But when they are overtaken and stopped by a gang of drunken rowdies, it turns out to be a false ambush. In the moonlight a huge "smirking" face "full of a guarded attention" asks politely for the price of a half bottle of vodka: "Guv'nor, sir, we're coming from a real good feast, a hitching, you know; we've married off one of our fellas, tucked him away, proper like. Our guys are all young and reckless, daredevils. . . . We'd gladly drink to your health and pay respects to your rank" (378). The danger passes, but the sketch leaves us with both an anticlimax and a nagging mystery. When it is later reported that a merchant had been robbed and slain on the road to Tula that very night, we are encouraged to hear a bit differently phrases like "coming from a hitching" and "tucked him away." It is a wise reader who can decide whether the knocking was truly an external threat or an internal panic. Despite this ambiguity, Turgenev's penultimate sketch most assuredly acquaints the hunter with a legitimate anxiety about the historic impatience of the Russian folk, thus presenting a second image of the native "soul" that is the complementary opposite of "Living Relics."

The most perceptive readers of Turgenev's Notes of a Hunter have understood that the individual sketches are part of a larger discourse that unfolds as a carefully supervised sequence of narrative units.[16] When Turgenev made additions to his canonical text in 1874, he clearly wished to reinforce the aesthetic principle of a conjunctive narrative syntax. In conjoining "Living Relics" and "The Knocking" just before the conclusion of his famous hunting sketches, Ivan Turgenev was leaving a parting word, giving one final emphasis to his vision of the paradoxical coexistence of contraries in the cultural ecology of rural Russia. The darkest enigma of the Russian folk was its mutual embrace of the meek and the mighty, accommodating both the Slavophiles' martyrs of long-suffering patience and the Westernizers' insurgent native rebels in one unpredictable and unencompassable cultural complex. *Notes of a Hunter* neither discovers nor captures the "soul" of Russia. But it does sketch with faithful attention the dynamic and fragile equilibrium of complementary opposites in the natural world and living culture of the Russian folk.

The publication of seven linked "plantation tales" in 1899 by Houghton Mifflin of Boston made Charles Chesnutt the first African American author to achieve literary visibility in high places. Yet the circumstances behind the initial appearance of *The Conjure Woman* have tended to cast Chestnutt's artistry into doubt. Responding with alacrity to a suggestion by the editor of *Atlantic Monthly*, Walter Hines Page, that a "skillfully selected list" of his short stories might make a book, Chesnutt forwarded twenty tales and sketches for Page to peruse along with two others already in his custody. When Page replied that Houghton Mifflin might consider a volume if there were enough "conjure stories," Chesnutt produced six new tales within six weeks. To later observers it has appeared that Chesnutt displayed undue haste in producing the desired commodity and in complying with the prestigious editor's guidance in selecting or excluding conjure stories for publication. The importance of being successful is a theme much in evidence in Chesnutt's journals; as early as 1880, he came to the realization that there was "something romantic, to the Northern mind, about the southern negro, as commonplace and vulgar as he seems to us who come into contact with him every day." [17] The fact that Chesnutt achieved his first success by working up a volume of Remus-like dialect tales has made his biographer suspect that, good as the black vernacular storytelling is, Uncle Julius is still the conventional "petted servant" whose role is to reaffirm "his endearingly mock-devious nature to an appreciative white audience." [18]

To suggest that *The Conjure Woman* is a text heavily subject to the mechanisms of market incentives is not necessarily to prove that it is an artistically compromised work of fiction. In fact, Chesnutt's early journals also speak to a precocious understanding of literary success that is far from naive or pusillanimous. An interesting paragraph dated May 29, 1880, elaborates on a sly missionary intent at work in the ambitious young writer:

I think I must write a book. . . . The object of my writings would be not so much the elevation of the colored people as the elevation of the whites, — for I consider the unjust spirit of caste which is so insidious as to pervade a whole nation . . . a barrier to the moral progress of the American people. . . . But the subtle almost indefinable feeling of repulsion toward the negro, which is common to most Americans—and easily enough accounted for—cannot be stormed and taken by assault. . . . their position must be mined, and we will find ourselves in their midst before they think it. . . . amusing them to lead them on imperceptibly, unconsciously step by step to the desired state of feeling." (139–40)

Taking our cue from this passage, it is quite likely that the Negro author who sold his wares to Houghton Mifflin in 1899 was a skilled negotiator in more than an economic sense. Although it is true that current literary taste is offended by the exclusion from *The Conjure Woman* of some of Chesnutt's most powerful and unmistakably allegorical Uncle Julius tales, it is wise to keep in mind that respected Russian authors also had to suppress social critiques that were less than oblique.[19] As Turgenev knew well, when the native tongue is speaking to a prejudiced master class it needs to be both blunted and forked. The censored tongue of Uncle Julius is both pointedly amusing and charmingly subversive.

Superficially conventional and entertaining, Chesnutt's cycle of seven conjure tales is also busily engaged in tricks of transformation and shape-shifting. *The Conjure Woman* simultaneously repeats and reverses available formulas, making a fixed reading of Chesnutt's intentions unnervingly difficult. Each story obediently follows the established literary protocol of the nostalgic post-Reconstruction "plantation tale": a white narrator picturesquely frames the speech-act of a venerable black uncle who relates in "darky" dialect a fanciful tale from slavery times. But Chesnutt also plays variations on that theme that create quite a spin on stereotypes. For one thing, the apparently innocuous naming of the two narrators sets up some rather uncomfortable associations. Julius is one of the typical names white minstrels in blackface gave to the "end man" who springs the jokes at the expense of the interlocutor or "straight man"; John is one of the standard names for the black trickster who strives to outfox Massa in slave folklore.[20] Any reader who catches these allusions will have a hard time deciding which of Chesnutt's rival narrators is the true trickster. Also, Uncle Julius repeats with a difference the

Uncle Remus stereotype; it matters that Julius is an ex-slave who was a "field nigger" immersed in the superstitions of conjury and the alternative medicine of "root-work." The tales that Julius tells are not pitched as clever children's stories, nor are they always transparent to John or the literate white reader. In each of Chesnutt's narratives Julius's old-time tale is motivated by an announced motive of John's that the story attempts to conjure away.[21] It may well be possible, as one recent critic has feared, to read Chesnutt's dialect fiction as politically limited because there is nothing to prevent the literal-minded reader from consuming it as trivial "darky" entertainment, yet that does not mean that Chesnutt was not also a pioneer of African American subversive indirection, or literary "signifying."[22]

"The Goophered Grapevine," the opening and first-written conjure tale in the 1899 collection, provides a good example of Chesnutt's tricky (or illusory?) complexity. Based on an off-color hoodoo story told to Chesnutt by his father-in-law's black gardener, the published tale puts the old wine of slave lore into a New South bottle.[23] The conjure story that Julius elaborates on metaphorically identifies the physical condition of the slave body with the (grape) culture of the South; thanks to the hoodoo of "Aunt Peg," he who eats of the Master's "goophered" grapes will have his vital signs wax and wane along with the vines. Chesnutt rehearses this fable from slave times in a new setting, however. A black voice with a long memory tells a cautionary tale to the new masters of the New South, a relocated Northern "pioneer" of industry, John, and his neurasthenic wife, Annie. Were it not for the advent of the Yankee carpetbaggers looking for cheap labor and land that "could be bought for a mere song," Uncle Julius would be the sole living retainer enjoying the once lucrative grapevines on the McAdoo plantation. But John "sees through" the goopher story as a warning not to purchase the hexed vineyard. So it would appear that the old negro's conjure tale has had little effect in the new times. The ex-slave's "shiftless cultivation" of the Southern vineyard is ended, and the new master is satisfied that the wages he will pay Julius as his coachman will be more than adequate compensation for any losses incurred. Thus the old conjure story has a happy ending—at least as framed inside the new master's narrative.

But it is Chesnutt, not John, who is the true master of this narrative that sets up a contest between two storytellers inside a specific historical frame. Several types of conjury are occurring simultaneously, and it is a complicated matter to decide whose magic (or trickery) is winning. On one level "The Goophered Grapevine," like the six stories that follow, observes a set formula: a shrewd old "darky" (actually a ginger-colored mulatto) is invited or permitted to regale his cultured, industrious listeners with outlandish stories that turn out to have been motivated by animal appetite or economic self-interest. But Chesnutt's first conjure tale also, as we have seen, highlights the appetites and interests of the literate outsiders who are moving in on Julius's territory. As Julius tells it, it was the white slavemaster, McAdoo, who first paid Aun' Peggy ten dollars to "goopher" his vines, thereby driving off the thieving slaves and earning "monst'us good intrus' " to the tune of fifteen hundred pounds of grapes. Next, McAdoo's white overseer protected his investment in a "noo Negro" by arranging for Aun' Peggy to remove the hex from the vines for Henry, the terrified grape-eater. Henry then magically flourishes exactly like the grapes, waxing so vigorous that McAdoo can sell his labor for fifteen hundred dollars each spring. This neat arrangement falters, however, when a Yankee comes to North Carolina and promises to double the yield with new techniques, "en ol' Mars [McAdoo] des drunk it all in, des 'peared ter be bewitch' wid dat Yankee" (41). The Yankee's cut-and-slash trimming of roots and vines proves to be the death of the old plantation, preceding by a few years the collapse of the Old South's culture. But he is replaced at the story's end by John and Annie, who bring an expanded agrobusiness "often referred to by the local press as a striking illustration of the opportunities open to Northern capital" (43). Looked at as a whole, Chesnutt's narrative exposes how whites have managed to exploit "black magic" to their own profit and how blacks have been exploited by "white magic" in its pursuit of "monst'us good intrus'." Julius's conjure tale has conjured up the bad old days of slavery, and Chesnutt's frame narrative has conjured up an insidious sameness between then and now. The ineffectuality of Julius's attempt to "goopher" John away from the lucrative grapevine subversively underscores the success of Chesnutt's conjury.

With his writer's ear for narrative pitch, John Edgar Wideman has noted how both Julius and Chesnutt are playing to multiple audiences by "keying" their speech-acts differently within the same interaction.[24] Beginning with the second tale of The Conjure Woman, "Po' Sandy," it becomes clear, even to John, that Julius's wildly extravagant stories are not merely stratagems to humor the Master out of his whims; "others,

poured freely into the sympathetic ear of a Northern-bred woman, dis-
close many a tragic incident of the darker side of slavery" (46). One of the
subtler dramas Chesnutt stages is the increasing divergence between the
Northern husband and wife in their hearing of what Julius's nonsense
is saying. What to John's ear is primarily a humorous ruse intended to
protect or improve Julius's economic standing is, in Annie's hearing, an
appeal to the curative power of empathy in uplifting the moral imagination. Gradually, the conjure tales of slavery become good medicine and
even a conversion experience for the enervated Annie. "Po' Sandy," for
instance, is an affecting, if gruesome, tale in which a slave husband's fer-
vent wish to be as rooted as a tree is magically granted by his conjure
woman wife; but when she, too, is called away on master's business before she can restore Sandy to human form, he is cut down and fed to the
local lumber mill. Annie gasps, "What a system it was under which such
things were possible!" while John wryly remarks, "What things? Are you
seriously considering the possibility of a man's being turned into a tree?"
(53). Annie here is obviously enlisted as Chesnutt's ally against an un-
imaginative reading of Julius's allegorical tale. When she hears the next
old-time story ("Mars Jeems's Nightmare"), Annie knows enough to in-
terpret it as a protest against her husband's not allowing any slack to
poor ignorant Tom, Julius's grandson.

The two penultimate stories in *The Conjure Woman* employ subtle paral-
lelisms between the external frame and the inner oral tale that suggest
Chesnutt's larger design of signifying on John while working to bring
about the conversion of Annie. "Sis' Becky's Pickaninny" is a "child-
ish" tale of slave magic that actually rescues Annie from "settled melancholy" and severe depression; not coincidentally, it also comments on
male horse-trading and female nurturing. A kindhearted master who
"nebber lack' ter make no trouble fer nobody" can't bring himself to
tell his choice domestic slave that she isn't on temporary loan but has
been sold for an irresistible piece of horseflesh. Distraught by her separation from little Mose, her nursing son, Becky's pain is temporarily alleviated by Aun' Peggy's conjure medicine. Consoling dreams are carried
by bird missionaries to the suffering mother, and a goophered hornet
brings swollen joints to the prize racehorse. But the bargaining men cannot be cajoled into relenting on their deal until the conjure woman ar-
ranges for Becky to find a bag of hoodoo at her door; believing that she is

hexed, Becky commences to waste away. As Julius tells it, her new master "wuz one er dese yer w'ite folks w'at purten' dey doan b'liebe in cunj'in, - but hit wa'nt no use" (91). Deciding "a lame horse wuz better 'n a dead nigger," the scales of justice are finally righted. Becky is returned to her son who, we are told, "could sing en whistle des lack a mawkin' bird, so dat de w'ite folks useter hab 'im come up ter de big house at night, en whistle en sing fer 'em." Although John dismisses Julius's offering as nothing but an ingenious fairy tale, Annie realizes that the "lie" is somehow true to nature, and we learn that her condition took a turn for the better from that very day "and she was soon on her way to ultimate recovery" (92). The white masters require near-death experiences before they will allow that black conjury might provide the healing made necessary by their cold calculations of economic advantage.

The arid realm of abstract rationality is parodied in Chesnutt's framing of the subsequent story, "The Gray Wolf's Ha'nt." John makes one last attempt to alleviate the awful boredom of which his wife complains. Displaying his genteel literacy, John reads with pleasure a philosophical passage that Chesnutt surely has planted as an ironic commentary, a satirical "metatext" that reveals an incomprehension of conjury's meanings:

> The difficulty of dealing with transformations so many-sided as those which all existences have undergone, or are undergoing, is such as to make a complete and deductive interpretation almost hopeless. So to grasp the total process of redistribution of matter and motion as to see simultaneously its several necessary results in their actual interdependence is scarcely possible. There is, however, a mode of rendering the process as a whole tolerably comprehensible. Though the genesis of the rearrangement of every evolving aggregate is in itself one, it presents to our intelligence . . ." (95)

Annie rightly interrupts what is rapidly becoming total "nonsense" in order to turn her attention to Julius, who is conveniently reporting for duty as family coachman and master of the African American talking-cure. His conjure tales have indeed dealt with "many-sided transformations" of existences and with redistributions of matter and motion that scarcely seem graspable. But Chesnutt no doubt hoped for eyes competent to see "simultaneously several necessary results in their actual interdependence." Unfortunately, it has taken a long time for readers to see the masked meanings underneath Julius's locally colorful speech and Chesnutt's deromanticization of slave times on the old plantation.[25]

"Hot-Foot Hannibal," the seventh and concluding conjure tale, has come in for much criticism, either as a disappointing bit of crowd-pleasing sentimentality or as a "Reunionist happy ending."[26] Despite its superficial resolution of difficulties, it is no less multilayered in implication, and it expands the reach of Julius's conjury. Now Julius works his verbal magic on the listening ears of Annie's younger sister Mabel, who has, to John's regret, just broken off a local match that "had promised to be another link binding" the Northern couple to "the kindly Southern people" (108). Without question, the tale of "Hot-Foot Hannibal" serves to admonish the impetuous and proud Northern belle, encouraging her to overcome a serious breach with her courtly Southern beau. It is clear, too, that Julius has conspired with the young gentleman's aims and with Annie's expressed sentiment in bringing about a healing of the threatened disunion. In accomplishing this reconciliation, however, Chesnutt also manages to respect the cunning indirection and lucid realism of the forked native tongue in which Julius speaks. For one thing, the tale's impact on Mabel depends on her vicarious identification with headstrong Chloe, an uppity domestic servant who is brought into the "big house" and who displays what proves to be a disastrous contempt for the unattractive promoted field hand, Hannibal. Chloe sees to it that the competent Hannibal is goophered to make room in the big house for handsome Jeff, but Hannibal has his revenge by tricking Chloe into a jealous rage that results in Jeff's being sold down river. Ironically, Chloe's hubris, as related by the former field hand, Julius, is precisely the trick that restores haughty Mabel to the arms of her disenchanted Southern lover. Significantly, it is a trick that works only when Julius manages to elicit the cooperation of a "balking mare" in delaying a journey that needs to proceed on "the long road" rather than the shortcut preferred by the Northern masters. Once the lengthy tale is told and the black driver gets the disputing parties on the right road, the desired reunion occurs. But what kind of ending has Chesnutt wrought?

Julius's narrative device brings about a happy ending replete with regional reconciliation, but at story's end his motives are unclear to John. There was an understanding that when the young people set up housekeeping in their big house, Julius had an invitation to enter their service. But "for some reason or other," he preferred to remain with John and Annie. Chesnutt implies that Julius will continue to take his chances with the older Northern couple. For some readers that ending underlines the success of *The Conjure Woman* as a narrative sequence in which the true profit of Uncle Julius's storytelling is revealed as a civilizing mission for the "elevation of the whites" above the spirit of caste.[27] Other readers have been careful to note that Julius does not always win or get what he wants, but that his tales of magical transformations in the "shadow language" of black dialect conjure up the unforgotten relevance of the slave past in the New South; at best, Julius's tales practice the survival art of African American signifying and "tonal semantics."[28] Perhaps what is most persuasive and most original about *The Conjure Woman* is Chesnutt's dramatization of the cultural contestation between a genteel and a vernacular understanding of the powers that shape and dominate the environment of the rural South.[29] Chesnutt, like Turgenev, invented a literary form that gave memorable expression to the unresolved tensions and antagonisms in representative encounters between articulate peasants and the literate masters who presumed to understand them.

Ethnographic writing that aims to recover the sophistication of a "native" tongue (or of folk medicine) will strive to perform rather than explicate the discourse of an alternative language. When a written text speaks in dialect or enacts a locally coded behavior it cannot remove all obscurities of meaning and motive if its true intent is to respect the play of cultural difference. The literature of ethnic "soul," in other words, must not demystify the aura of something intangible and inexpressible even as it provides narrative access to the "other" within the body of a nation. A strategic subversion of popular genres of literary ethnography was initiated by Turgenev and Chesnutt, who deliberately complicated prevailing understandings of the rural Russian and black folk. This practice of creative ethnography took an even more radical form when it was embraced by a writer from within the vernacular culture that had become an object of study. Zora Neale Hurston could claim by birth to have been "pitched headforemost" into "the crib of negroism," and it was she who fully undertook the subversion of standard scientific ethnography. *Mules and Men* anticipated as early as 1935 much current thinking about the perilous "positionality" of all attempts at cultural observation.[30] Yet it also has been cited as a sourcebook for a regressive cultural nationalism that promotes a timeless mystique of "authentic" negroism located in the Southern rural folk.[31] Clearly, this is a work that illustrates some central tensions that result when one's home territory has become a field of cultural inquiry.

Mules and Men displays at first glance all the customary credentials and apparatus of a scholarly explication of African American folklore: a preface by Dr. Boas certifying Hurston's ability "to penetrate through that affected demeanor by which the Negro excludes the White observer"; a special typeface separating the documentary material from the surrounding narrative; explanatory footnotes, a glossary of terms, and even useful appendixes that reproduce authentic songs and hoodoo recipes.[32] Yet on closer examination the inadequacy of the supplementary scholarly protocols is patently obvious. There is an arbitrariness about Hurston's explanatory notes that borders on the playful or the deceptive. Take, for instance, the opening paragraph of appendix 3: *Paraphernalia of Conjure*: "It would be impossible for anyone to find out all the things that are being used in conjure in America. Anything may be conjure and nothing may be conjure, according to the doctor, the time and the use of the article" (277). Next comes a list of thirty-eight items of conjury, concluding rather blasphemously with the Bible, "the great conjure book in the world" (280). But anyone who has read Hurston's idiosyncratic work to the end will realize that what may at first appear frivolous is actually quite to the point. The truth is that the effectiveness of conjure, like the significance of the "big lies" the folk tell, is elusively circumstantial and situational.

Hurston's introductory words to her anthology playfully forewarn the reader of the tonal shifts and slippage of secure meaning that will follow. Paraphrasing (or parodying) Psalm 122, Hurston allows she was "glad when someone told me, 'You may go and collect Negro folklore'" (1). But this gracious permission from higher authority allows nothing truly new to her, except that she now can reflect on what she has always been doing by looking through "the spyglass of Anthropology." It matters, of course, that Hurston doesn't say "telescope," since it is not only a removed view she has been encouraged to take but also an alien perspective on home territory. And, as if to emphasize that self-alienation, she speaks of returning as Lucy Hurston's daughter to her "native village" (2). Can this double self, the daughter-detective, remain "just Zora to the neighbors" while also serving as our trusted informant? Surely it will be a tricky business to remain an insider and yet work for the benefit of the outside world. The reader is quickly made to understand that "folklore is not as easy to collect as it sounds" because "the under-privileged" are reluctant to "reveal that which the soul lives by," because "the Negro" is particularly evasive, and because "we" smile and tell something "that satisfies the white person" who "doesn't know what he's missing." Suddenly the reader has grounds to suspect the primary source of information. Our guide reveals herself as an insider who identifies with a culture that has learned to say something without telling all: "The theory behind our tactics: 'The white man is always trying to know into somebody else's business. All right, I'll set something outside the door of my mind for him to play with and handle. He can read my writing but he sho' can't read my mind' " (3). In Barbara Johnson's apt words, it is impossible to tell whether Hurston here is *describing* a strategy or *employing* one.[33] Even so, Hurston's tricky writing does serve as a fair introduction to the resistant culture of a denigrated people, a culture in which speech and behavior is a strategic performance to gain a degree of position and power.

As an anthology of folktales and rites of conjure *Mules and Men* was unique in its time for situating its unglossed primary "texts" within culturally embedded scenes depicting the interlocutive exchange between the ethnographer and the informants. When the book was going to press in 1934, Hurston was eager for Dr. Boas to understand that this "unscientific matter" of "the between-story conversation and business" had been made necessary by the commercial instincts of the publisher.[34] Yet two years earlier Hurston had herself taken responsibility for "folk tales with background so that they are in atmosphere and not just stuck out into cold space. I want the reader to see why Negroes tell such glorious tales." Although Boas apparently had to be placated for the interjection of Hurston's own vivid narrative presence, it was Boas who as early as 1927 had encouraged his "native" pupil to record what she alone could capture: "When we talked about this matter I asked you particularly to pay attention, not so much to content, but rather to the form of diction, movements, and so on."[35] Even if her book took liberties with the disciplinary protocols of academic anthropology, Hurston was enough of a "Boasian" to understand that the performative dimension was a substantive component of the communicative code of her homefolk.

Mules and Men offers an earful and an eyeful of black-on-black interaction. Unlike the guardedly indirect or cloaked meanings cleverly inserted into the cross-class and cross-racial dialogues presented by Turgenev and Chesnutt, Hurston's speakers swap open-faced "lies" in a public culture that thrives on competitive verbal improvisations within established speech genres. Features like metaphoric substitutions or comic exaggeration that might be ascribed to the conditioned defensiveness of a subordinate population are found to flourish inside the segregated space of blackness. One important implication of Hurston's dramatic "polylogue" of verbal combatants is to suggest that even the home talk of Southern black folk is an oblique language full of tonal meanings and sound effects. This is borne out in the many tongue-wagging contests that relish fanciful language within specific social and sexual contexts. A work party addresses black-white labor relations by exchanging recycled "John and Massa" stories; a fishing party fills its idle hours rehearsing a repertory of animal fables; and the dance hall becomes a convention of male "woofers" spouting courtship trash. Some oral tales exchanged among the folk are metacommentaries on their unique mode of speech. One story signifies on the uppity daughter who comes home "finished up" from schooling and cannot describe in a letter how her father makes a mule move by saying the word "(clucking sound of tongue and teeth)" (41). And there is the marvelous fable about how God put the snake on earth to "ornament the ground" but agrees to let him have "poison in his mouf" for protection when it becomes clear that everything treads on him and kills off his generations (97). Hurston's "folk tales" need no interpretation for those on the inside, and the outsider is not given any help. An alert reader, though, might learn to share the oral culture's evident delight in the protective ornamentation displayed on every page of Hurston's anthology. Or as one wise old insider puts it: "There's a whole heap of them kinda by-words. . . . Everybody can't understand what they mean. Most people is thin-brained. . . . Some folks is born wid they feet on the sun and they kin seek out de inside meanin' of words" (125).

Everywhere that Hurston roams black men and black women adorn their lives and labor with a verbal and bodily style that plays variations on received forms. Public recognition requires proof of competitive excellence in modifying a traditional genre of performance. A "lie" is not a successful "lie" if " 'taint no such a story nowhere" or if the teller "jus' made dat one up herself" (30). This powerfully conveyed vision of black folk attaining autonomy through ingenious reappropriations of given formulas and material paraphernalia is consistent with Hurston's more overt theorizings about race and culture.

The author of *Mules and Men* had devoted considerable thought to what made her people different. In "Characteristics of Negro Expression," published in 1934, Hurston's keen aesthetic appreciation for the look and sound and movement of Southern black life results in a remarkable variation on Alexander Crummell's earlier argument alleging the superior adaptability of the Negro race. Hurston, too, rings changes on the American reverence for originality by attaching special cultural merit to mimicry. Positing the existence of a racial "will to adorn," she bluntly states: "Whatever the Negro does of his own volition he embellishes." [36] Well in advance of scholarly studies of black English or African polyrhythms, Hurston was citing specific African American transformations of grammar, song, and dance to argue that the Negro race possessed a gift for dramatic improvisation:

> What we really mean by originality is the modification of ideas. . . . So if we look at it squarely, the Negro is a very original being. While he lives and moves in the midst of a white civilization, everything that he touches is reinterpreted for his own use. . . . Paul Whiteman is giving an imitation of a Negro orchestra making use of white-invented musical instruments in a Negro way. Thus has arisen a new art in the civilized world, and thus has our so-called civilization come. The exchange and re-exchange between groups. (838)

It is significant that Hurston associates her race with an authentic, even "primitive," talent for mimicry and opposes that natural improvisatory genius to the civilized, secondary art of imitation. Hurston's infectious glee in the destabilizing verbal and ritual magic of the black South is ultimately consistent with a biological type of racialist thinking.

The larger drama, the overarching narrative of *Mules and Men*, is truly about "black power." Hurston's recovery of the native tongue and of "hoodoo" magic celebrates an individual and collective empowerment unimaginable in Turgenev's and Chesnutt's unresolved dramatizations of hidden culture wars. Sensitive feminist readings of Hurston's narrative of cultural reimmersion rightly point to the increasing personal and spiritual authority accumulated by Zora's narrative persona as she competes with the "big liars" of the deep South and earns the "crown of power" as a New Orleans conjure woman.[37] Yet there is another story about power relations embedded in the full textual mechanics of *Mules and Men*. Hurston's book is also a "metaethnography," a commentary on what it takes to collect the empowering materials—the forceful crafts of verbal signifying and ritual hoodoo mastered by the black folk of the enslaved American South. Empowerment in the world of the rural black South does not come cheaply and, once attained, is precarious.

Measured by her own narrative, Hurston's success in recovering the power of "black magic" depends on a combination of patronage, trickery, and great strength of will. To win her credentials fully, the daughter-detective must rely on powerful patrons to authorize her quest and protect her life and welfare. To be credible as an ethnographer, Hurston requires the support of Dr. Boas and of her wealthy white "godmother," Mrs. Rufus Osgood Mason; to be viable among her informants, she requires the confidence of the "native" keepers of the lore; to be secure in her local status she needs the physical protection of "Big Sweet" in the sawmill camp and the spiritual blessing of Luke Turner, the direct descendent of Marie Leveau, the legendary New Orleans "queen of conjure." Sustaining her position requires a good deal of protective ornamentation and a mastery of improvised masks of identity and meaning. Although she may look at first like a turncoat to her people, "a revenue officer or a detective of some kind," she does not betray the secrets of manufacture behind the goods that she illicitly presents to the outside world. *Mules and Men* is an "inside job" pulled off by a native daughter who pretends to be a "bootlegger on the lam," but it isn't finally a robbery of her people's property. Hurston's remarkably deft book manages to display the powers of the "native tongue" without providing enough of a translation so that nonnatives can fully master it. Hurston's narrative *affirms* the existence of a racial gift for the "black arts" of conjury and subversive mimicry. In the end the reader is left mesmerized by the performance of Hurston as "Sis Cat," who has learned to wash up her act and put on company manners *after* she has swallowed the rat.

To her credit, Zora Neale Hurston refused to prettify the devices and stratagems of folk empowerment that she had acquired as an understudy to Southern black traditions. Whether she exaggerated the racial purity or overestimated the social power of the resilient and resistant oral culture of America's segregated black folk remains, quite legitimately, a matter of much dispute. What Hurston and her literary predecessors Turgenev and Chesnutt unquestionably did demonstrate was the cultural integrity and expressive sophistication of a substandard veiled discourse that was only fully accessible to its native speakers, the descendants of Russian serfdom and black American slavery. Whether a latter-day recovery of that native tongue—the historic Russian or African American vernacular—is essential to preserve the authentic ethnic "soul" of the nation has also become a matter of intense debate. As we shall see, culturally aware Russians and African Americans have not always agreed that what made them a special people was the existence of a shared folk legacy.

5 UNDERGROUND NOTES

Double-Voicedness and the Poetics

of National Identity

Literary history sometimes produces the impression that a collective identity has been encapsulated in one specific expressive form. It may well be that "identity politics" relies on the prior formulation of identity poetics. It has often been noted, for instance, that the tradition of African American writing has its foundation in a specific autobiographical genre, the slave narrative. The invisibility of the race's basic humanity was in part rectified by the capacity of literate black individuals "to tell a free story" about the African American condition.[1] But a more intimate view of the full humanity of America's veiled nation required that African American writers create credible representations of interior discourse. It became necessary to experiment with a form of utterance that could convey an inner race-conscious sensibility through an invented autobiographical narrative.[2] Modern African American literature, not unlike the Russian literary tradition, necessarily gravitated toward the problematic poetics of a specific and peculiar genre, the "notes of a native mind" or the national confessional novel.

In his seminal study, *Problems of Dostoevsky's Poetics*, Mikhail Bakhtin named and celebrated that writer's "polyphonic novelistic discourse" in terms that recognized it as nothing less than Russia's national narrative voice: "All the elements of novelistic structure in Dostoevsky are profoundly original; all are determined by that new artistic task that only he could pose and solve with the requisite scope and depth: the task of constructing a polyphonic world and destroying the established forms of the fundamentally *monologic* (homophonic) European novel."[3] The underlying notion here (as in Bakhtin's brilliant discussion of *Notes from Underground* as an internalized and unresolved polyphonic utterance) is that Dostoevsky had invented an innovative non-European form of discourse that could only have emerged from a specifically Russian sensibility, one finely attuned to a national culture in critical dialogue with itself. And, in fact, a few pages later Bakhtin makes a claim for the "Russian-ness" of this internally plural discourse: "Here in Russia the contradic-tory nature of evolving social life, not fitting within the framework of a confident and calmly meditative monologic consciousness, was bound to appear particularly abrupt. . . . In this way the objective preconditions were created for the multi-leveledness and multi-voicedness of the poly-phonic novel" (20). Whether or not one is disposed to agree with Bakh-tin's culturally specific attribution of a "dialogic imagination" to Rus-sia's national consciousness, the literary history of the Russian novel has demonstrated a strong attachment to the theme of the reflexive or "su-perfluous" hero whose characteristic mode of expression is a confes-sional narrative of rich inner ambivalence and irresolution.

A well-documented shock of recognition occurred among African Americans once *Notes from Underground* became widely available in trans-lation. Readers familiar with DuBois's portrait of the American Negro's "double consciousness" could hardly remain unmoved by Dostoevsky's famous confessional monologue of a symptomatic personality whose every word voiced a socially constructed pathology. It is no secret that Dostoevsky's portrait of a divided mind provided one important prece-dent for the embattled racial psyches so memorably depicted in Richard Wright's "The Man Who Lived Underground" (1944) and Ralph Ellison's *Invisible Man* (1952).[4] In this chapter, however, I wish to propose that African American writing had independently evolved its own parallel ex-ample of a culturally symptomatic confessional monologue as early as 1912. Independent of Dostoevsky, James Weldon Johnson devised a re-markably similar portrait of a representative antihero in *The Autobiography of an Ex-Coloured Man*. Both Russian and African American writing had ar-rived at a point of psychic crisis when it became imperative to give liter-ary form to the presence of an "underground" self-consciousness. Sig-nificantly, these newly representative "native speakers" were giving full voice to the cultural hybridity of Westernized Russians and urbanized American Negroes. If the truth be told, the national soul no longer pos-sessed a single authentic native tongue; instead, it confessed to the per-plexities of an internalized dual identity.

When Fyodor Dostoevsky returned to Petersburg after his involuntary exile among Russian commoners and convicts, he rapidly rejoined the ranks of the empire's third estate, seeking to shape public opinion in a tumultuous time. With the financial and intellectual support of his brother, Mikhail, Dostoevsky was able to launch an independent journal, *Vremia* (Time), that became the herald of a new movement in the annals of Russian cultural nationalism. The public announcement of the new journal in September 1860 prophesied that the imminent abolition of serfdom would initiate a transformation as vast in its national consequences as the Petrine reforms—namely, "the fusion of the educated class and its representatives with the nation's folk element."[5] Without rejecting or regretting the historic separation of Russia's Westernized elite, the new journal accepted as its task the necessary and opportune "reconciliation of civilization with the folk element": "we return unbowed to our native soil" (18:36). By virtue of such phrasing, the new movement was rapidly labeled *pochvennichestvo*, or the "native soil party," but the term carries misleading implications of nativism for English speakers. It is essential to keep in mind that the "native soil" conservatism of the Dostoevsky brothers was a dynamic and teleological vision of an emerging Russian nationality that would gradually unite the standards of the "enlightened" Europeanized intelligentsia with the traditional communalist ethos of the *narod*, the spontaneous fraternalism of the Russian folk.[6] The *Vremia* group hailed the advent of an emancipated Russia in forward motion, seeing it as a unique nation on the verge of achieving national fraternity and independent status in the pantheon of world civilizations.

A closer look at the public pronouncements made by the journalist Dostoevsky reveals the emotional urgency of a thinker subject in equal measure to euphoria and anxiety. It will be remembered that the author of *Notes from the House of the Dead* alternated between exhilaration and despair in his depiction of attempts at fraternization across the "abyss" (*bezdna*) that divided the cultivated elite from the commoners. In the articles that advocate the "native soil" vision of a spiritually reunified Russia, intense emphasis is placed on the *necessity* of fusion, and it is clear that the specter of dissension and division lurks just beneath the encouraging rhetoric of the pundit's prose.[7] Dostoevsky's proclamation of a "new Russia" that is "gradually being felt" in the age of emancipation is predicated on one fervently held but evidently precarious article of faith: "The Russian spirit is broader than class enmity, class interests and prerogatives. . . . it is a general spirit of conciliation, the basis of which resides in our upbringing" (PS, 18:50).

All the rudiments of Dostoevsky's position were on view in the first number of *Vremia*. In a lengthy introductory article of January 1861 Dostoevsky added his distinctive voice to the nationalist chorus: "We believe that the Russian nation is an extraordinary phenomenon in the history of all mankind" (54). His version of Russia's exceptionalism was a specific variant of earlier notions, however. Like the Slavophiles, he invoked the mythic notion of Russia's pacific and communal foundation of state power, free of European violence and factionalism.[8] But like Chaadaev, he embraced the history of Petrine Westernization as necessary for assimilating the universal standards of a pan-European civilization on a "neutral soil." What lent uniqueness to Dostoevsky's cultural nationalism was precisely its ingenious blending of Slavophile particularism and Chaadaevan civilizationism in a broadened definition of what constituted Russian nationality:

> Everyone will at least agree with us that the Russian character may be sharply differentiated from the European; in it one may distinctly observe a talent for higher synthesis, a capacity for universal reconciliation and panhumanism. . . . [The Russian] sympathizes with all of humanity regardless of differences of nationality, blood or soil. . . . He guesses by instinct the panhuman trait even among the most sharply differentiated peoples. . . . Every Russian can speak all languages and master the spirit of each foreign tongue in its nuances as if it were his native Russian language —which does not occur among Europeans *in the sense of a general national ability*." (55)

By this rather unusual definition, the essence of the Russian nationality was its innate cosmopolitanism. By physiology and culture, Russians possessed more than any other national group a putative gift for polyglot speech and universal empathy. The capstone of this argument was, for Dostoevsky, the monumental achievement of the national poet, Pushkin, whose very existence confirmed the inspiring idea of a Russianness that incorporated and superseded the boundaries of Western civilization. To elevate Pushkin to the status of national paragon was also to locate the embodiment of nationality in the literate culture of an emerging Russia. Dostoevsky was shifting the very ground of national identity away from its customary roots in the earthy soil of the folk.

The ambition and the stresses implicit in Dostoevsky's "native soil" idea of a united Russian culture are in plain view in two programmatic essays of 1861 titled "Pedantry and Literacy." In these essays Dostoevsky makes clear his understanding that the spread of literacy is the indispensable prerequisite for genuine emancipation and union with the native soil. Without access to letters and enlightened learning the former serf masses cannot participate equally in the development of an integral Russian nationality. But Dostoevsky, the former inmate of Omsk prison, also understands better than anyone else how wide and deep is the gulf (*yama*), the chasm (*propast'*) that separates the educated from the illiterate population of Russia. A history of serfdom and selective privileges for a Westernized elite has so alienated the common peasant that "mistrust is part of his flesh and blood" (19:7). In Dostoevsky's Russia the Europeanized educated class has come to realize that its mentality and its literature is distinctly Russian, yet it doesn't know how to approach the people so that they will accept the benefits of its consciousness and learning. Nothing, however, is more important than raising the entire nation to a common literacy and shared cultural understanding. Dostoevsky's answer to what seems an insurmountable dilemma is born of a desperate confidence in the literary potential of a divided nation.

Dostoevsky shrewdly ridicules, in an invented dialogue, the presupposition of many educators that they are not as "native" as the peasants they would enlighten. When Dostoevsky voices the suggestion that the literary achievements of nineteenth-century Russia have captured in poetic truths the evolving self-consciousness of the national identity, he is interrupted by a critical challenge: "Where is the national character in all this. . . . I mean, you know, fairy tales, folk songs, legends, and so on and so forth?" (12). To which Dostoevsky makes a pointed and unconventional reply: "You, it seems, directly equate nationality with folksiness. . . . Why, by what right should nationality belong only to the common folk? Does true nationality disappear with the development of the people? . . . Were the Greeks of the age of Pericles no longer as Greek as they had been three hundred years earlier?" (14). This reasoning opens up the possibility that a contemporary artist can be a "national poet" who articulates the undeveloped consciousness of the "native soil." Not surprisingly, Dostoevsky is already predicting in 1861 that the Russian people would learn to "recognize themselves" in the poetry of Pushkin if they could be brought over into literacy.[9] Dostoevsky was very close to asserting that an operative sense of nationality was dependent on an adequately complex literary discourse. The imagined community of the nation rested precariously on the spread of literacy. Unfortunately, the Russians faced the peculiar problem of overcoming the resistance of a rightly suspicious peasantry sealed off in its own protective culture of orality. Dostoevsky was enough of a psychologist to understand how tenuous was the hope of instilling a love of high literacy among a people resentful of their treatment as inferiors: "There is nothing a man understands so quickly as the tone you take in addressing him, your attitude toward him" (19:28).

Dostoevsky's second lengthy essay on "Pedantry and Literacy" launched a withering attack on well-meant "bookish" attempts to uplift the peasant masses. In the process, Dostoevsky revealed his own shrewd and sober awareness of the psychology of the "insulted and injured." The notion of distributing instructive and simplified "readers" to newly liberated villagers is anathema to Dostoevsky. The least whiff of condescension or paternalism will be detected by the common folk, and they will understand the message of such "readers" — "to make them read it because it is shameful to be an illiterate and uneducated peasant, shameful before the eyes of the benevolent and charitable gentlemen who were finally forced administratively and officially to promote enlightenment among the ignorant peasantry" (19:52). (It is worth noting that the colloquial Russian phrase for the ignorant peasantry is *chornyi narod* — literally, the "black folk," they who historically worked the black soil.) Though it may seem counterintuitive, Dostoevsky urges his educated countrymen to understand that it takes literary skill to approach the common people; to allure them into a love of letters one must "remove any thought of guardianship by their masters" (19:45). Dostoevsky's reading of the peasantry's mind makes it more susceptible to the indirection and complexity of literary literacy than to the blandishments of didactic and practical letters. But this is another way of saying that Dostoevsky intuited that the alienated and ironic self-consciousness of Russia's Westernized intelligentsia was analogous to the alienated and mistrustful consciousness of the denigrated Russian peasantry. The "native soil" had spawned a nationality that had internalized a double awareness of itself, but the barrier of literacy had kept the two halves of the nation from identifying with one another. Dostoevsky soon applied himself to making Russia's peculiar dual identity speak its mind in a shocking confessional narrative.

In retrospect, the classic literary expression of a peculiarly modern unhappy self-consciousness, of a relentless inner dualism, is unquestionably Dostoevsky's *Notes from Underground* (1864). Over many years, it has meant many conflicting things to many readers: a philosophical tract in defense of human freedom; a case study in existentialist psychology; a satire against scientific determinism; a rogue's progress that exposes a pathological irrationalism. But first and foremost, as Bakhtin so sensibly pointed out, this famous text is, from beginning to end, a speech-act of a most unique and peculiar sort. It is a written confessional self-definition in which each of the narrator's confident assertions is directed at an internalized other and then immediately qualified by "a loophole": "From the very first sentence, the hero's speech has already begun to cringe and break under the influence of the anticipated words of another with whom the hero . . . enters into the most intense internal polemic." [10] A wriggling uncertainty is present in the famous opening phrases: "I am a man who is ill. . . . I am a spiteful man. A decidedly unattractive man am I." [11] The very form of this utterance is paradoxical; the narrator's discourse is avowedly solipsistic and self-directed, yet it constantly addresses absent interlocutors. We are in the presence of an odd and inauthentic communicative gesture: the confessional soliloquy. Such an autobiographical act must necessarily be both endless and futile. Why? Because the initial impulse to confess one's inner self is motivated by a need for open acknowledgment of an unexpressed identity, but confirmation of that previously invisible self cannot be achieved in solitude. To be sure, a confessional narrative may arise from motives of pride or shame. The speaker could be seeking either affirmation or compassion; he might be struggling to achieve self-justification or self-acceptance. Ultimately, though, confession is the imploring of an other's understanding, but Dostoevsky's pathetic narrator is writing underground notes to himself, beseeching a self-absolution that can never be granted. No wonder, then, that one of the few genuine realizations this compulsive scribbler eventually arrives at is the depressing revelation: "This is no longer literature, but corrective punishment" (5:151).

But of course *Notes from Underground* is literature because the closeted diarist has been placed on public display by the professional writer, Fyodor Dostoevsky. In a signed footnote that greets readers of the first page of the narrative, Dostoevsky states: "Such persons as the compiler of these *Notes* not only exist in our society, but indeed must exist, considering the circumstances under which our society has generally been formed." Despite the fact that the underground man constantly writes to assert his autonomy and his belief (for better or worse) in his rebellious individuality, he is presented to us as a socially constructed phenomenon. Thus what Dostoevsky has placed on exhibit is a *symptomatic* antiheroic personality whose every unique word embodies a social pathology. The linguistic and grammatical quirks so brilliantly outlined in Bakhtin's discourse analysis are themselves placed within a larger frame of social reference that accounts for the narrator's representative act of evasive confessional self-definition. As we read Dostoevsky's excruciating transcript of a mind that experiences itself as an occupied zone, we begin to suspect that the underground man is, as Joseph Frank so aptly put it, a "parodistic persona" whose convoluted autobiography "exemplifies the tragi-comic impasses resulting from the effects of [outside] influences on the Russian national psyche."[12] This sense that Dostoevsky's fictional confession is exhibiting a Russian variant of a more widely shared modern self-consciousness has impressed generations of English-speaking readers (and writers) ever since Constance Garnett's popular translation became available in the early 1920s.

Dostoevsky's unhappy citizen of Petersburg, that "most abstract and intentional city on earth," is forever measuring his puny self-esteem against the grandiose architecture and cruel symmetries of a European mentality that distorts and obscures his given nature. In the *Notes* themselves, we watch an unsuccessful and unpersuasive rebellion against two internalized images of man that have plagued the narrator from his youth well into middle age. In the first part of the Petersburg diary we overhear a tirade of self-justifying "philosophizing" against the smug calculations of a Western rationalism that defines mental maturity as "enlightened self-interest." But this prolonged argument with utilitarian measurements of reasonable conduct is finally a defensive screen erected to hide the narrator's deep-laden insecurity about measuring up to other imported Western notions, particularly the seductive "bookish" ideals of romantic heroism and willed self-transcendence. As Slavic scholars of Dostoevsky have pointed out, the underground man is conducting a bitter critique of two sharply contrasting Western ideologies that had attracted Russian thinkers in Dostoevsky's lifetime.[13] First, withering irony is directed at scientific materialism's utopian systems of rational behavior modification, then bitter mockery is hurled at the sublime egotism promoted by the poetry and prose of literary romanticism. Dostoevsky's voice from the Russian underground launches a powerful double attack against imported Western theorems that suggest human nature can be shaped by a "rational egoism" or by an "egoistic altruism." But Dostoevsky also saw fit to entangle this direct protest in the twisted coils of an unattractive and pathetic personality. As the narrator rightly suggests at the delicate moment when he turns from the philosophical and anthropological arguments of part 1 to the intimate biographical details of part 2: "There is, incidentally, a whole psychology in all this" (5:166).

It can be called, for the sake of brevity, the psychology of postcolonial resentment. More than anything else, the humiliated pride of the underground man rages against his frustrated attempt to demonstrate that he is self-determined, that his identity is willed and autonomous. His tirade against utilitarian and deterministic theories of human conduct reaches its self-defeating climax when he claims that everywhere and always man's "most advantageous advantage" is his *need* to exercise his "independent volition no matter what it costs or where it leads" (5:113).[14] Oddly, the claim that man's autonomy is not to be denied rests on an argument from necessity—there is an obligatory or compulsory need to defy predictions of behavior. As Bakhtin's close attention to the language of Dostoevsky's diarist shows: "The work does not contain a single word gravitating exclusively toward itself and its referential object; there is not a single monologic word. . . . precisely in this act of anticipating the other's response and in responding to it he again demonstrates to the other (and to himself) his own dependence on this other" (229). The underground man's endless campaign to refute any and all imagined rejoinders to his self-assertive monologue results in a compulsive irrationalism that is as far from an assertion of human freedom as "whim" or "spite" (two of his favorite reasons for acting) are demonstrations of free choice.[15] The underground man settles protectively into his own solipsistic mousehole because he cannot bear to expose to public view evidence of that swarm of "contrary elements" within him that demands to be acknowledged as his "living life." The character who foolishly imagines that his free will can be demonstrated by desperate rejections of all conceivable self-characterizations is the same character who foolishly thinks he displays his indifference to others by stamping his feet as he parades his turned back on those who spurn him. Most pathetic of all, the underground character feels shame and hostility even in the presence of the genuine empathy extended to him by the humiliated prostitute, Liza, who is capable of accepting and understanding the inner contradictions of a suffering self-consciousness. Dostoevsky's underground notes express the interminable misery of one who forever feels his twoness and yet refuses to accept the divided consciousness which he culturally inhabits.

Something very much like Dostoevsky's culturally symptomatic display of a self-disguising confessional narrative emerged out of African American writing in 1912. In that year, a curious document titled *The Autobiography of an Ex-Coloured Man* first appeared. Written anonymously, the book seductively hinted at some dark mystery made transparent. To heighten that appeal, a preface issued by the publishers promised that the work would live up to its titillating title: "In these pages it is as though a veil had been drawn aside: the reader is given a view of the inner life of the Negro in America, is initiated into the 'freemasonry,' as it were, of the race." [16] Making obvious allusion to DuBois's pathbreaking but more opaque *Souls of Black Folk*, the publishers were offering their readers a quite different book—a "dispassionate" narrative that would make "no special plea for the Negro" while helpfully unriddling the sphinx-like thoughts of Negroes in relation to each other and to the whites. At the same time, the book was also being promoted for not treating "the coloured American as a *whole*," offering instead a "composite and proportionate presentation" of all the various groups of Negroes. Thus the advertising for this apparently straightforward book already indicated something rather tricky—the work purported to unveil both "Negroness" and the true multiplicity of Negroes in America. As things turned out, the book had even more surprises in store than its first readers could have imagined.

When Alfred A. Knopf published the second edition of the *Autobiography* in 1927 at the height of the Harlem Renaissance, the reading public learned that the original document was actually a novel, the fictionalized confession of a racial antihero. Its true author was a young multitalented lawyer, diplomat, and songwriter, James Weldon Johnson, who in writing the book anonymously had taken on the colors of a "chameleon" who had chosen to pass for white. The text was thus exposed as a complex act of subtle duplicity, since both the fictional narrator and the actual author were in different ways and for different reasons passing for what they were not. To compound the various levels of masked identity, Johnson himself had dictated almost verbatim the language of the original preface signed by "THE PUBLISHERS," thus miming the desires of white outsiders peering in on the secrets of an exemplary Negro autobiography.[17] Johnson and his nameless protagonist both knew what it meant to be a crossover artist, yet only one of them could truly be said to have repudiated his color.

Although the bland surface of the ex-colored man's prose is wholly unlike the agitated scribblings of the underground man, Johnson is, like Dostoevsky, practicing a double-voiced narrative irony that exposes the moral failure of an antihero in the very form of his speech. *The Autobiography of an Ex-Coloured Man* is written in a deliberately evasive, "colorless" prose designed to deflect attention from some rather startling contradictions and shifts of attitude.[18] The first two paragraphs of Johnson's novel already serve as fair warning that the narrator is "divulging the great secret" of his life without quite understanding or caring to understand his motives in doing so. He says he may have been led by the impulse of "the un-found-out criminal to take somebody into his confidence," even though that act is likely to lead to his undoing. Alternatively, however, his urge to confess might simply express the thrill of exposing a transgression in public. Is his primary motive, then, unconscious penitence or a perverse pride in personal bravado? At the start of the confession, we are offered something like the complexity of Raskolnikov, but without his mental energy or inclination to be introspective — "back of it all, I think I find a sort of savage and diabolical desire to gather up all the little tragedies of my life, and turn them into a practical joke on society. And, too, I suffer a vague feeling of unsatisfaction, of regret, of almost remorse, from which I am seeking relief . . ." (3). This trailing off into unexamined or ignored ambiguities becomes the true signature of Johnson's studiously faceless narrator; he regularly settles for self-protective imprecision instead of revealing his true colors. But Johnson also cleverly sees to it that his narrator's prose quietly betrays what it is he chooses not to see, what it is he identifies with, but disowns.

Much as Dostoevsky managed to both impersonate and undermine the voice he heard emanating from Russia's underground self-consciousness, Johnson dons the mask of his ex-colored man in order to tell a double-voiced tale in which he can, in African American parlance, "signify" on the career of a self-betraying Negro American artist. Reading Johnson's invented narrative, we eavesdrop on the rationalizations offered by a fair-skinned African American who has chosen to pursue the path of self-interest by passing for white and by denigrating or denying his visceral attachment to colored culture. As Eric Sundquist has shrewdly remarked, James Weldon Johnson is "ragging" on a failed double of himself, narrating the story of a biracial composer who has sold himself short and given up on negotiating between two oppositional cultural worlds.[19] In 1906, Johnson had abandoned an eminently successful collaboration with his brother, John Rosamund, as popularizers of "coon song" musicals on Broadway in order to accept public service as a U.S. consul in Latin America. During this hiatus in his artistic career, he seems to have become anxious about the degradation of African American talent involved in the commercialization of Negro expressive culture. Before he left for Venezuela, Johnson had begun to circulate draft chapters of a future novel to his chosen literary mentor, Brander Matthews, Columbia University's cosmopolitan professor of dramatic literature.[20] In the completed manuscript, Johnson's fictional protagonist, despite great musical talent, becomes a virtual house servant who provides "novelty" entertainment to a bored millionaire and his guests by turning classical music into "rags." But Johnson's composition in prose, like sophisticated ragtime music, kept up a subtle syncopated exchange between two simultaneous and contrasting lines, playing a standard "rags to riches" American success story against buried allusions to slave narrative subtexts while containing both themes within a single picaresque narrative form.[21] Johnson's debut performance as a novelist was itself emblematic of a hybrid African American artistry that demands a nuanced appreciation of its own unique voice.

Johnson's "colored" narrator is depicted as the product of a hidden biracial connection. In his childhood, he was carefully taught by his kept and well-kept middle-class Negro mother to identify with the white patriarch who sponsors him behind the scenes but disclaims his paternity. It is tempting to view Johnson's protagonist as an ironic representation of the "progressive" Negro elite in post-Reconstruction America; he proudly wears around his neck a hollowed-out gold piece given him by his absentee white father. This necklace insidiously suggests the yoke of his collusion with neoslavery, his acceptance of a false worth offered by white patronage. Later, too, when the young musician finds his niche as a cultural valet to his millionaire "good patron," his own account suggests sickening compliance with degrading but profitable "darky" employment:

> I soon learned that my task was not to be considered finished until he got up from his chair and said: "That will do." The man's powers of endurance in listening often exceeded mine in performing—yet I am not sure that he was always listening. At times I became so oppressed with fatigue and sleepiness that it took almost superhuman effort to keep my fingers going; in fact, I believe I sometimes did so while dozing. During such moments this man sitting there so mysteriously silent, almost hid in a cloud of heavy-scented smoke, filled me with a sort of unearthly terror. He seemed to be some grim, mute, but relentless tyrant, possessing over me a supernatural power which he used to drive me on mercilessly to exhaustion. But these feelings came very rarely; besides, he paid me so liberally I could forget much. (121)

In this scene Johnson precociously registers a deep anxiety over racist exploitation of "colored" entertainment in a liberal Northern economy. His prose also uncannily suggests a falsely benevolent and ghastly variant of the "white terror" that dominated and paralyzed so many Southern blacks.

It matters a good deal that Johnson's white-identified narrator imbibed from his Southern mother's improvised songs a cultural blackness that he forever associates with his "natural" expressive genius: "I used to stand by her side and often interrupt and annoy her by chiming in with strange harmonies. . . . I remember I had a particular fondness for the black keys" (5). Indeed, throughout his many travels and chameleonic shifts of attitude toward the lower-class blacks he encounters, Johnson's narrator cannot repress his visceral response to vernacular black culture. Significantly, his prose only becomes colorful when it conveys in supple sentences the highly original, bicultural artistry of African Americans dancing the cakewalk, throwing the "bones," playing ragtime, preaching their sermons, and singing their gospel songs. Ironically, the narrator's profound attachment to the genius of his people is revealed to him in Europe when an enthusiastic German pianist plays variations on ragtime themes "in every known musical form": "I had been turning classical music into rag-time, a comparatively easy task; and this man had taken rag-time and made it classic. . . . I gloated over the immense amount of material I had to work with, not only modern rag-time, but also the old slave songs" (142–43). This inspiration gives the pallid narrator the courage to recover his boyhood pride in the "colored" race and to defy the taunts of his cynical white patron: "My boy, you are by blood, by appearance, by education and by tastes a white man. . . . This idea you have of making a Negro out of yourself is nothing more than a sentiment; and you do not realize the fearful import of what you intend to do" (144–45). Undeterred, the narrator transplants himself back to his native South. Outside Macon, Georgia, he attends a "big meeting" at which he discovers, like DuBois before him, the powerful combined cultural force of the Negro preacher and the song leader. By a happy coincidence (or deft symbolic touch) the inspirational duo is named John Brown and "Singing Johnson," suggesting a glorious blending of the militant and the aesthetic strains in the legacy of the Southern spirituals: "So many of these songs contain more than mere melody; there is sounded in them that elusive undertone, the note in music that is not heard with the ears" (181). Sadly, though, Johnson's narrator is not made of the stuff needed to realize his dream of becoming an acknowledged composer of Negro classical music.

The crucial difference between a genuine African American artist like James Weldon Johnson and his false double is revealed in the advice the ex-colored narrator offers black people in the paragraph preceding his description of a horrific lynching that drives him in terror and shame from identifying with blackness: "In many instances a slight exercise of the sense of humor would save much anxiety of soul. . . . If the mass of Negroes took their present and future as seriously as do most of their leaders, the race would be in no mental condition to sustain the terrible pressure which it undergoes; it would sink of its own weight" (183). This attitude is perfectly consistent with the occasional sniffs of condescension that expose Johnson's narrator as at best a halfhearted champion of Negro equality:

> A novel dealing with coloured people who lived in respectable homes and amidst a fair degree of culture and who naturally acted "just like white folks" would be taken in a comic-opera sense. In this respect the Negro is

much in the position of a great comedian who gives up the lighter roles to play tragedy. No matter how well he may portray the deeper passions, the public is loath to give him up in his old character; they even conspire to make him a failure in serious work, in order to force him back into comedy. In the same respect, the public is not too much to be blamed, for great comedians are more scarce than mediocre tragedians; every amateur actor is a tragedian. (168)

Johnson's narrator can imagine but cannot embody a serious assertion of the meaning of color in American culture. As a practicing musician his greatest success is achieved by playing Mendelssohn's "Wedding March" in ragtime; as a racial politician, his best advice to American blacks is that they, in effect, "lighten up." No wonder Johnson's pale and bloodless narrator chooses to become an "ex-colored man" rather than carry the serious burden of his full identity. In the hierarchy of values reflected in the bleached and bland language of Johnson's antiheroic narrator, cultural blackness needs to be underplayed or, if expressed, only allowed to perform entertaining variations on white themes and melodies.

Appropriately, the final chord in the narrator's movement toward self-betrayal occurs at a piano. He pledges his love to a classic white beauty at a "progressive card party" by "involuntary closing" Chopin's Thirteenth Nocturne on a major triad instead of the minor chord it requires (208–9). In a futile attempt to resolve a complex internal tension, he strikes a fraudulent final harmony, "thus silencing the minor key of his black life" and renouncing the music of his black soul.[22]

An extensive critical literature has been produced in the effort to define the precise degree and direction of the irony present in the evasive sentences and strange non sequiturs that characterize Johnson's narrator.[23] Some readers detect a consistent authorial irony at the expense of the narrator's reliability; others protest that the naive narrator is, ironically, often a rather reliable index to Johnson's view of the class and racial conflicts in American society. The interpretive difficulty is much like that which faces the reader of *Notes from Underground*: how are we to understand a patently antiheroic protagonist who often voices opinions we think we recognize as the author's, but that occur within a large-scale narrative riddled with contradictions and corrosive ironies?[24] Good readers will understand, whether they have read Bakhtin or not, that Johnson and Dostoevsky are writing sentences that bear double messages, that speak for the narrator and the author in a tricky hidden dialogue. Like Dostoevsky's underground diary, Johnson's narrative belongs finally to the genre of parody, but it is parody of a complex type in which an unresolved contest of implications replaces a simple undermining of any one character or style of expression.[25] The entire speech-act of these fictional autobiographies demonstrates a truth about cultural identity that cannot be summarized in simple dualisms (either/or) or crude ironies (this, not that). Looked at in this Bakhtinian manner, the discourse of Dostoevsky's underground man articulates the mentality of a representative self that experiences itself both as a cultural construct and as moral agent. Similarly, the ex-colored man's confession offers testimony to the difficult truth that he is not essentially either black or white, though social forces conspire to make him choose to pass for one or the other.[26] James Weldon Johnson composed The Autobiography of an Ex-Coloured Man in a "double-voiced discourse" that inscribes into its prose the indelible features of an African American expressive tradition whose hybrid forms of speech and music speak for a substantial and sophisticated culture that has been denigrated, yet cannot finally be denied.

Independent of English translations of Dostoevsky's Notes from Underground, and well in advance of Bakhtin's discourse analysis, African American writing had brought forth a literary form that closely intersected with the Russian genre of the culturally symptomatic confessional monologue. On reflection, it should not seem too surprising that "double-voiced" narratives emerged from the midst of two different nationalities that were similarly entangled in an inextricably dual identity that was partly Western and partly not. Although their stylistic symptoms differ widely, both texts expose to view the cultural hybridity of a painfully emerging identity that speaks in several tongues.

What finally makes Dostoevsky's underground man and Johnson's ex-colored man pathetic and pathological examples of an antiheroic self-betrayal is quite simply their shared inability to accept and creatively affirm their internalized biculturalism. At the same time, it is worth noting the difference between these two denials of an ineradicable biculturalism—in the Russian case, it goes unacknowledged, but in the African American instance it is deliberately hidden. In an earlier draft of Johnson's novel, the last (and perhaps too conclusive) line was: "I know now that the very soul-trying ordeals that I have avoided would have brought out of me all the best that was in me." [27] Johnson's ex-colored man is conscious of his deceptions and self-deception, though he tries to hide them from view. But the underground man is unconscious of his compulsive self-evasions, though his prose betrays them at every turn.

Dostoevsky saw fit to celebrate Pushkin as Russia's national genius precisely because that poet had discovered an artistic shape and a compelling moral in the anguish of his hero Onegin's divided loyalty to rustic Russia's unvarnished beauty and Petersburg's urbane glamour: "With surprise and veneration and, on the other hand, almost with a touch of derision, we first began to understand what it meant to be a Russian. . . . all this happened only when we began to be properly conscious of ourselves as Europeans and realized that we too had to enter into the universal life of mankind" (PPS 19:10). Fyodor Dostoevsky and James Weldon Johnson were the first imaginative writers in their national cultures to give full expression to the internal ruminations of a symptomatic postcolonial double-mindedness. After them, much Russian and African American writing has continued to emerge from "soul-trying ordeals" that voice the pain of divided minds straining to accommodate the birth of a twin sensibility, a multiple culturedness that more and more has seemed to be the true measure of each nationality. On the evidence of Dostoevsky's and Johnson's symptomatic confessions of a problematic cultural hybridity, the national "soul" was sole no longer.

6 NATIVE SONS AGAINST NATIVE SOUL

Maxim Gorky and Richard Wright

It is surely an irony, if not an embarrassment, that the two major modern autobiographers with the closest family ties to the legacy of Russian serfdom and American slavery firmly rejected nationalist ideas of ethnic exclusivism or cultural separateness. Raised in intimate and bruising contact with folk who still bore the evident scars of bondage, Maxim Gorky (1868–1936) and Richard Wright (1908–1960) embraced a revolutionary politics and vociferously resisted what they had experienced in the oppressed and oppressive culture that had spawned them. Each one carried into maturity the large psychic burden of the alienated insider, restlessly seeking to account for the sources of the rage and rebellion that set them apart from their closest relatives. Native grandsons of former serfs and slaves, they rejected the cult of native "soul" however defined. Both men struggled mightily against the temptation of nationalist intellectuals to sentimentalize or glorify a home culture that had historically endured abuse and accommodated servility.

Reviewing *Black Boy* in 1945, Ralph Ellison noted the resemblance in theme and tone between "Richard Wright's blues" and the antecedent literature of Russian serfdom: "The extent of the beatings and psychological maimings meted out by Southern Negro parents rivals those described by nineteenth-century Russian writers as characteristic of peasant life under the Czars." [1] In the same essay, Ellison cited Dostoevsky's *House of the Dead* as one of Wright's "literary guides" in capturing the psychic distortions of lives lived under oppression, but added that characteristically "Wright *recognized* and made no peace with its essential cruelty." Wright's scathing account of his escape from a deadening home life in the "Black Belt" and his liberation by means of insubordination and literacy was a deliberately ironic twentieth-century reprise of Frederick Douglass's narrative of the life of an ex-slave. But Wright's autobiography was no less a reflection of his powerful identification with the life and writing of Maxim Gorky. Coming to social consciousness in

Depression-era Chicago's John Reed Club at the height of the Popular Front campaign to unite the thinking proletariat of the world, the young refugee from America's "lower depths" could not help but be aware of the Russian writer's legendary life and inspirational example. Gorky's name was promoted widely in pamphlets, newsprint, and, above all, in the world-famous autobiography in both its translated and cinematic versions.[2] It is not surprising then that Wright, like Gorky, should have turned to autobiography as his most effective weapon in beating back the retrograde partisans of folk wisdom and national "soul." Gorky's *Childhood* (1913) and Wright's *Black Boy* were each a continuation by superior artistic means of polemics they had waged in the years immediately preceding the composition of their own exemplary lives.

Between 1905, the year of the brutal suppression in Petersburg of Father Gapon's peaceful workers' demonstration at the Winter Palace, and 1913, the year in which Gorky published the influential account of his own formative years, the young writer had emerged as an obsessive berater of Russia's literary giants, Tolstoy and Dostoevsky. This extraordinary assault was, as we shall see, not entirely free of the psychological complication now known as "anxiety of influence"; nonetheless, the public terms of Gorky's hostility toward Russia's cultural colossi were (and should be) taken seriously. Those terms were moral and political. Gorky's allegation was that Russia's greatest writers had conspired to betray their people's much-deferred faith in justice and social reconstruction. His complaint was most famously articulated in a lengthy tirade of 1909, "The Disintegration of Personality": "After the fall of hundreds of young and splendid people, and after a decade of heroic struggle, the greatest geniuses of a land of slaves exclaimed with one voice: 'Submit.' "[3] A few years afterward, Gorky wrote rapturously to a literary critic who had in his estimation finally understood the peculiar "melancholy" that constituted a "*national disease* of the spirit":

> What I am saying is that this is the first time I have encountered in such acute and precise form the sad, yet much-needed and amazingly timely indication of an innate inclination of the Great Russian towards an Oriental passivism which, in combination with the renowned "breadth of the Russian soul" — or rather with the shapeless and chaotic nature of that soul —

gives us that "dashing nihilism" which is so typical of us, and yet is always so baneful and especially destructive.[4]

Here Gorky actually seems to be subscribing to a negative version of Russian "soul," abhorring some fatal genetic predisposition toward reckless fatalism; yet the diagnosis also makes a very pointed allusion to some grandiloquent Dostoevskian phrasing that has obviously made the "disease" even more pernicious. Whatever ails the collective Russian will is, in part, a literary ailment.

By 1913 Gorky was fulminating in two angry articles against the Moscow Arts Theater for staging adaptations of novels by Dostoevsky and thus promoting a contagion of "Karamazovism." In no uncertain terms Gorky ridiculed the notion that Dostoevsky was a prophet of national salvation; rather, he was Russia's "evil genius" who "deeply understood and presented with relish two diseases bred in the Russian by his monstrous history: the sadistic cruelty of a thoroughly disillusioned nihilist, and its opposite, the masochism of a beaten, frightened creature."[5] The intensity of this denunciation displays fascination as much as antipathy; indeed, Gorky's struggle with Dostoevsky amounted to a lifelong attempt to exorcise a private as well as a national demon. Tolstoy had piously encouraged among his adherents the spiritual passivity of "nonresistance to evil," but Dostoevsky had exacerbated an active adoration of suffering that ran deep through centuries of painful Russian history. As Gorky meditated on his own life, he could not forgive the one literary predecessor who had made intellectually seductive the unfortunate Russian propensity for an "anarchism of the defeated" that permitted saintly peasants, craven sensualists, and underground intellectuals to wallow helplessly in a chaotic, unjustifiable world.[6] So it came to pass that Gorky offered his *Childhood* to Russian readers as an antidote to Dostoevsky. His own biography could serve as a living refutation of that redemptively suffering Russian land imagined by Dostoevsky.

Richard Wright, too, was embroiled in literary controversy in the years preceding his emergence as the visible black standard-bearer of proletarian realism. Like Gorky, he was in revolt against what he regarded as a pernicious degradation of the folk by the self-appointed tribunes of a native culture. In Wright's case, however, the battle was joined in order to defeat an inadequate appreciation for the seriousness (in all senses) of the resistant subculture of America's black underclass. In the autumn of 1937, the ire of Richard Wright overflowed in two eruptions against the Harlem Renaissance and the person he regarded as its most seductive representative, Zora Neale Hurston. What is especially interesting in retrospect, aside from the intense enmity between this opposed pair of black Southern writers, is Wright's utter contempt for any form or shape of "puttin' on de massa." All the devices of linguistic evasion and indirect aggression that were cause for celebration in Hurston's world are for him nothing but shameful displays of impotence. Aligning himself with a notion of resistance that was proudly gendered masculine, Wright's "Blueprint for Negro Writing" and his dismissive review of *Their Eyes Were Watching God* demonstrate a symptomatic hostility directed at black writing that dresses itself up in ethnic frills. Although conceding that Hurston could write well, Wright accused her of primping up a picturesque primitivism: "Her prose is cloaked in that facile sensuality that has dogged Negro expression since the days of Phillis Wheatley. . . . Miss Hurston *voluntarily* continues in her novel the tradition which was *forced* upon the Negro in the theater, that is, the minstrel technique that makes the 'white folks' laugh."[7] Wright's personal distaste for clever writing that threatened to make Negro folksiness sentimentally appealing to envious and condescending whites led him to join the public contempt of American leftist journals for the so-called renaissance of the Negro arts. His young man's literary manifesto, which coincided with the attack on Hurston, cruelly satirized the Negro literati as castrati: "They entered the Court of Public Opinion dressed in the knee-pants of servility, curtsying to show that the Negro was not inferior, that he was human, and that he had a life comparable to that of other people. For the most part these artistic ambassadors were received as though they were French poodles who do clever tricks."[8] Much like Gorky, Wright adopted a rhetoric of degeneracy to impugn those who had, in his estimation, distorted the real features of the masses. The lives of the folk amounted to much more than some colorful collective melodrama shuttling between laughter and tears.

Although it might seem that Gorky was pained by a debilitating cult of Russian suffering, whereas Wright was pained by the cultivation of an effete and entertaining blackness, they each were advocating a similar literary revision of the representation of the historic folk. Indeed, Wright's "blueprint" for a literature of the black masses closely resembles Gorky's 1934 address to the First All-Union Congress of Soviet Writers over which he presided.[9] Wright was calling for a selective integration of the "progressive" aspects of Negro folklore and religion into a consciously refashioned narrative of collective consciousness that would promote in the native readership a revolutionary attitude toward reality. Gorky's famous speech, which helped consolidate the official definition of "socialist realism" as the historically concrete depiction of reality in its revolutionary development, was itself deeply committed to a normative and purified reading of Russian folklore that was his own invention.[10] Likewise, Wright kept himself at arms' length from the indiscriminate "conspicuous ornamentation" of black religion and folkways that he took to be so fashionable in current black writing. Instead, he embraced along with Gorky what he foresaw as a more empowering and accessible history-making art of mass culture:

> Negro writers must accept the nationalist implications of their lives, not in order to encourage them, but in order to change and transcend them. . . . a deep, informed, and complex consciousness is necessary; a consciousness which draws for its strength upon the fluid lore of a great people, and moulds this lore with the concepts that move and direct the forces of history today. . . . all the complexity, the strangeness, the magic wonder of life that plays like a bright sheen over the most sordid existence, should be there. To borrow a phrase from the Russians, it should have a *complex simplicity.*[11]

As we shall see, more than a shared revolutionary ideology is in evidence here. The mystery of an uplifting exposure to oppression informed the lives these two writers led and the books they wrote.

Richard Wright's first writings emerged from a biography that bore many striking and uncomfortably close resemblances to Gorky's well-known life history. Both writers suffered an abused and peripatetic childhood in the midst of a squabbling clan of downwardly mobile former serfs and sharecroppers. As children they led vagabond existences along the major river of the nation's heartland; at an early age deprived of fathers and disappointed in mothers, they shuttled in and out of temporary households dominated by sporadic violence and a stultifying piety. Wright's reading of his own life was undeniably affected by his intimate awareness of Gorky's emblematic autobiography. It is instructive to measure carefully the formal similarities and tonal differences between *Black Boy* (subtitled *A Record of Childhood and Youth*) and Gorky's *Childhood* (*Detstvo*).

Both volumes, as their titles indicate, deliberately expand the personal memoir of formative experience into a much more portentous narrative shape; each work takes on the gravity of an exemplary life, charting a pilgrim's progress out of the slough of despond. Gorky's title signaled a conscious allusion and challenge to Tolstoy's *Childhood* (1852), the prototypical Russian "pseudo-autobiography" in which a gentrified myth of childhood awareness was elaborately reconstructed in the representative perceptions of a narrator who functioned as a transparent pseudonym for the real author.[12] With this strategy, authoritative generalizations about the process of coming to consciousness could be inferred from what were obviously the fictionalized particulars of a "genuine" childhood experience. When Gorky allowed his famous fictional name to underwrite the acute observations of the endangered child, Aleksei Peshkov, who was his actual former self, he was not only reversing Tolstoy's strategy, he was offering a countermyth to the prevailing literary image of a child's dawning self-awareness. Richard Wright was performing a similar repetition with a crucial difference when he employed the testimonial genre of the African American autobiography to compose something close to his own version of "poor Richard's almanac," a survival manual boldly titled *Black Boy*. It is certainly appropriate to read Wright's now famous book as a pointed reiteration of Frederick Douglass's prototypical slave narrative of 1845, especially given its celebration of a rise to literacy that rescues a self-emancipated man from a native "black world" that is nothing but an extension of slavery. Yet an equally compelling case can be made for reading *Black Boy* as an African American autobiography composed in conscious and active dialogue with what was generally accepted as the paradigmatic text of proletarian self-development—namely, with the work that Erik Erikson aptly named "the Bolshevik legend of Maxim Gorky's youth."[13]

Although Erikson's perceptive reading of Gorky's autobiographical myth is derived primarily from an analysis of Mark Donskoi's film of 1938, his argument is more faithful to the literary text than is suspected by those many readers, inside and outside Russia, who insist on sentimentalizing Gorky's portrait of his nurturing, folksy grandmother. Briefly stated, Erikson claims that the author's childhood persona embodies a "protestant" refusal to participate fully in the conventions of his home culture:

> Each scene and each significant person thus represents a temptation to regress to the traditional morality and the ancient folkways of the people. . . . By far the greatest temptation, the one which accompanies Alyosha to the very end, is that of finding refuge in his grandmother's peace of mind and becoming part of her calm conscience. . . . she obviously symbolizes the primitive trust of the people, their ability to survive and persist, and yet also their weakness in enduring what will ultimately enslave them." [14]

Readers of Gorky's remarkable childhood memoir immediately confront, as did Wright's later readers, an uncomfortably intimate domestic scene in which maternal discipline protectively stifles a traumatized child. The opening scene already frames the central circumstance of Gorky's childhood: premature exposure to the most brutal facts of life accompanied by the pacifying consolations of folk wisdom. A terrified four-year-old child witnesses in rapid succession the corpse of his father and the labor pains of his grieving mother as his grandmother holds him close, stilling his questions and literally cloaking him:

> "And why should I shush?"
> "Because you're making too much noise," she said, laughing.
> The way she spoke was caressing, cheerful, rhythmical. We became firm friends from the first day, but now I wanted her to take me out of that room as soon as possible. [15]

Later, at his father's grave site, the child and the grandmother both notice several trapped frogs desperately scrambling to climb out of the rapidly filling pit:

> "Will the frogs get out?"
> "No, it's already too late," she answered. "God be with them!" (11)

These tiny episodes already contain subtle undercurrents of the affection and resistance that are characteristic of the adult narrator's ambiguous attachment to his lulling nurturance among the historic Russian folk.

Much of Gorky's autobiography is told in the voice and perspective of a child deeply immersed in the turbulence and calm, the anarchy and quietism of the "dark people" that Turgenev's hunter had watched so attentively in the days of serfdom. Gorky's artistry guarantees that his

readers will stand, as Helen Muchnic observed, alongside that astonished boy "in a dark corner, gazing in tense and troubled incomprehension on the tragically sordid scene that unfolds." [16] But this contempla-
tive child-witness is supported by and sometimes interrupted by another
voice that belongs to the more impatient writer who stands behind the
retrospective adult narrator. At the beginning of the second chapter, it
is Gorky himself who intrudes to make clear the ambition behind this
patient re-creation of a child's baffled responses and vacillating emotions in a typically teeming Russian household: "Truth is grander than
pity and I am not writing about myself but about that close, suffocating
atmosphere of oppressive impressions in which lived, and lives to this
very day, the ordinary Russian person" (17). Much, then, depends on how
effectively Gorky's narrative cultivates the reader's sympathies and an-
tipathies as it reconstitutes the representative insults and injuries of a
Russian boyhood. Yet the greatest achievement of Gorky's writing rests
on its persuasive presentation of a still-conflicted adult mind as it actively recalls the unresolved conflicts of a battered childhood. And that is
why the body of critical opinion has not been able to reach a stable consensus about Gorky's final attitude toward the vast world of the illiterate
and semiliterate Russian folk in which he was raised.

To be sure, the careful sequence of episodes in *Childhood* does follow
Erikson's outline of a proletarian's progress. The child withdraws from
and gradually rejects traditional peasant behaviors that collude with a
folk culture thriving on punitive discipline, formal piety, outbursts of
uncontrolled rage, and a disabling resignation to suffering. The development of a "protestant" personality resistant to the mentality of traditional Russia can be charted by the casualty list of sympathetic figures victimized by the Kashirin clan of former serfs with whom Alyosha
lives. Early on the child is literally shielded from the grandfather's savage routine of ritual whippings by "Gypsy," an adopted foundling whose
strapping physique takes much of the intended punishment. The first of
several "intercessor" figures, Gypsy is an outcast who pays the ultimate
price for assimilating to the domestic culture of the household; given
shelter as a reliable beast of burden within the family dye-works, he soon
adopts the reckless abandon of the Kashirin males and the self-oblivious
compassion of the grandmother. Faithfully serving the extended family
with his compulsive thievery and martyrlike obedience, Gypsy is finally
crushed under the weight of a burial cross he has been ordered to carry

to the grave of an uncle's battered wife. Like Alyosha's large, soft grand-mother whom he adores, Gypsy has learned too well how to be an expert at tolerating cruelty and minimizing suffering.

A quite different ally of the child in the Kashirin home is a lodger nicknamed "Good Deal" (*Khoroshee delo*) for his constant comment when-ever he is invited to tea. Gorky is careful to depict him with the pointed beard, spectacles, and "books in the new typography" that indicate the presence of a Russian *intelligent*, or progressive intellectual. With equal care "Good Deal" is portrayed as an enthusiast for the grandmother's magnificent oral rendition of the folktale, "Ivan the Warrior and Miron the Hermit," urging that it be written down as "terribly, truly Russian." Gorky obviously concurs, making sure to insert into his text the entire eighty lines of this folk poem about a too-obedient warrior who ac-cepts his master's decree to behead a solitary champion of truth and peace and who then himself dies waiting for the hermit to finish his last prayers for humanity: "This was, you see, his punishment / For heeding the evil command / And for hiding behind another's conscience" (83). Here we can easily detect Gorky at work busily winnowing authentic folk materials for suitable kernels of progressive content. "Good Deal" himself, however, is not so fortunate as to be appreciated by Alyosha's family. The solitary intellectual and amateur scientist is ostracized, even by the grandmother, as bad company for Alyosha: "Watch out that you don't hang around him too much; God knows what kind of man he is" (85). Although the future writer's would-be tutor in secular learning gets summarily banished from Alyosha's family as a godless and dangerous character, Gorky as author reserves the right to speak a proper farewell: "Thus ended my friendship with the first of an endless series of aliens in their own country who are its best people" (90).

Toward the end of the memoir the young Aleksei Peshkov becomes increasingly embittered and abandoned. The grandparents' family tears itself apart in ugly dissension and falls into penury. Alyosha's beautiful but remote mother remarries and is brutally abused before the child's eyes while the grandmother, to solace her woes, takes increasingly to drink. In one crucial late sequence of events the rebellious child mocks the obligatory recitation of pious and pedantic lessons, then becomes appalled by his grandmother's submission to and suppression of her husband's savagery, and takes sweet revenge by cutting off heads from the illustrated saints' calendar by which his grandfather regulates his daily prayers. Finally, in chapter 12, Gorky lessons his readers with a parable of his own. Evoking one more time the sinister image of the burial pit that yawned open at the beginning of his childhood, Alyosha is now seen actively undertaking a reconstruction of his environment. The reader witnesses a precocious experiment in perestroika, as the future revolutionary uproots and overhauls a nasty backyard pit in which one of his adult tormentors had committed suicide. Alyosha transforms the unsightly bloodsoaked earth into a "garden project" (*postroiki v sadu*) that he proclaims to be his sanctuary and "first independent deed" (142). As Gorky's *Childhood* ends, the unsponsored boy is about to be thrust forth "into the world," yet he is clearly ready to leave his folk home behind for a new community of his fellows, the dispossessed of the earth. Even so, it is less than clear that Gorky's writing has made a clean break from its roots in the ancient subculture of the Russian folk.

A profound ambivalence permeates the form and content of Gorky's *Childhood*. Depending on the critical lens through which it is viewed, the exemplary life of Aleksei Peshkov has been described as a parable of enlightenment, a mutation of the traditional Russian folk epic, and as a "secular auto-hagiography." [17] This confusion about the fundamental genre of the work is virtually inevitable given the narrative's evident uncertainty regarding the role of the folk's lore in contributing to the formation of Gorky's young rebel from the banks of the Volga. A critical measure of this unresolved tension is found in the unforgettable presentation of Alyosha's earthy grandmother. At times it seems as if this nurturing matriarch brings into the battered child's life a redemption of *bliny* and *byliny*, of sweet pancakes and heroic tales: "I had been as if asleep, hidden in a dark corner, but she appeared, awakened me, led me out into the light, wrapped everything around me into one unbroken thread and wove everything into a many-colored lace" (14). Yet these beautiful images associated with Arina Kashirina soon get entangled with many threads of meaning. Speaking to the child, she explains away her husband's greedy exploitation of Gypsy's compulsive thievery with a hand-loomed folk saying: "It's all, Lyosha, complicated lacework spun out by a blind hag, and how are we supposed to make out the design in it?" (37). To cite another memorable image, the grandmother's luxurious hair is glorious and sheltering in the small child's eyes. But he also sees it become a convenient means of abuse when she is dragged by it and battered with her own hairpins. Very subtly, that mantle of hair becomes associated with the seductive potential in folklore and folk religion for a paralyzing enchantment: "I used to take her heavy braids into my hands and wrap them all around my neck as I listened attentively, without moving a muscle, to her endless stories that never satiated me" (43). The implication is perhaps made more directly at other moments in Gorky's narrative when it is obvious that the grandmother's traditional peasant piety richly embroiders scenes of patriarchal brutality and saintly endurance in colorful images and rhythms of speech. As we have also seen, her vast repertory of folksongs and oral tales could serve to inspire a patient courage in those whose fate it was to undergo suffering. By itself, however, the musicality and fantasy so dear to the vernacular culture of the Russian folk did not encourage active resistance to the customary evils of serfdom and their cruel residue in peasant society.

The adult narrator who occasionally intrudes on the faithful account of Aleksei Peshkov's childhood recollections is often painfully of two minds. The bitter truth that Gorky knows confuses him. Is it an affliction or an inspiration to his readers? At the end of the penultimate chapter, after the particularly ugly scene of spousal assault and battery on Alyosha's pregnant mother, Gorky pauses in wonderment at his own activity:

> As I recall these vile abominations of barbarous Russian life, I stop at times and ask myself: is it even worth it to speak of them? And then, with renewed confidence, I answer yes, it's worth it, for it is the living loathsome truth and even today it hasn't ceased to exist. And that truth must be known to its very roots so that it can be ripped by its roots from the memory, from the soul of man, from our oppressive and shameful life.
>
> And there is another more affirmative reason compelling me to depict these abominations. Although they are repulsive and cause pain, perhaps crushing the life out of many sensitive souls, the ordinary Russian is sufficiently healthy and young at heart to overcome them, and overcome them he will. (152–53)

This is, of course, a reprise of the metaphor of the "garden project." Alyosha the child and Gorky the writer are both determined to be healthy minded when confronted with the "beastly rot" that is the residue of serfdom. The oppressive truth (and the truth of oppression) can fertilize the mind and nourish the will to beautify life. But this willful leap of faith is uncomfortably close to a Dostoevskian awareness of the stimulating appeal of suffering. The chapter that records the first appearance of the rebel in young Aleksei Peshkov concludes with a sobering admission: "Long afterwards I understood that the Russian people, because of the poverty and squalor of their lives, generally love to divert themselves with woes, playing with them like children, and they are rarely ashamed to be unhappy. Amid endless monotony suffering comes as a holiday, and fire is an entertainment; on a blank face even a scar is an adornment" (120). Gorky may have liberated himself personally from the seductive fatalism and piety of the Russian folk, but he could not undo the emotional bonds that kept him captive to their culture's penchant for extremes of stoicism and rebellion. That is why he struggled all his life to attack "Karamazovism" at its roots.

Richard Wright's searing account of his Mississippi childhood appears to have been written as a deliberate assault on the pieties of black American "soul talk." It also would appear to have been composed with Gorky's prototypical autobiography firmly in mind. Certainly Wright's own description of *Black Boy* in an interview of 1945 accords in the main with Gorky's project, except for what is characteristically his more extreme, more categorical repudiation of any cultural nurturance whatsoever: "I wrote the book to tell a series of incidents strung through my childhood, but the main desire was to render a judgment on my environment. . . . That judgment was this: the environment the South creates is too small to nourish human beings, especially Negro human beings." [18] Like Gorky's *Childhood*, *Black Boy* dramatically frames a long series of traumatic episodes between a four-year-old's encounter with horrifying domestic "primal scenes" and the narrator's emergence, in premature adolescence, as a modern rebel. There is also, as in Gorky's work, a grand narrative strategy that channels a flood of recovered childhood impressions within the supervisory reflections of an adult voice. Despite these formal and generic resemblances, however, the dominant tone of Wright's narrative is far more alienated from its folk origins than anything we find in the recollections of "Maxim the Bitter." To cite Robert Stepto's rather oblique summation of *Black Boy*: "Expressions of literate mobility slowly take form, then accompany, and then supercede expressions of illiterate mobility." [19] In other words, Richard Wright seems intent on writing off any indebtedness to the unlettered Southern black culture of revivalism and survivalism.

Conscious life begins in Wright's autobiography with a representative incident in which the disruption of domestic decorum leads to the beating of a black boy. Hushed into silence by his mother and closed off from the natural world behind long fluffy white curtains kept immaculate by an ailing near-white maternal grandmother, an impatient, bored black child ignites with lit broomstraws "the hems of the curtains" that he has been forbidden to touch. In this earliest memory, young Richard's subconscious nearly succeeds in sweeping away the respectable matriarchal black religious home in which he is narrowly confined. Ironically, the terrified boy seeks refuge for his willfulness by "hiding under a burning house." Once caught, he is severely beaten by his mother. Wright's narrative quickly associates this first punishment with an entire environment dedicated to the suffocation of instinct and the stifling of curiosity. As a consequence of his battering, young Richard suffers an obsessive delirium: "Whenever I tried to sleep I would see huge wobbly white bags, like the full udders of cows, suspended from the ceiling above me. . . . I could see the bags in the daytime with my eyes open and I was gripped by the fear that they were going to fall and drench me with some horrible liquid." [20] This is, to be sure, a most peculiar wet dream, the life-squelching nightmare of a black male child horrified at the prospect of being nurtured to death by an overwhelming maternalism.

Before the long first chapter of *Black Boy* concludes it becomes clear that Wright means to evoke, through the pallid features of the pious grandmother and the transparent deficiencies of young Richard's parents, the punitive protectiveness of family life in a black underclass that has been utterly intimidated by the overhanging specter of a white terror. The constant supervision of language and disciplining of conduct administered through the black matriarchy and church is revealed for what it is in Wright's eyes: a misbegotten home remedy of self-restriction to ward off the ironfisted blows of Southern racism. But an equally appalling denial of adequate nurture results from the failure of black males to help lift their sons into true manhood. Furious to find himself abandoned by a father whose only remaining potency is sexual, young Richard forever associates the paternal image with biological and spiritual hunger. Having somehow survived the deprivations of his childhood, the adult writer has lived to pen a devastatingly antipastoral portrait of the

Negro South. This is epitomized in the painful description of the artist's father that concludes Wright's introduction to "Part One" of his life,
"Southern Night":

> I was to see him again, standing alone upon the red clay of a Mississippi
> plantation, a sharecropper, clad in ragged overalls, holding a muddy hoe
> in his gnarled, veined hands. . . . though ties of blood made us kin, though
> I could see a shadow of my face in his face, though there was an echo of
> his voice in my voice, we were forever strangers, speaking a different lan-
> guage, living on vastly different planes of reality. . . . I stood before him,
> poised, my mind aching as it embraced the simple nakedness of his life,
> feeling how completely his soul was imprisoned by the slow flow of the
> seasons . . . how fastened were his memories to a crude and raw past, how
> chained were his actions and emotions to the direct animalistic impulses
> of his withering body. (40)

Not since Alexander Crummell's appalled view of the unredeemed souls
of America's black peasantry had there been an indictment of the poverty
of a native birthright to match Richard Wright's account of his literary
ascent up from human bondage.

Black Boy is relentless in its enumeration of the privations that the
future author endured on home soil. In a notorious parenthetical aside
early in the second chapter, Wright's adult distress rivals the shocking
cultural despair of nineteenth-century Russia's foremost "Westernizer,"
Peter Chaadaev: "Whenever I thought of the essential bleakness of black
life in America, I knew that Negroes had never been allowed to catch the
full spirit of Western civilization, that they lived somehow in it but not
of it" (45). Indeed, for many African American critics, Wright's stature
as a militant black writer has been difficult to reconcile with his refusal
to be culturally black or to embrace with pride "intra-racial ritual com-
munications."[21] Here is where Wright's conflict with Hurston is most
in evidence. Although it would not be true to say that Wright's writing is
uninfluenced by black vernacular forms, they are put in their place as, at
best, deflections of pain and suppressions of inexpressible feelings and
thoughts.

Unlike Hurston, Wright feels the need to translate the euphemisms,
barbs, and metaphors of "tribal" speech into a more public and direct
language that dares to say what it thinks and express all that it feels.
Young Richard is immersed in a ritualized language of black "talkin' and

testifyin' " that is shown to be a ghettoized speech of restricted limits and deflected rage. The text of Black Boy is sprinkled with "folk ditties" and male-bonding routines like the "dozens," but Wright takes care to expose the aimlessness and racialist bravado of what finally amounts to little more than "trash talk": "And the talk would weave, roll, surge, spurt, veer, swell, having no specific aim or direction, touching vast areas of life, expressing the tentative impulses of childhood" (95). The genuine lyricism of childhood—those moments of experience that elevate the imagination and expand the range of emotion—can in Wright's book only be captured by Whitman-like litanies or prose "chants" that retrospectively express the solitary musings of young Richard in the lush natural world of rural Mississippi.

As for the raptures and transformative power of the evangelical black religion, young Richard felt only the duress of being herded into a protective communal corral: "During the passionate prayers and the chanted hymns I would sit squirming on a bench, longing to grow up so I could run away, listening indifferently to the theme of cosmic annihilation, loving the hymns for their sensual caress . . . and the trembling sense of fate that welled up, sweet and melancholy, from the hymns blended with the sense of fate that I had already caught from life" (130–31). The sources of self-affirmation and cultural resistance that Hurston or even DuBois had located in the jubilation and jivin' within Southern black culture were mostly lost on the black boy who became its most famous native son.

Wright's alienation from his "soul-folk" is perhaps most visible in his disdain for "Shorty," the rotund elevator operator who qualifies as "the most colorful of the Negro boys on the job." The distance and disappointment Wright feels are fully present in his introductory paragraph: "Psychologically he was the most amazing specimen of the southern Negro I had ever met. Hardheaded, sensible, a reader of magazines and books, he was proud of his race and indignant about its wrongs. But in the presence of whites he would play the role of a clown of the most debased and degraded type" (268). Shorty boasts, successfully it turns out, that he can get a quarter from the first white man he sees. Announcing his hunger and his need, Shorty refuses to perform his assigned duty: "Can't go no more, Mr. White Man, unless I get my quarter." Wright realizes that Shorty is playing up to the "element of sadism" involved, speaking as he does "in a tone that sounded like crying" and offering to do anything for that quarter: "Shorty giggled, swung around, bent over, and poked out his broad, fleshy ass. "You can kick me for a quarter," he sang, looking impishly at the white man out of the corners of his eyes." After receiving full force the white man's foot on his rump, Shorty yesses massa's demand to open the door, but first picks up the quarter and puts it into his mouth and chortles, "This monkey's got the peanuts." Had Hurston related this episode, the "cheekiness" of Shorty's irreverence would not go unnoticed; the servant manages to "moon" the master while also exposing the brutality a white Southerner feels entitled to indulge before giving a black man "his quarter." But Richard Wright is a somber literalist when it comes to defending black dignity and manhood: "I witnessed this scene or its variant at least a score of times and I felt no anger or hatred, only disgust and loathing" (269). Significantly, it is Shorty who enviously bids adieu to young Richard as he lights out for what will prove to be the not-so-free territory of the North. Shorty admits he will either die, kill, or be killed in the "goddamn South" he will never manage to leave. Richard Wright, however, is able to move on and write the memoirs of an ex–black boy: "This was the culture from which I sprang. This was the terror from which I fled" (303).

What, then, has made Wright so different? It is no trivial matter that young Richard's first defiance of his home culture's paralyzing injunction against expressing the truth of his own emotions and experience occurs when he cajoles a schoolteacher who boards with his family to read out loud the story she is reading, *Bluebeard and His Seven Wives*: "They could not have known that Ella's whispered story of deception and murder had been the first experience in my life that had elicited from me a total emotional response. . . . I had tasted what to me was life, and I would have more of it, somehow, someway" (46–47). In a controlling environment overwhelmingly female and pious, the literary word enters with murderous intent, authorizing masculine aggression and confirming previously censored fantasies of revenge. Wright's autobiographical writing is positively eloquent about the literal empowerment literature can bring to the wretched of the earth who have been dispossessed of the cultural means to speak effectively to the world at large. Much like Douglass before him, young Richard employs subterfuge to learn the literacy that enables him to free his imagination and finally his body from the "southern night." Curious to know firsthand something of the man who had called down on himself the scorn of the South, Richard forges a library request with the collusion of his ally in persecution, a "Pope lover" Irish Catholic who holds a borrower's card: "Dear Madam: Will you please let this nigger boy have some books by H. L. Mencken?" (291). Before leaving Memphis, Wright had already armed himself with Mencken's gift for "fighting words," and he had begun to identify his own life story across the color-line with the lonely waifs and wanderers of the European naturalist novel.[22] In the recently restored second part of Wright's autobiography, *American Hunger*, we learn that the mature writer never ceased to admire the inseminating ejaculation that the literary word represented to his imagination: "I strove to master words . . . to make them melt into a rising spiral of emotional stimuli, each feeding and reinforcing the other, and all ending in an emotional climax that would drench the reader with a sense of a new world" (330). Clearly, the nightmare of drowning in a suffocating mother culture had been overcome, but one cannot ignore the desperate intensity with which Richard Wright clung for dear life to the weapon of the literary word.

Although Gorky's rebellion against the passivity and fatalism he detected in the souls of Russian folk was less extreme than Wright's rejection of his home culture in America's Black Belt, the two writers shared a common secret about psychic survival in an environment that punished the uncensored expression of inner being and insubordinate instincts. That secret was, quite simply, that the book, standard literacy, was more of a lifeline to full humanity and free expression than the culture that was the birthright of former serfs and slaves. Few writers have been as eager as Gorky and Wright to testify to the central importance of literacy in getting a true purchase on life itself. In the essay "How I Studied" (1918), Gorky waxed lyrical on the subject: "The more I read the closer books bound me to the world and the more vivid and significant life became for me. . . . Like some wondrous birds out of fairy tales, books sang their songs to me and spoke to me as though communing with one languishing in prison; they sang of the richness and variety of life. . . . Each book was a rung in my ascent from the brutish to the human."[23] Literacy for Gorky was the spiritual equivalent of Jacob's ladder. Wright's voice was no less enthusiastic, though characteristically more prosaic: "I read Dreiser's *Jennie Gerhardt* and *Sister Carrie* and they revived in me a vivid sense of my mother's suffering; I was overwhelmed. . . . It would have been impossible for me to have told anyone what I derived from these novels, for it was nothing less than a sense of life itself. All my life had shaped me for the realism, the naturalism of the modern novel, and I could not read enough of them" (295). These powerful testimonials offer living proof of a rather odd paradox—men of the people who become social revolutionaries and "slice of life" realists are the greatest believers in the power of books and literacy to emancipate lives from the shackles of the people's own cultural reality.

Richard Wright never imagined there could be much comfort or support for his hard-earned self-awareness in an aesthetic of blackness. Nor could he imagine an adequate defense against the dehumanizing pressure of white terror in the refuge of cultural separatism. It is understandable that "native sons" like Richard Wright and Maxim Gorky continue to cause resentment for daring to assert, or at least to imply, that human dignity cannot be fully nurtured within any vernacular subculture of colonized and illiterate folk. Perhaps one simply has to be as radically alienated as a Mississippi black boy or an orphaned Russian "river rat" to feel the desperate importance of rebellion and to call out to others to transcend the limits of a given cultural identity and reach up for the power to express an essential, inalienable, universal humanity. In any event, it was with good reason that Gorky and Wright spoke up as they did and when they did against the temptation to adulate the bruised historical "soul" of a long-oppressed race. Liberation of the folk's full humanity and historic potential would arrive with the spread of mass literacy and free access to the world's library of humane letters. Armed with the fighting words of a color-blind and cross-cultural humanism, native sons could lend their minds and muscle to an international brotherhood of ex-colonial souls, the no longer wretched of the earth.

7 EURASIANS AND NEW NEGROES

The Invention of Multicultural Nationalism

In the immediate wake of Europe's first world war there appeared, within a few years of one another, two collective manifestos by young Russian and African American intellectuals announcing radical reconceptions of each group's collective cultural identity. These proclamations were the harbingers of two new nationalist movements that attempted to come to terms with their people's long historic experience with geographical diffusion and cultural hybridity. The Russian "Eurasianists" first announced themselves in a collection of essays titled *Exodus to the East (Iskhod k vostoku)*, published by a refugee press in Sofia, Bulgaria, in 1921. What became known as the "New Negro Renaissance" received its public debut on March 1, 1925, in a special "Harlem" issue of *Survey Graphic*; by November, an expanded, lavishly illustrated version of that collection appeared in book form emblazoned with the proud title, *The New Negro*. These two events had no direct connection with one another, yet they each took place against a similar historic backdrop and together they illustrate a remarkably parallel development in the reconstruction of received notions of national and racial identity. More importantly, their differences speak to some essential distinctions between modern Russian and African American understandings of cultural pluralism and ethnic "soul."

It matters that each movement took shape in a diaspora—under the pressure of geographical displacement and mass migration in the turbulent wash of war and revolution. Huge social and political events had forced a readjustment of perspective regarding the historic identity of Negroes and Russians. African Americans had to account for a mass exodus from the cultural homeland of the South and the consequent urbanization and modernization of rural black folk. Émigré Russians had to assimilate the brute fact of the Russian revolution and the consequent vulnerability of their national culture to aggressive Westernization. What distinguished the Eurasians and New Negroes and made

them different from all previous theorists of ethnic identity was their ingenious attempt to reconcile cultural diversity with cultural nationalism
by celebrating hybridity while also retaining the right to promote pride
in ethnic exclusivism.

In each movement one major thinker led the way in defining a concept of multicultural nationalism that could claim to be the reconstituted essence of the native soul. And in each case a movement that once
seemed short-lived has exhibited remarkable powers of resuscitation.
The "Harlem Renaissance" is current once again in various attempts
to formulate a credible black aesthetic.[1] Meanwhile, "Eurasianism" is
being publicized and revived in contemporary post-Soviet efforts to invigorate a non-Western conception of "Russianness."[2] It is, therefore, of
more than academic interest to focus on the careers and thoughts of the
two academics who galvanized these precocious multicultural nationalisms of the 1920s.

It may at first seem surprising to learn that the chief instigator of one
of Russia's most vehemently anti-Western nationalisms was an internationally acclaimed linguist and a founding father of Prague Structural-
ism. Prince Nikolai Sergeevich Trubetzkoy (1890–1938) was the scion of
two branches of Imperial Russia's highest aristocracy and a wunderkind
of comparative philology and religions. His philosopher-father, author
of *The Doctrine of the Logos*, was the first elected rector of Moscow University. His uncle Evgeny was a prominent art historian who was much celebrated for explicating the compositional features of Old Russian icons.
The young prince's family was heavily steeped in both Western learning
and Orthodox piety; consequently, his own erudition ranged from scientific ethnography to mystical theosophy. Trubetzkoy began his scholarly career at age fifteen with a sophisticated analysis of ancient Paleo-
Siberian ritual practices encoded within a Finnish song text. Before his
student years concluded, he was already a recognized expert in Finno-
Ugric and Caucasian languages and philology. Significantly, the future
"Eurasian" and father of comparative phonology devoted his earliest
studies to the cultures of small nations and to the elaborate syntactic systems and structures of mind present within the obscure languages of so-
called Asiatic Russia.[3]

It should be, then, somewhat less surprising to discover that this refugee scholar of non-Western languages launched from his first perch out-

side revolutionary Russia an astonishing indictment of Eurocentrism. Trubetzkoy's pamphlet-sized screed, Europe and Mankind (Evropa i chelove-chestvo) appeared in Sofia in 1920 and rapidly became the talk of the Russian émigré community. We now know that it was, by design, the prologue to Eurasianism avant le mot. In a remarkably frank letter of March 7, 1921, to his lifelong correspondent and colleague, Roman Jakobson, Trubetzkoy announced his grand intention:

> This book was conceived by me a long while ago (in 1909–10) as the first part of a trilogy bearing the title, A Justification of Nationalism. . . . The thrust of this book is strictly negative. It does not offer any positive, concrete guidelines. . . . What is essential in the book is the rejection of egocentrism and "excentrism" (the positing of a center outside the self—in this case, the West). And I have indicated the chief requirement that flows from this . . . is a revolution in the consciousness and world-view of the intelligentsia of the non-Romano-Germanic people. . . . The essence of this revolution in consciousness consists in the total defeat of egocentrism and excentrism and in the transition from absolutism to relativism. . . . In Russia and Asia popular Bolshevism is not the uprising of the poor against the rich, but of the maligned against the maligners. For the Russian "folk" the word "bourgeois" does not signify a rich man, but a man from another culture who imagines himself superior precisely by virtue of belonging to that culture.[4]

Prince Trubetzkoy's slim volume may well rank among the first "third world" critiques of Western ethnocentrism. It certainly posts its theses like an evangelist seeking converts. The book opens by defiantly announcing that its ideas "for most educated Europeans . . . are viscerally unacceptable," but it recruits all those who share its convictions "to rally together as a united detachment" to develop its ideas and put them in practice. Moreover, the author proclaims that the ideas in it "pertain not only to Russians but to peoples whose origins are in neither the Romance nor the Germanic groups, but who have in some way adopted European culture."[5] Finally, the book's concluding words have the distinct ring of an ideological war cry: "There is only one true opposition: the Romano-Germans and all the other peoples of the world—Europe and mankind" (64).

The argument sandwiched between these crude clarion calls is deft and sophisticated. Trubetzkoy's pamphlet had its origin in postwar disillusionment with the pretense of Western objectivity: "The Great War and especially the subsequent 'peace' shook our faith in 'civilized mankind' " (2). Trubetzkoy's fundamental complaint was that modern Russia's hard-won and much-vaunted culture had been victimized by a particularly invidious form of imperialism that eroded its foundations from within: "In evaluating European cosmopolitanism one must always remember that terms such as 'humanity,' 'universal human civilization' and so forth, are extremely imprecise and that they mask very definite ethnographic concepts" (6). To the eye of the informed ethnographer, so-called European cosmopolitanism is more correctly called *pan-Romano-Germanic chauvinism*, and despite vocal Western claims to enlightenment "all cultures [past and present] maximally differentiated from contemporary European civilization are lumped together by European scholars as 'primitive' " (28). What Trubetzkoy the comparative ethnologist knows is that every European nation was once a congeries of dialectal and ethnographic groups that came to be subsumed through history and conquest into a larger unity, a particular "supraethnographic humanity" based on a common stock of cultural assets. In this conception of Europe, however, the dominant Romano-Germanic culture presumed itself to be the highest evolutionary stage of humanity. The fundamental egocentricity of Eurocentrism is especially appalling to the careful student of small cultures whose complex social and semantic systems go unrecognized by chauvinistic Western scholars of "universal history." Long before Levi-Strauss, Trubetzkoy was proclaiming "the mind of the 'savage' is full, despite the fact that the materials filling it are utterly different from those filling the head of the European. . . . the intellectual baggage of the 'savage' and the European must be viewed as neither comparable nor commensurate" (32).

Yet it is not ultimately an anthropologist's defense of 'primitive' cultures and the cause of cultural relativism that most inflames the ferocious argument with the West in *Europe and Mankind*. Trubetzkoy's deepest anger is directed at the "fifth-column" (to use an anachronistic term) within historically non-Western cultures: the Europeanized and assimilationist intelligentsia. With devastating cogency he points out that genuine assimilation requires a culturewide responsiveness to innovation within a community's historic inventory of assets and practices, and thus all Westernizing nations are doomed to uneven development, permanent backwardness, and a worsening perception of inferiority.

Trubetzkoy's analysis goes a long way toward explaining why modern Russia found itself obsessed with generational conflict and managed, without a proletariat, to produce the first successful communist revolution:

> A most grievous consequence of Europeanization is . . . the dismemberment of a people's national body. . . . every generation in a nation that has borrowed a foreign culture has its own particular culture, and the distinctions between "fathers and sons" will always be sharper than in a nation whose culture is homogenous. . . . It follows that the different parts of a Europeanized nation (classes, estates, professions) represent various stages in the assimilation of Romano-Germanic culture. . . . Social, material, and professional differences are much greater in Europeanized nations than in Romano-Germanic nations precisely because ethnographic and cultural distinctions have been added to them. (49–50)

The cultural elite will find it impossible to keep pace with the rate of innovation occurring in the "civilized" world and, in desperation, will goad the lagging nation into periods of "leaping" evolution that will necessarily be followed by periods of "stagnation" to restore order to the disrupted culture. In short, Trubetzkoy sought to demonstrate to a generation of rudely displaced Russians that the "consequences of Europeanization are so deleterious and appalling that it must be considered an evil" (54). The urgent task ahead was to revolutionize the consciousness of the Westernized intelligentsia so that it fully appreciated the *relativity* of the benefits of European "civilization." To that end the campaign of the "Eurasianists" became dedicated.

One of the first enthusiastic reviews of *Europe and Mankind* came from the pen of a specialist in economic geography, Pyotr Savitsky, who rapidly became Trubetzkoy's collaborator and cofounder of the Eurasianist program. What he brought to the ethnographer's anticolonialist ideology was the leaven of realpolitik. Savitsky wanted to counter the aggressive universalism of Western civilization without renouncing its empirical science and technology, and he thought he detected a power base in the spacious resources of Russia that made it relatively speaking the foremost non-Western oppositionist culture. He rightly anticipated that Trubetzkoy's militant cultural pluralism was powerless without activating a new form of Russian nationalism that presented itself as "the example for non-Western humanity that can benefit from the ideas."[6] At the end of his review, Savitsky was already pointing toward the Eurasian exit from the dilemma of Russia's subjugation to a supposedly superior Western civilization. The very process of Europeanization, he alleged, had finally elicited a dialectical "self-assertion" (*samoutverzhdenie*) of Russia in the form of the fervid utopianism and continental scale of "popular Bolshevism." With Savitsky's assistance the Eurasianist program would embrace the unfolding revolution in the name of Russia's cultural and geographic prerogative to federate the oppressed non-Romano-Germanic masses of the third world between Europe and Asia.

In August 1921 an unprecedented form of Russian cultural nationalism expressed itself from within the Western diaspora of refugee intellectuals.[7] In its first shape it was a rather unsystematic assemblage of ten essays by four coauthors cryptically titled *Exodus to the East: Premonitions and Accomplishments. An Affirmation of Eurasians.* The introduction to the volume fully participated in the apocalypticism common to all Russians at that moment in time: "We know that an historic spasm separating one epoch of world history from the next has already begun. We do not doubt that a shift of the West European world is arriving from the East."[8] But observers then and since also detected in this same volume a striking discontinuity with all previous conceptions of Russia's place in the world—and correctly so. The crux of the difference was revealed at the end of the introduction: "We are 'nationalists' but of a wider and broader sort than the European conception; even ethnically our nationalism spreads as broad and far as the forests and steppes of Russia. . . . Merging with the life and culture of our native and environing elements, we are not ashamed to declare ourselves *Eurasians*" (vii). Something truly remarkable was occurring. Facing a Russia in flames and famine after the final collapse of the White army's resistance, one group of Russians cast off by the revolution refused to be demoralized and, in fact, reaffirmed the creative potential within Russian culture.[9] Here was a patriotic faith that could even surmount the apparent triumph of godless Bolshevism. Yet the strain of that effort was visible in the discordant contents of the volume.

Trubetzkoy and Savitsky were joined in the first declaration of Eurasianism by two fellow travelers who would prove to be less committed to what was most original about the emerging ideology. The talented musicologist Pyotr Suvchinsky saw in the Bolshevik cataclysm a Nietzschean "music of time" and forecast the emergence of a new humanity forged in the perfervid religious and artistic spirit of Russian utopianism.[10] He greeted the disruptive forms and neologisms of Russian Futurism and later became one of the tragic returnees who reconciled themselves to Soviet rule. A quite different temporary ally was the sophisticated intellectual historian and future theologian, Georgy Florovsky.[11] He forcefully renewed the traditional Orthodox and early Slavophile critique of Western rationalism and legalism and saw in the trauma of the revolution a reassertion of the "nonhistoric" and unworldly impatience of Russian spirituality with the limits of reason and precedent. He soon broke from the Eurasian movement and became a distinguished philosophical proponent of the Orthodox faith in the West. To the extent that *Exodus to the East* provided a wholly new direction for Russian nationalist thought, it was set in motion by the creative intellectual synergy between Trubetzkoy and Savitsky.

Together the philologist and the geographer established for the first time the grounds for locating the linguistic and ecological substratum of Russia's historic culture in the vast Eurasian continent between Europe and Asia. Two articles by them became the basis for the later evolution of Eurasianism as it spread in a series of publications from 1921 to 1937.[12] The original "affirmation of Eurasians" concluded with two interlocking and complementary theses: Trubetzkoy's "The Upper and Lower Layers of Russian Culture" and Savitsky's "Continent-Ocean (Russia and the World Market)." Trubetzkoy's contribution marshaled his considerable erudition in historical linguistics to deliver a wholly uncustomary reading of the basis of Russian culture: "Thus from an ethnographic point of view, the Russian people are not purely Slavic. The Russians, the Ugro-Finns, and the Volga Turks comprise a cultural zone that has connections with both the Slavs and the 'Turanian East,' and it is difficult to say which of these is more important" (96). Reaching well beyond the esoteric details of comparative etymology, Trubetzkoy proceeds to connect the structural features of the Russian folk's music, dance, ornamentation, and material culture to specifically non-Western modes of expression. For instance, he notes (as Paul Robeson would later acknowledge with great excitement) the presence of the pentatonic or "Indo-Chinese" scale at the basis of all traditional non-Western song. More radically, Trubetzkoy separates Russian rhythm and choral polyphony from all other Slavic as well as Romano-Germanic forms of singing. There is even a passage in which Trubetzkoy speaks of the body language of Russians in a manner that anticipates much later "Afrocentric" accounts of a poly-rhythmic black aesthetic:

> Romano-Germanic dances are characterized by the obligatory presence of "cavaliers" and "ladies" dancing together and holding each other, which permits them to make identical rhythmic movements with their feet only. Russian dances are in no way comparable. . . . even if two people are dancing, they may be of the same sex and may dance in turn rather than simultaneously; and they do not hold one another. Consequently, rhythmic movements can be executed not only with the feet but with the arms and shoulders. (94)

By the time Trubetzkoy has adduced all his evidence it is clear that the "lower layer" of Russian culture is profoundly non-Western and is not even purely Slavic; it carries in its blood a distinctive admixture of the peoples of the Eastern steppe and it responds to ancient Eurasian cultural patterns in its daily life. As for the "upper layer," until its forcible Westernization under Peter the Great the Russian nobility had derived its literacy and spirituality from Eastern Christendom. If, then, the revolution is truly to succeed in reconstructing Russian culture, it must create a new "choral" union based on the people's firm ethnoreligious foundation in Byzantium and Eurasia.

Savitsky's addition to this newly drawn "culture zone" of Eurasian Russia was to suggest that it had potentially the support of a large and viable ecological niche. The concluding essay in the volume sketched out a preliminary draft of Savitsky's geopolitical design for an autonomous Eurasian continental economy—an odd premonition of Stalin's "socialism in one country." Although commerce in an imperial age was quickest and cheapest by sea, the apparent disadvantage of landlocked Eurasia had a natural solution. Relying on the findings of climatologists and soil scientists, Savitsky urged Russians to appreciate the Middle Continent's latitudinal regularity and gradual transition among four diverse ecological zones—tundra, forest, steppe, and desert bordered one another without obstruction on the vast Eurasian plain, allowing for an exchange of resources outside the colonialist world market. On very earthly as well as spiritual grounds, then, Russia had always been identified with Eurasia: "The economic future of Russia lies not in the aping of the 'oceanic' policy of others, but in the comprehension of its 'continental nature' and in an adaptation to that nature" (125). This, too, was an unconventional appeal, asking Russians to withdraw from the mistake of Imperial (and pan-Slavic) emulation of European power politics and prestige.

As Trubetzkoy and Savitsky further refined their ideas, Eurasianism became a powerful ideology, a seductive hybrid variant of traditional Russian cultural nationalism. Trubetzkoy developed a pluralistic "culturology" that situated historic Russia at the very center of a distinctively Eurasian "language union" and "cultural zone."[13] His vast learning and profound perception of structural features led to a revolutionary theory in linguistic science—namely, that genetically unrelated languages can evolve family relationships as a result of territorial convergence, just as protracted contact among ethnically diverse populations surely results in cultural transfers. Roman Jakobson, Trubetzkoy's younger colleague, revived the flagging Eurasian cause in 1931, when his research led him to conclude that all the Eurasian languages shared in common an absence of tonality combined with a distinct separation of palatalized and "hard" consonants.[14] Savitsky could barely restrain his imagination as he contemplated this discovery. He thought it not accidental that a fellow Russian had perceived this process of "organic" fusion of contingent "continental unions": "Would it be impossible, following in your steps," he wrote to Jakobson, "to do in the realm of phonological geography what the Russians have done in soil science, that is, to draw a new map of the world . . . to produce, so to speak, a *Eurasianization of the globe?*"[15] Savitsky's quick leap from phonetics to geopolitics illustrates what had always been a besetting problem with the Eurasianist embrace of pluralism and diversity. Even in the first declaration of the Eurasians, Savitsky and Trubetzkoy had detected in Russia's eclectic language and Eastern Christian religion a privileged distillation of "non-Westernness." As Savitsky put it in announcing "The Turn to the East": "To translate it all into the language of reality, it means that there has appeared on the stage of world history a new cultural-geographical entity that has yet to play its leading role."[16] Underneath all the theorizing about cultural relativism and Russian hybridity one can still hear the heavy tread of a missionary nationalism—the "march of civilization" is simply migrating to a new Eurasian home.

A quite different blending of cosmopolitanism and ethnic particularism was accomplished by the leading theorist and self-proclaimed "midwife" of the contemporaneous New Negro movement in America. Alain LeRoy Locke (1886–1954) was in many respects the ideal candidate to give his generation's response to DuBois's call of April 1920: "A renaissance of American Negro literature is due: the material about us in the strange, heart-rending race tangle is rich beyond dream and only we can tell the tale and sing the song from the heart." [17] Locke was so perfect an embodiment of the "Talented Tenth" that he might well have become the anointed favorite of DuBois. The product of generations of Philadelphia free black schoolteachers, Locke was destined by talent and temperament for cultural ascendancy. Replicating DuBois's own rise to prominence, he entered Harvard without advanced standing yet graduated magna cum laude in philosophy within three years. In 1907, Alain Locke became the first African American Rhodes scholar; although his career at Oxford and Berlin did not result in an advanced degree, like DuBois before him he persisted despite the racial and academic obstacles thrown in his path. Locke began teaching at Howard University as an instructor in philosophy and education in 1912, then returned to Harvard with an Austin Dissertation Fellowship (1916–17), where he completed his doctorate, titled "Problems of Classification in Theories of Value." Back again at Howard, the young philosopher agitated for courses in race history while also founding the literary journal, *The Stylus*, in which Zora Neale Hurston was first published. All things considered, Locke might well have struck DuBois in 1920 as the right young man to promote the postwar Negro cultural renaissance. Yet by 1925, when Locke had become the intellectual impresario who produced the premiere appearance of the "New Negro," relations with the elder statesman of African American cultural nationalism were publicly strained.[18] Locke, in the felicitous phrase of his biographer, was a "multivalent man" whose intellectual, social, and sexual life was involved in mediating a complex array of conflicting values.[19] And that made him and his assertion of "Negroness" new in an unprecedented manner that made DuBois exceedingly uncomfortable.

The young intellectual who was recruited to coordinate the Harlem-based movement had learned to hold many conflicting tendencies in a sophisticated balance. Philosophically he had come of age in the not-so-genteel atmosphere of the great public exchanges at Harvard between Josiah Royce, William James, and George Santayana. At the same time he had been more than brushed by the "ancestralism" and aestheticism of

Harvard Anglophiles like Barrett Wendell and Irving Babbitt. Well before his encounters at Oxford with the bigotry of Southern Rhodes scholars and the oratory of commonwealth anticolonialists finally forced Locke to confront "the heart-rending race tangle," the Harvard undergraduate had been exposed to entanglements of a different order from the color-line. The young philosophy major who proposed to read "The Greats" at Oxford obviously felt the appeal of a normative neoclassicist human-ism; yet it was also apparent that Locke had already been drawn, inside and outside the classroom, toward an experientially based relativism of values. Part Idealist and "Tory," Alain Locke also knew himself to be a modernist aesthete, eager to be identified as a "cosmopolite" with a taste for "art for life's sake."[20] As his voluminous correspondence makes visible, the celebrated black American Rhodes scholar arrived in England determined to fashion for himself a differently colorful per-sona—that of an Edwardian dandy. But the new Negro who returned from that European sojourn would be both a "race man" and a gay blade, simultaneously an advocate of cultural nationalism and sophisticated urbanity.

To understand better why Alain Locke was selected to lead the cam-paign to introduce the American public to the "New Negro," it helps to consider the range and quality of his earliest writings. His first note-worthy publication arose from a paper, "Cosmopolitanism," he read to the Oxford Cosmopolitan Club, itself a gathering of border-crossing individuals of color on the periphery of British culture.[21] Already the young African American was calling for a "rational cosmopolitanism" that would be complementary and not antagonistic to an informed na-tionalism. True cosmopolitanism, he maintains, does not rest on the ca-nonical Western syllabus of a universal, hierarchical education but is in-stead predicated on the exercise of imaginative empathy. As opposed to a civilization of museumlike exhibits and a nationalism identified with fixed frontiers, Locke calls for a heightened sense of the contras-tive effect of one cultural tradition on another: "The sense for paral-lel but not equal values is the true criterion of cosmopolitan taste."[22] Although more modulated than Trubetzkoy's later tirade, Locke, too, ac-cuses the European mind of having lost a sense of its own incommen-surability with other mentalities, "so the sympathy we avow each other is suspicious and often a false analogy rather than a sense of contrast understood." In the stimulating company of Oxford's select diaspora of commonwealth scholars, Locke had come to value parallel developments within an asymmetrical world of cultural difference.

Upon returning to the United States, Locke's first publication was a lecture significantly titled, "The Negro and a Race Tradition." Here one can detect the beginnings of what Leonard Harris has referred to as Locke's theory of "ethnogenesis," meaning the deliberate symbolic construction of cultural invariants to support group norms for a nation in formation.[23] Addressing the American Negro Society in 1911, Locke acknowledges in the "Afro-American of culture" a choice of two heritages: a racial consciousness and a race-memory. The latter depends on the interrupted transmission of a cultural mentality, the former on a promised acquisition of constitutional and human rights. Those concerned with race education face an enormous challenge: "We have to justify and rationalize a comparatively accidental + contradictory body of tradition + coordinate + bring to solidarity a very disconnected + heterogeneous lot of people." [24] The openness with which Locke speaks of the *construction* of a race tradition would perhaps not have been quite so possible before the advent of Jamesian pragmatism or the expectation he shared with Van Wyck Brooks, his Harvard classmate, that the "American temperament" was finally outgrowing Puritanism in the new century. In any event, Locke's rhetoric departs from the standard moral-political "uplifting" of the race and reaches instead toward a cultural reconstruction of the American Negro: "We are an experiment in a land of experiment. . . . we should not think our intellectual + spiritual problems wait upon the solution of our practical problems, when there was every reason to believe that a theoretical change of attitude might circumvent certain stubborn facts + gain a moral victory for the race long before a corporate + practical success was demonstrated." Even before he made a name for himself as Howard University's resident patron of the arts, the young "cosmopolite" and aesthete from Oxford had placed his best hope for racial progress on an expansion of the African American cultural horizon. Unlike DuBois, or even James Weldon Johnson, Alain Locke was convinced that the aesthetic could be the political.

Locke needed an institutional basis of support, however, to publicize his vision of the complex expressivity of an emerging Negro culture. It was his good fortune to find an ideal ally in Charles S. Johnson, the chief editor of *Opportunity: A Journal of Negro Life*, the newly established organ of the National Urban League. Johnson's bold leadership from 1923 to

1928 transformed the style of black activism in America by creating a rival approach to the civic-minded militancy of DuBois's NAACP journal, *The Crisis*. Johnson came to New York by way of the University of Chicago, where he imbibed from Robert Park a new culturally sensitive sociology dedicated to surveying the subjective and experiential diversity within specified social groups.[25] Guided by a strict fidelity to the varieties of Negro experience, Johnson became, by everyone's account, the stage manager of the Harlem Renaissance and, through the literary contests sponsored by *Opportunity*, the dispenser of its most coveted awards.[26] It was Johnson who immediately sought out Locke as a contributor to his new journal, appointing the erudite Howard professor "special foreign correspondent" in 1923. Obviously pleased with Locke's extensive literary connections and impressed by his awareness of cosmopolitan and anticolonialist currents in European treatments of Africa, Johnson approached Locke on March 4, 1924, with a new idea: . . . "It was proposed that something be done to mark the growing self-consciousness of this newer school of writers. . . . We want you to take a certain role in the movement. We are working up a dinner meeting, probably at the Civic Club, to which about fifty persons will be invited. . . . You were thought of as a sort of Master of Ceremonies for the 'movement.' "[27] This letter launched Locke's career and brought the "New Negro" into national prominence.

The Civic Club Dinner of March 21, 1924, was the masterstroke of Johnson's organizational genius. For the first time most of New York's prominent publishers and literati (white and black) were assembled in one room; they were invited to hear the "Younger School of Negro Writers" showcased by the likes of Carl Van Doren and Horace Liveright, the establishment promoters of a second American Renaissance. Before the toasting had ended, Locke was approached by Paul U. Kellogg, the editor of *Survey Graphic*, to supervise a special issue of his magazine devoted to the new black writing and arts. This gesture symbolized the linkage of Afro-America's "New Negro Renaissance" with the postwar flurry of cultural nationalist movements among emerging nationalities. The "Harlem" issue of *Survey Graphic* in March 1925 was the fifth in a distinguished series devoted to publicizing the social and cultural resources of newly self-determining peoples. Significantly, the volume that became *The New Negro* had been preceded by anthologies of art and reportage on the rise "from serfdom to self-help" in Czechoslovakia, Ireland, Russia, and Mexico.[28] Kellogg and Locke clearly sensed a parallelism among the various contemporary experiments in formulating and redefining nationhood.

From its initial conception, the "Harlem" issue was to represent a self-consciously modernist and internationalist approach to the achievement of race progress. In the month before publication, Kellogg was encouraging Locke to emphasize a departure from old "economic-educational" and "political" solutions proposed by Booker T. Washington and Du-Bois: "We are striking out along new lines in this Harlem number. . . . We are interpreting a racial and cultural revival in the new environment of the northern city."[29] As Locke drafted his opening essay, he added a revealing sentence to his discussion of Harlem, "the Mecca of the New Negro": "Our comparison lies, therefore, less with the [conserving organism] of a ghetto than with those nascent centers of self-expression and self-determination which are playing a creative part in the world today—what Dublin has become for New Ireland or Prag [sic] for the new Czecho-Slovakia."[30] The "New Negro" in Locke's understanding was taking shape in a race capital that thrived on cosmopolitanism.

Two months before the "Harlem" number hit the streets, Albert Boni had contacted Kellogg about the rights to reprint materials in an entire book about the New Negro; it was understood that Alain Locke would preside over the expanded volume. The tome that resulted is much more national in scope than its Harlem predecessor and so unwieldy in its representation of constituencies and perspectives that it defies summary.[31] Yet Locke's thumbprints are all over *The New Negro: An Interpretation*. He manages to be a guiding presence, so much so that his interpretation provides an unmistakable ideological orchestration to its massed chorus of voices. He interjects himself five times, dominating the opening pages and providing editorial leads for the sections dealing with the creative arts and cultural expression. Although the book was, among other things, a current sociological survey of diverse Negro types and institutions in urban America, it was Alain Locke's new conception of Negro identity that was the real news for an older generation of African American race leaders.

"Negro life is not only establishing new contacts and founding new centers, it is finding a new soul"—the message could hardly have been more direct.[32] Alain Locke's "Foreword" contrasts with DuBois's "Forethought" to *The Souls of Black Folk* in being so dramatically forward-looking. Locke is fully confident that the Negro at present speaks more articulately than ever before for a race that is only now constituting itself in modern times: "The galvanizing shocks and reactions of the last few years are making by subtle processes of internal reorganization a race out of its own disunited and apathetic elements" (xvii). Dispersions and relocations on a national and international scale have created an internal transformation of the Negro mind that is the best evidence of a new figure on the world stage: "Whoever wishes to see the Negro in his essential traits, in the full perspective of his achievement and possibilities, must seek the enlightenment of that self-portraiture which the present developments of Negro culture are offering" (xv). Yet Locke does not deny that this emerging Negro American culture, however separate, is part of a wider maturation and sophistication of America itself and of other formerly provincial peoples.

In the title essay, "The New Negro," Locke explains how it can be that the time has arrived for the Negro to cease seeing himself as a stereotype or a "problem," as a sociological shadow of his empirical self. There is no longer any reason to equate a Negro essence with any one geographical section or cultural segment. Harlem is so much on the mind of the younger generation because it symbolizes the urbane self-knowledge made possible by the effects of urbanization on a previously disaggregated and culturally diverse people. The Negro can finally find himself in his full dimensions in Harlem—it is truly "the laboratory of a great race-welding" (7). It is also, in its interaction with Manhattan, the place where sentimental or prejudicial myths about Negroes can give way to better informed assessments of the inner differentiation and artistic endowments of the race. Ultimately, there can be no revaluation of the Negro or healing of the American nation without a broader cultural recognition of what the race in all its multiplicity contributes to the growth of the American mind.

In "Negro Youth Speaks," we learn that artistic discourse is uniquely the medium capable of articulating the complex wholeness of a people, "forecasting in the mirror of art what we must see and recognize in the streets of reality tomorrow, foretelling in new notes and accents the maturing speech of racial utterance" (47). Locke's celebration of the rising generation of Negro artists should not be mistaken for mere avant-gardism. His essential point is that the historic moment has finally arrived when the "conditions of a classical art are almost at hand." Never before have Negro artists been so happily released from "the hampering habit of setting artistic values with primary regard for moral effect" (48) or so liberated from the conscious burden of racial representation. At the same time, no other generation has been as well situated to "evolve from the racial substance something technically distinctive, something that as an idiom of style may become a contribution to the general resources of art" (51). Locke claims, in a remarkable phrase, that race has become for the younger generation "an idiom of experience, a sort of added enriching adventure and discipline, giving subtler overtones to life" (48). Thus the New Negro artist will be more than a modernist in blackface, will in fact no longer be a "cultural nondescript": "Our poets have now ceased speaking for the Negro—they speak as Negroes" (48). Negro identity is thus most perceptible as a developing array of cultural idioms, and it asserts itself by relying on an "emotionally welded" race-gift of vital expression.

A sophisticated theory of "cultural racialism" informed Locke's concept of the new Negro arts. In a major philosophical statement published in 1924, Locke contended that race and culture are mutually independent variables that "are in no way organically or causally connected," yet this "does not deny that race stands for significant social characters and culture-traits or represents in given historical contexts characteristic differentiations of culture-type." [33] Locke's position on racial theory might perhaps be described as "phenomenological essentialism." That is to say, Locke understands the sense of race to be a social construct, but he maintains that once it is established and becomes a matter of social heredity a sense of race must be regarded as "one of the operative factors in culture since it determines the stressed values which become the conscious symbols and tradition of the culture" (194). In short, a peculiar selective preference for certain culture traits is reinforced by societal racism such that "it becomes an accepted, preferred, and highly resistant culture complex that seems to be and often is self-perpetuating" (198). Locke thus has his own version of the "conservation of race" argument, but one that allows for ethnic remolding within the dynamic development and fluctuating social pressures of actual historicity. As a philosophical thinker Locke keeps his credentials as a cultural relativist without erasing race or racial culture-types as operative categories of analysis and praxis.

Returning to the text of *The New Negro*, we see that modernity, for

Locke, promotes an unprecedented and opportune clustering of the expressive idioms of the entire African diaspora. In the two substantive essays that follow on his opening proclamations, Locke provides an aesthetic education for the emerging black arts movement. "The Negro Spirituals" and "The Legacy of the Ancestral Arts" build the foundations for a truly cosmopolitan articulation of the Negro's message to the world. The construction of a "race tradition" that commands respect requires more than accommodation to middle-class values; it requires an appreciation of "primitive" African American spirituals as sophisticated music and of "savage" African art as classically disciplined. Locke expands considerably on the claims made by Du Bois for the legacy of the sorrow songs. The technical distinctiveness of the Negro spirituals has great potential to be heightened rather than whitened: "Just as soon as the traditional conventions of four-part harmony and the oratorio style and form are broken through, we may expect a choral development of Negro folk song that may equal or even outstrip the phenomenal choral music of Russia. . . . It can therefore undergo without breaking its own boundaries, intricate and original development in directions already the line of advance in modernistic music" (208–9). Similarly, Locke was a leading voice in urging African Americans to appreciate and cultivate, as European modernists had, the "distinctive idiom both of color and of modelling" achieved in Africa's decorative and sculptural arts: "The Negro physiognomy must be freshly and objectively conceived on its own patterns if it is ever to be seriously and importantly interpreted. Art must discover and reveal the beauty which prejudice and caricature have overlaid" (264).

In his earliest writings for *Opportunity*, Locke had been celebrating the "cosmopolitan humanism" of African art and letters and calling for an informed "Africanization" of America's black elite: "We can safely predict a great reappraisal when Africa is eventually seen, as it must be . . . with the artist's eye. Thus we look at our own culture, or we could not endure the sight of it." [34] It is fair, then, to assume that Alain Locke's program for *The New Negro* amounted to a campaign to sophisticate and hyphenate the common understanding of what it meant to be African American in the twentieth century. This goal could only effectively be achieved through the construction of a Negro arts movement that consciously developed the idiomatic varieties of racial expression into new cultural forms that articulated a nationality in the process of formation.

African Americans had the potential to express artistically the multicultural and cross-cultural interaction of a democratic American civilization that had yet to honor its own dynamic diversity. Being African American was a complex fate, but it promised a bright future in which one could uphold race pride and be a multiculturalist, too.

The Russian Eurasians and the Harlem "New Negro" movement each added an uncustomary ingredient, a cosmopolitan spice, to previous thinking about the cultural specificity of their ethnic identity. However, these new varieties of "multicultural nationalism" were the products of two very different mentalities, each struggling to adjust an old essence to modern circumstances. Trubetzkoy and Locke are both diasporic theorists of nationality, but they speak from very different situations and to very different ends. As James Clifford has rightly cautioned us, "diaspora" is itself a traveling term that is loose in a world of complicated transnational migration and contact patterns.[35] The Russian Eurasians found themselves recently dislocated from a homeland, separated by a political taboo against return; they exemplified the longing and nostalgia of an exclusivist expatriate minority community unreconciled to and alienated from the "host" cultures in which they were dispersed. They were uncomfortable exiles committed to reinhabiting imaginatively and eventually physically a homeland that could conceivably be reclaimed, if not restored. The Harlem-based "New Negro" movement found itself at the nexus of a transnational migrant circuit in which the historic dispersion of a race was being reaggregated in the contact zone of a modern metropolis. The so-called Harlem Renaissance was the cultural expression of an intranational and postnational racial affinity group of border-crossing "cosmopolites." These "New Negroes" inhabited a country of the mind, a projected site of multicultural solidarity, of diversified unity that, not so oddly, resembled the unrealized cultural ideology of the polymorphous American "host." Thus the geocultural "situatedness" of these new Russian and African American theories of ethnic identity made them very dissimilar, even though these movements were both responding to the cultural dislocation brought on by the postwar dismantling of Eurocentrism in politics and the arts.

If we ask what was genuinely new about these two varieties of cultural nationalism that sprang up in the 1920s, in each case we see an unprecedented cultural embrace of the non-Western component within Russian and Negro identity. There were, to be sure, previous examples of bicultural universalism advanced by Russian and African American nationalist thinkers. Dostoevsky's last public address in June 1880 on the occasion of a huge Pushkin festival was a moving reiteration of his prophetic sense that Russians were destined to fulfill the "universal responsiveness" so evident in the national poet's "all-European and pan-human" faculty of reincarnating in himself the spirit of other nationalities.[36] And DuBois always predicated the wholeness of America's national identity on its full acceptance of the already bicultural gifts of its African American coworkers in the kingdom of culture. But the Eurasians and the New Negroes shifted all previous arguments for the acquired biculturalism of Russians and black folk in a radically new direction.

From its first formulation, Eurasianism pushed the disassociation of Russia from Europe further than even the most radical pan-Slav thinker.[37] Nikolai Danilevsky had begun in 1869 the process of remapping Europe as a mere peninsula of the Asiatic continent whose natural geographical center was occupied by the peacefully expanding empire of the Slavic people. But the Eurasians also discarded cultural affinities with the rest of the Slavic world and reinterpreted Russia's language and culture as the ethnographic center of an autonomous Eurasian civilization that was a non-Western multicultural geopolitical entity reasserting itself in the final overthow of Western colonialism. Trubetzkoy's essay of 1925, "The Legacy of Genghis Khan," extended the Eurasian argument to include a proclivity for state power that consolidated rule, as the Tatar overlords and their Muscovite successors had, under the undeniable authority of one head and a single faith. It was difficult to ignore the fact that the Eurasian movement contemplated a nativist non-Western alternative to Bolshevism that would lay claim to a unified geographical world that roughly coincided with Imperial Russia as of 1917. Eurasianism was finally very much a Russocentric construction of "multicultural nationalism" that ironically mirrored the "chauvinistic cosmopolitanism" of the Romano-Germanic hegemonic West it opposed. This Russian version of cultural pluralism masked a regressive essentialism that sought to resuscitate an imagined non-Western "soul" of the historic Russian folk. Were it possible for that to be accomplished, a Eurasianized Russia would assume, by ethnographic right, its leadership role as the model and vanguard of an emerging third world between Europe and Asia.

By contrast, the "New Negro Renaissance," at least as evoked in theory by Alain Locke, could claim that its multicultural nationalism was consistent with the progressive and pluralist orientation of cosmopolitan modernism. In part a product of the cultural relativism and democratic pluralism of Wilsonian America, Locke's vision of a Negro nationality in formation was hospitable toward the diasporic diversity and sociological multiplicity of the race's contemporary identity. More than any predecessor, Locke was open to the construction of a race tradition that would permit the articulation of the many cultural roots and routes of the "Black Atlantic" in modern and hybrid forms. The New Negro mentality was not only part rural and part urban, part Southern and part Northern, but a developing cosmopolitan consciousness learning to express out loud and in public the "barbarian yawp" of its rich idioms derived from African, Caribbean, and American Negro experience. The urbane and "multivalent" African American intellectual could see himself as potentially representative of the most "mixed" and miscegenated New World identity, as the "midwife" of a neo-Africanized American nationality coming of age in the twentieth century. There is more than a touch of vanguardism and of cultural racialism in this African American version of multicultural nationalism.[38] Nonetheless, Alain Locke's New Negro ideology looked forward to the emergence of a vital cultural pluralism within a reconstructed racial and national identity—a dream still deferred and still actively alive.

8 PRESERVING THE RACE

Rasputin, Naylor, and the Mystique

of Native "Soul"

In an increasingly multicultural world of permeable borders and hyphenated identities, it might seem that timeless or uninflected concepts of ethnicity would have disintegrated, having been shredded by constantly rubbing up against the transient populations and intrusive technologies of modernity. Such has not been the case, however. In the latter part of the twentieth century, calls for ethnic purity and racial identity have intensified even as the very terms *race* and *ethnicity* have been interrogated and deconstructed. This paradoxical result should discourage but not startle theorists of group interactions and cultural processes. Alain Locke's understanding of the historical dynamics of racialism included the expectation that "at least a temporary accentuation" of racial emphases and cultural typologies would occur "in conditions of increased contacts and increasing complexity of surrounding culture elements."[1] The same disruptive forces of demographic migration and cultural exchange that helped bring into being the Harlem Renaissance and Eurasianism also have encouraged reaffirmations, in modified form, of ethnic essentialism among African American and Russian intellectuals. Cultural nationalism, in fresh currents of Russophilia and Afrocentrism, surges once again in a revived literature of Russian and African American "soul."

Two popular contemporary novels dramatize particularly well the problematic status of an endangered cultural essence by staging compelling mythic versions of the conflict between a vulnerable communal identity and hostile surrounding forces. Both Valentin Rasputin's *Farewell to Matyora* (1976) and Gloria Naylor's *Mama Day* (1988) literally construct an island refuge of ethnic "soul" and tell of its dramatic encounter with a "mainstream" world that threatens to inundate it. Moreover, both novels center on the pathos and power of a representative matriarch who embodies the core of an ancestral way of being that soon may be supplanted by an uncomprehending modernity. The structural similarity and similar cultural resonance of these two influential fictions make them irresistible points of comparison between contemporary Russian and African American versions of "preservationist" literature. Yet, as was true of each nationality's variant of "multicultural nationalism" in the 1920s, here, too, some sharp distinctions must finally be drawn. Although Rasputin and Naylor each participate, generally speaking, in a neoconservative restoration of cultural essentialism and although their texts both perform a cultural resistance to the erosion of ethnic and racial particularism, their differences reflect some important divergences between the mentalities of contemporary Russian and African American "nativist" writers.

Bolshevik vanguardism was a secularized state-sponsored variant of the impatient missionary nationalism that had inspired Russia's first Westernizers to anticipate the possibility of a great leap forward into the radiant future of civilization. But the grim realities of forced collectivization and industrial shock therapy had finally produced, by the 1960s, an unofficial countercultural school of "village writers" (*derevenshchiki*) whose pledge of allegiance was to the tattered banner of a radiant past.[2] According to census reports, the Soviet Union ceased being primarily an agrarian society sometime between 1959 and 1962.[3] Anticipating that historic demographic shift, Soviet intellectual culture had already begun to turn an attentive eye on the economic health and human vitality of the dwindling rural sector. One of the earliest indications of this intensified concern for a correct measurement of agrarian Russia's condition was the appearance of "documentary" sketches and diaries in which the voices and opinions of local collective farm officials were amplified by talented Soviet writers.[4] Soon afterward, this largely analytic literature of farm management and rural reform was radically transformed by the bold introduction into Soviet literature of an older narrative genre, the Turgenevan peasant sketch, in which literary vignettes from the Russian countryside once again served as powerful lyrical reminders of an ignored cultural alternative.

It was Aleksandr Solzhenitsyn who first enriched the modern rural sketch with intertextual allusions to classical precedents of Russian narrative prose. When the early Solzhenitsyn is remembered, it is usually in connection with the movingly restrained, bellwether text of the de-Stalinization campaign, *One Day in the Life of Ivan Denisovich* (1962). But the most permanent legacy Solzhenitsyn left behind for later Soviet public culture was contained in the modest shape of two "peasant sketches" — the well-known "Matryona's Home" of 1963 and the unjustly neglected "Zakhar's Pouch" of 1966, the last officially published writings of his brief Soviet career. Through these influential rural vignettes, Solzhenitsyn gave birth to contemporary "village prose," transforming the genre from reformist satire on local conditions to a truly "oppositionist" quest for authentic national cultural values.[5] Solzhenitsyn understood that the full pathos of rural traditionalism within an officially antihistoric state could best be conveyed by reinventing the forms and structures of the great nineteenth-century narratives of the Russian countryside. With unmistakable clarity, "Matryona's Home" evoked the aesthetic and humanitarian precedent of Turgenev's *Notes of a Hunter.* An episode from the normally hidden recesses of peasant Russia is related through the special sensibility of a literate outsider who is fond of rambles through the remote hinterland. Solzhenitsyn was well aware of the legendary fame of Turgenev's sketches in hastening the emancipation of the serfs. By analogy, his peasant sketches of the 1960s can be perceived as appeals to the Soviet intelligentsia to liberate the human and cultural substance of the agrarian folk from the facile stereotypes and ignorant contempt of a modern ruling class. A decade later, the meteoric literary success of the young Valentin Rasputin offered proof that Solzhenitsyn's call had been heard.

Rasputin's emergence as the true inheritor of Solzhenitsyn's radical traditionalism can be explained as a conjunction of sociology and sensibility. Rasputin's particular biography attached him to a location that had been spared, until recently, the rude disruptions of officially mandated Soviet progress. His native Siberian region had not undergone the mass relocation and collectivization that transformed the inherited peasant culture of the black earth districts of Russia and Ukraine. But Rasputin's generation was destined to witness a delayed catastrophic shift in the demography and ecology of central Siberia. Born in 1937 on the banks of the Angara River in a village that now overlooks the man-made Sea of Bratsk rather than an expanse of communal farms, Rasputin lived to see his home territory transformed by a large outflow of local youth and a heavy influx of outside technicians. Although himself a product of modern Siberia, being a university-trained journalist and the son of a peasant father who went off to war and later found employment in a timber collective, Rasputin remains deeply attached to the communal and matriarchal values that sustained his "natural" childhood and stable existence during the traumatic years of Russia's wartime deprivations and losses.[6] It might be claimed that his upbringing gave him both an imagination of disaster and a reliance on traditional forms of resistance and survival.

Certainly Rasputin's literary sensibility and narrative techniques express a profound neoconservatism that continues Solzhenitsyn's earlier initiative. He is best known to the Russian public for five novella-length works written between 1967 and 1985, all of which strategically exploit prerevolutionary literary subtexts even as they address pressing contemporary issues.[7] In formal terms, his fiction represents a contemporary revival of the traditional and rather unique Russian prose genre of the *povest'*: an extended, nonnovelistic narrative characterized by nonlinear and digressive narration. And in thematic terms, too, his art has concerned itself with dramatic revivals at a moment of near-extinction. What preoccupies Rasputin's imagination is the sorry spectacle of peasant communities facing catastrophic endings (financial, familial, and legal) without any reliable aid or understanding from the "upper level" of the socioeconomic order. But perhaps what most distinguishes Rasputin among his generation of "village prose" writers is his extraordinary vision of the delicate symbiosis between Russia's nature-given landscape and traditional Russian modes of nurturance. That subject is most memorably dramatized in works that touch on one central trauma Rasputin's imagination keeps revisiting: the socially commanded inundation of rural Russian villages by the floodwaters of progress and hydroelectric power. The young journalist who was assigned to cover the story of the flooding of his native village and the construction of the Ust'-Ilimsk Sea has become the major post-Soviet literary champion of conservationism and cultural conservatism.[8]

As a writer, Rasputin's first excursion back to his point of origin occurred in 1972. In that year he published a thinly fictionalized autobiographical "sketch of a journey" titled Downstream, Upstream (*Vniz i vverkh po techeniiu*). It is a skillfully meandering narrative that records both a geographical and a psychological drift back home of a young Siberian writer, Viktor, after a five-year absence. Rasputin's leisurely account evokes archetypal scenes from the Russian literary past, especially those that convey the theme of reimmersion in an evaporating provincial world. There is certainly a structural parallel to *Childhood*, Gorky's fond yet ambivalent memoir of his formative years up and down the Volga in an ancestral world of undying customs and superstitions. Yet despite this subtle attachment to prior reminiscences of Russian cultural legacies, Rasputin's sketch ends abruptly with Viktor's anxiety-ridden departure from a riverside home in which he can no longer find mooring. Ultimately, *Downstream, Upstream* poses some painful unresolved questions about a writer's attempt to find stability in his violently reconfigured homeland.[9]

The opening paragraph speaks with evident irony about an end to all that "senseless, exhausting scampering from store to store" that is the curse of Moscow life: "It all ended at once, as if it had been cut out of Viktor's life as soon as he entered the cabin and put down his suitcase; and now all that stretched ahead was that light and pleasant indolence that had been agitating him with its promise of leisure and freedom." [10] Like many an earlier would-be Russian Rousseau, Viktor is saying good-bye to city life and hectic modernity, but it is also obvious that he is driven by a city-bred illusion of rustic peace. Once launched on the smooth, slow current toward home, Viktor is lulled into a transparently sentimental state in which he spins fragile daydreams. He resurrects an adolescent shipboard romance that actually ended without regrets back in the city, away from the water. He romanticizes a small country family of perfectly matched young parents, and he fantasizes a secure respite from his restless travels: "Only in his native village, with his father and mother, he knew his rest would be complete. . . . he would plunge into that life as into a second childhood" (245). These stereotypical images of rural life and a tranquil past rapidly vanish, however. As Viktor descends the river closer to home, the waters become more agitated and the memories they evoke take on sudden depth.

In fact, Viktor's earliest and keenest recollection of his formative years is a powerful memory of the sublime force with which the Angara River broke loose from its ice cover precisely on his sixth birthday: "The little boy kept crying, without wiping away the tears, and kept looking and looking at the river, at its noisy festive liberation that began in the night, amid the thunderstorm, far from people's eyes" (250). A childhood spent in close touch with Siberian nature connects the dawn of environmental awareness with a respect and awe for the often violent cycles of natural renewal. In his inner depths, Viktor knows better than to rest on a dream of endless rural calm and felicity. Nurtured in a farming village on the banks of the ever-shifting river, Viktor's mentality is shaped as much by transcendental ecstasies as by traditional routines. The home territory Viktor knows in his marrow is a land alien to the secular rhythms and reasons that dictate the hectic pace and fugitive pleasures of city life.

The closer Viktor comes to renewed contact with his native landscape, the higher his anxiety rises. We learn, rather belatedly, that Viktor's last trip home was on the day before the flooding of the reservoir and the relocation of his village. Even as he has been floating downstream, he has been reluctantly registering the changes that make this voyage something less than a return journey. Passing an island, Viktor is reminded that all the little floating worlds near his childhood home have been erased from sight and mind. Oddly, the nearer he approaches his point of origin, the more intensely he recollects images of extinction from five years ago:

> Viktor walked up to what was left of the hut and stood before it for a long time, as at a grave. . . . Only a few huts stood quietly, the rest had either been torn down or were being taken down; bare, exposed rafters stuck out awkwardly; the gaps where the pushed-out windows had been stared lifelessly yet commandingly into the street . . . and cooling out in the open, puzzled and chilled, as if after a fire, sat domestic Russian stoves left to the whim of fate. (261–62)

The casting outdoors of the very symbol of Russian rural warmth and hospitality seems to mark the end of a culture; indeed, the local folk describe the scene Viktor recollects as nothing less than "the passing away of the world [*svetoprestavlenie*]." Apocalypse seems to have outpaced Viktor, arriving before he can manage to touch home soil once again.

But Rasputin also sees to it that Viktor recalls a tormenting dream he experienced two years before, after he had published a story about an old man dying "with all the requisite sighs, moans, thoughts and sensations." In that dream, the old man (who resembles Viktor's grandfather) "arose from his nonexistence" and reprimanded the young author for daring to write about "what you just cannot know, no way" (267). It is difficult not to detect in this an ironic self-reference to Rasputin's own presumptuousness in writing about the death of a representative village matriarch in *The Last Phase*, which itself was published two years earlier. On the verge of Viktor's return to the ashes of a village culture, he is haunted (as are Rasputin's readers) by the possibility that writers can be guilty of pronouncing final sentences without adequate authority.

It is important not to minimize the shock of nonrecognition that Viktor undergoes when he finally arrives at his downstream home. Compared to what it once was, it is a flattened and degraded world. The river has been swallowed up in a vast pool: "From edge to edge the water lay supine and muffled in one ungraspable expanse, pressing its weight upon the forlorn, low-lying shore; the sky above it was vacant" (271). Uninspiring and unforbidding, this flat water is invaded by motorboats that bounce and drone among the waterlogged stumps of former forests. "No pure and ancient mystery hovered on high over these waters. . . . the feeling of eternity departed, closed shut under a tight lid" (280). When Viktor finally lands on his native shore, he steps onto disenchanted territory. Although his kinfolk meet him, he cannot recognize his village or find his own home amid the row houses that blend together in the new streets of the workers' settlement. Disorientation and cultural displacement appear to have overtaken the writer's homeland.

Rasputin, however, subtly qualifies the pessimism that his maladjusted alter ego experiences. In a skillful variation on Turgenev's "Bezhin Meadow," Viktor gets lost in a suddenly foreign-looking familiar landscape. Like Turgenev's hunter, Viktor loses his bearings, yet also stumbles on an unsuspected world of surviving natural and cultural wonders. Picking his way past distorted landmarks that leave him feeling unconnected to his childhood, Viktor suddenly wanders into a newfound meadow that resuscitates his sense of old Russia: "Here it was spacious, radiant, and festive. Growing separately, so as not to block one another's light or draw the earth's moisture from one another, stood in fashionable majesty two fat magnificent birches with broad-spread and heavy-bedecked boughs, exactly like two grand ladies. . . . and it was so remarkable and joyous here that you wanted to weep from this inexpressible, unworldly happiness" (298). Like Turgenev's hunter, Viktor also comes across a scruffy peasant lad who inspires sagging hopes; navigating through the dangers of a treacherous sunken forest, the boy leads the returned writer to the fresh water that still flows within the stagnant "sea" of the man-made reservoir. The village samovars require that tea be brewed from a daily supply of this clear river water. There is, then, some evidence that those who still inhabit the ravaged village culture have adapted to a life that contains some vestiges of Siberia's former graces and grandeur.

As for Viktor, however, he is now truly a displaced person. His absence has meant that he cannot locate the remaining natural sources of cultural identity that still sustain his kin as they continue to observe the rhythms and routines of "downstream" rural life. "He was right next to those places and yet at a distance all the same . . . a different land lay before him, reminding him at precious few moments of the land on which he had grown" (304). *Downstream, Upstream* beautifully expresses the uncomfortable exile of a native son whose own life is unmoored from a much-loved homeland that seems washed away in a flood of Soviet modernity. Even so, total cultural extinction in Rasputin's resistant Siberia was clearly a bit premature, at least in 1972.

Within another four years Rasputin completed a second literary evocation of his endangered home territory. In 1976 he published the provocatively titled *Farewell to Matyora.* The sensational success of this tale, as measured by its many reprintings and its release as a major film in 1982, speaks eloquently to an increasingly widespread anxiety about the cultural extinction of Russia in the latter days of the Soviet Union. But underneath the plot's dire events there is strong encouragement for a conservationist conservatism that is anthropological as well as ecological. Commonly acclaimed or denounced as an affecting vision of catastrophe, Rasputin's novella does not yield as much ground to victorious modernity as is often thought.

As Rasputin imagines Matyora, it is a rich, arable island in the middle of the Angara River; its land has been worked collectively for over three hundred years. The story focuses on the events of one final summer prior to the inundation of the island required by the construction of a vast hydroelectric project. The plot thus revolves around a central conflict between Leninist progress as defined by the famous slogan, "COMMU-NISM IS SOVIET POWER PLUS ELECTRIFICATION," and the aged remnants of old-style Russian communalism. This struggle is narrated largely through the remarkable language and die-hard perspective of the last holdouts, the resident custodians of the condemned island. The result of the "what" and the "how" of Rasputin's telling is a harsh panoramic view of what figures as the immolation of Russia's folk culture by

Soviet Prometheanism. Without violating the languid, dilatory narrative style of a Russian *povest'*, Rasputin writes of a near-apocalypse. The author's own prose sets up a powerful current of literary antimodernism that successfully counters the official Soviet culture's recklessly heroic pursuit of technological progress.

In the act of naming and inhabiting his fictional island, Rasputin creates a magnetic field of cultural affiliations. Matyora is, like Solzhenitsyn's Matryona, etymologically rooted in the ancient earthbound culture of "Mother Russia," but Rasputin's island also harbors the hoary masculine tradition of salty speech known as *mat*, or "mother-talk." [11] Local legend relates that the island's name actually derives from the continent (*materik*) from which it long ago emerged. This cluster of connotations is most appropriate, since Rasputin's island is a microcosm of the Old Russian continent and its ancient agrarian culture. It is home both to a representative peasant matriarch, Darya Pinigina, and to her compatible opposite, the old heretic, Bogodul, whose name means "blasphemer."

To Rasputin's credit, he relies on more than verbal associations to convey the island's endearing traditionalism. The narrative functions as a virtual handbook of ethnographic "thick description" of the customs and rituals of unmolested village life. Early on there is a memorable depiction of that central rite of Russian hospitality, tea drinking from a samovar: "Darya kept pouring from the samovar into her glass, from her glass into the saucer, sipping gently and carefully, savoring the tea, not swallowing right away, neatly licking her lips and slowly, dreamily talking, as though not choosing her words but taking them out at random, talking and talking, not taking the conversation in any one direction, but bending it this way and that." [12] This elaborate sociable routine is a perfect epitome of the inefficient, labor-intensive, and therefore unhurried and meditative flow of the ancient communal life. Darya, Bogodul, and the few remaining elders of the island collective are accustomed to hard seasonal labor, but it is "peaceable work," it allows the time and space for undirected gossip and reminiscence and it promotes the slow accretion of a shared, context-specific identity. Like Darya's rich peasant speech, which is filled with additive particles to provide rhythm and emphasis to proverbial formulas, this "samovar life" affords plenty of margin for play and enjoyment within a rigidly patterned existence based on the cycles of nature and ancestral duties and expectations. [13] The narrator's voice merges with the mentality of Matyora's matriarchy in affirming that a "table without a samovar at its head is no table at all, but a feeding station for birds or animals without savor or ceremony. Three masters have been honored for ages in a household—the person who heads the family, the Russian stove, and the samovar" (81–82).

Rasputin's island is also permeated with a degree of animism that is intended to startle the modern reader. Behaviors that at first seem merely quaint superstitions, like the pervasive belief in "wood demons" and "house spirits" or the custom of not wrapping up a samovar in the house when it is taken outside so that it can see where to return, gradually signify a reverence for the power of environment in lives led close to an age-old homeland. Without warning, the narrator enlists himself among those who see invisible hovering presences. The sixth chapter suddenly lurches into the territory of "magic realism" with the introduction of a small nocturnal animal who presides as the all-seeing "Master" of the island. This guardian spirit is sensed by all who are native to Matyora, and in turn his keen earthbound sense foresees the destiny of all the beings and structures that occupy the island. He hears the silent houses and the quiet land preparing for the end of their natural days of service to the world, yet paradoxically the "island was preparing to live a long time" (58).

In stark opposition to this endangered preserve of old Russian folk-ways is the Soviet mainland culture, which is determined to renovate Siberia by erecting a quickly assembled hydroelectric paradise of worker settlements and state farms. Perhaps because of its vivid scenes of desecration, *Farewell to Matyora* has been described as depicting "a process of national matricide," concluding with "a grotesque, cinematic image of post-Apocalypse Russia: smoke-blackened tree stumps." [14] Undeniably, Rasputin's narrative features memorable episodes in which the profanation of cultural icons occurs as a direct consequence of rational central planning. From the initial battle scene in which a ragtag band of senior citizens momentarily halts the legalized vandalism of gravestones by a team of sanitary engineers to the climactic harrowing and arson of the island's homes and landscape by order of the project supervisors, it is clear that Matyora is being submerged by an occupying army of progress that is as wasteful and impious as the Tatar horde. That analogy is boldly drawn in Darya's picturesque language; the outside invaders are directly addressed as "heathens" (*pogantsy*), they camp in a "horde" (*orda*), and the "rack and ruin" they bring about is described as "being carried off to Tartary" *(pomchalo v tartarary)*. It is as if the latter-day Bolsheviks have indeed become Eurasians who are trampling underfoot the true soul of Russia.

In the end, however, Rasputin refuses to imagine the total extinction of his symbolic preserve of Russian cultural antiquities. Despite its title, *Farewell to Matyora* performs something less than an obituary to Old Russia. Darya succeeds, in the most moving chapter, in laying her homestead to eternal rest exactly as ancestral voices at the family graveyard instruct her to do. She washes and sanctifies the family home as if she were "dressing" a corpse for proper Orthodox commitment to the earth and posterity. She says farewell by "putting in order" domestic life precisely as timeless tradition has always required.

Despite the worst assaults of the marauding horde, the island's presiding totem stands unfallen while the advance of Soviet modernization proceeds apace:

> Matyora, both the island and the village, was impossible to imagine without the larch tree in the common pasture. It rose and towered over all the rest like a shepherd towers over his flock spread out on grazing land. It did resemble a shepherd conducting his ancient guard duty. But no one, no matter how literate, referred to that tree, despite the gender of larch as "she," no, it was a he, the "tsar-larch"—it stood so eternal, powerful, and mighty. . . . And apparently it had grown so high and so strong that it was decided in the heavens for the sake of general order and measure to shorten it. Without its crown the larch squatted and seemed weaker but, no, it had not lost its powerful, majestic aspect; it became very likely even more awesome and imperious. It's not known when the superstition was born that it was the tsar-larch that held the island firm to the river's bottom, to solid ground, and that as long as it stood so would Matyora. . . . The sole standing survivor, the insubordinate tsar-larch, continued to rule over everything around it. But everything around it was empty. (159, 165)

In this invented parable, the enduring tsar-larch is rhetorically crowned with the aura of the medieval Muscovite princes, those stern and necessary protectors of the national faith against the heathen overlords. The semantic and political implications of Rasputin's truncated but unbowed shepherd-tree are rather far-reaching, implying as they do the persistence on ancient Russian territory of a sheltering authoritarian presence.

In the last pages of the original text an obscuring fog besets the landing party that has the assignment of removing the remaining unvanquished residents from their island refuge. As the motor launch approaches, its sound is drowned out by the agonized wail of Matyora's tutelary spirit: "Its putt became clearer and then moved away again, and then once more, sharper and clearer, rose the voice of the Master." [15] It is surely noteworthy that the landing party never reaches its destination. In a daring and provocative departure from the norms of secular Soviet realism, Rasputin concluded his dire allegory of Russia's cultural and environmental death with a native touch of "magic realism." An old Russian legend (and an opera by Rimsky-Korsakov) relates how the "shining city of Kitezh" sank uncorrupted to the bottom of a lake at the time of the first Mongol invasion, preserving like Atlantis an unspoiled civilization from destruction by foreign hands. According to that legend, the sunken city's pealing bells could still be heard every Midsummer Eve. Likewise, by reviving ancestral myths and animist beliefs common among the faithful Russian folk, *Farewell to Matyora* offers its readers the tenuous but tenacious hope that the communal and authoritarian spirit that once sustained the old village culture has not entirely passed from the Russian soul.

Like Solzhenitsyn before him, Rasputin performed a literary conjury that restored a fond but faded vision of the Russian homeland as permanently rooted in a mothering earth and a sheltering forestland. Not quite sunk from sight is a peaceable kingdom of communes in communion with ancestral Slavic custom and the Russian God. Cultural survival for these conservative nationalists requires nothing less than an extrasensory perception of the indissoluble bond between Russia's ecological and ethnic health. Despite the ravages of savage Soviet progress, the violated Russian landscape still retains the physical and cultural features that the Westernizers have forgotten or attempted to obliterate. A restored sight of the enduring motherland is quite literally seen as the secret to preserving the race.

Toward the conclusion of a remarkable public conversation in 1985 Toni Morrison turned to her younger colleague, Gloria Naylor, and proudly acknowledged a hard-won achievement: "It's possible to look at the world now and find oneself properly spoken of in it. . . . This is *our* work and I know it is ours because I have done it and you know it is be-

cause you have done it. . . . It's a marvellous beginning. It's a real renaissance."[16] What is celebrated here is nothing less than the literary
emergence of yet another new Negro voice—one that finally speaks of
the bondage and bonding that African American women *know* they have
shared in the untold history of their endurance. Naylor herself acknowledges, rather like Rasputin in the Russian context, that she is the grateful follower of strong predecessors within a historic outpouring of actively affirmative ethnic writing. Her name, like Rasputin's, has become
inextricably linked with a contemporary variety of conservationism and
cultural nationalism.

Not until 1977, when she was a twenty-seven-year-old undergraduate at Brooklyn College, was Gloria Naylor exposed to writing by black
women; but after reading poems by Gwendolyn Brooks and Toni Morrison's *The Bluest Eye*, she immersed herself in the entire tradition that
lay behind her. By the time she finished her bachelor of arts degree in
English in 1981, she had already completed her first novel, *The Women of
Brewster Place*; in 1983, Naylor received a master of arts in African American studies from Yale University, having analyzed the history and artistry
of her antecedents with a thoroughness impossible before the advent of
black studies in the academy. By 1988, Naylor unleashed that formidable
learning in a public assault on the restrictions that had been imposed
on black female self-expression despite the advances of the civil rights
movement and the assertiveness of the black arts movement. Raising
her voice in the controversy surrounding Alice Walker's *The Color Purple*,
Naylor documented how generations of African American writers had
conspired to look at black females with glazed eyes. Overly conscious of
surveillance by the white gaze, most black male writers had either whitened or luridly colorized female sexuality while holding black women's
writing accountable "for 'proving' that the Afro-American community
contains harmonious and loving couples."[17] Signaling her own rebellion against the constraints of a Euro-American standard of family values
and femininity that had until recently been corseting the literary image
of America's black women, Naylor enlisted herself in the campaign of recovery performed by the "motherline" of African American writing since
Hurston's time—in Susan Willis's definition, "the journey [both real
and figural] back to the historical source of the black American community."[18] In the same year she passionately defended Alice Walker, Naylor
joined the distinguished company of Paule Marshall and Toni Morri-

son by unveiling her own multigenerational monument to black womanhood, *Mama Day.*

Naylor's credentials for conjuring up the deep matrilineal roots of
African American culture were earned at home well before her graduate training. Her personal history, it has been suggested, takes on a
mythic dimension, representing her people's passage in modern times;
although conceived in the South, she was born and raised in New York
City, yet she remained embedded in an extended family that sustained
the manners and memories of the Mississippi sharecropper village from
which both her parents and grandparents had migrated.[19] Religion, too,
played a particularly formative role in the development of Naylor's sense
of place. In 1963, that horrendous year of assassinations and church
bombings, Naylor's mother became a Jehovah's Witness and her daugh-
ters rapidly followed suit. From 1968 to 1975 Gloria Naylor was an active
Witness, preaching the truth of a world utterly corrupt and awaiting
Armageddon. Although admitted to Hunter College, her commitment
to an apocalyptic faith prevailed, and she removed herself from secular education until 1975, when she finally became disillusioned with the
rigidity and righteous pessimism of her prophetic sect. Well into young
adulthood, Gloria Naylor's family and faith had given her access to a special realm of being that enabled her to be in the city but not of it, to be of
the world but not in it. The fact that the young writer's imagination had
been homeschooled in values that defied the norms of secular humanism
simply cannot be ignored.

As we shall see, Naylor's big novel about the survival of a nurturing
matriarchy on an autonomous island of Southern black folk demands
to be read as an allegory about cultural politics. In interpretations of
it, Naylor is usually located at the intersection between black feminism
and Afrocentrism, where so much contemporary academic criticism has
been produced. Yet Naylor has been careful in interviews to keep a distance from political labels, and her text would seem to resist enlistment
in a separatist campaign. What swims into view as her magic island takes
on its full dimensions is a deep respect for the restorative power of material culture and oral tradition to surmount tragic loss and to heal ruptures inflicted by time and circumstance. And this trust in the curative
value of what is passed on by tongue and hand from generation to generation amounts to a "womanist" appreciation for cultural process that
is less ethnocentric than it at first appears to be.

In the tradition of DuBois, Naylor opens her world of black folk with a challenge to the reader to listen well: "Willow Springs. Everybody knows but nobody talks about the legend of Sapphira Wade. A true conjure woman: satin black, biscuit cream, red as Georgia clay: depending on which of us takes a mind to her. . . . It ain't about right or wrong, truth or lies; it's about a slave woman who brought a whole new meaning to both them words, soon as you cross over here from beyond the bridge." [20] The very mode of narration has "crossed over" several customary boundaries: it is situated somewhere between literate and oral discourse, and it speaks in a communal voice about an ancestral tale that silently exists in multiple mental variants and lies outside ethical and empirical norms. "Mixing it all together and keeping everything that done shifted down through the holes of time," the narrative gives the reader a myth of origins for an anomalous island culture of unassimilated Euro-Africans that survives in splendid detachment just off the coast of Georgia and South Carolina. In a further gesture of disorientation, Naylor makes this exceptional Gullah-like subculture of freed landowning Africans the central focus of a modern African American love story that is being recollected in the novel's present and the reader's future time, 1999. This bold defiance of all the rules of standard narrative plausibility is reminiscent of the unapologetic disruption of scholarly practices perpetrated by Hurston in *Mules and Men*. In a similar send-up of obtuse book learning, the reader is forewarned not to approach Willow Springs in the manner of "Reema's boy," who returned to his home island burdened with ethnographic rationalizations and a useless tape recorder. His "extensive field work" results in a one-purpose explanation for the expressive oddities of the local dialect: whatever might appear to be nonsensical or ignorant speech was to be appreciated for "inverting hostile social and political parameters. 'Cause, see, being we was brought here as slaves, we had no choice but to look at everything upside-down" (8). This is a wicked cut, indeed, since Naylor is clearly willing to parody the trendy "cultural studies" understanding of black vernacular speech as a reactive medium "signifying" on or reversing standard white discourse.

By contrast, Naylor's narrative offers the flexible reader access to alternative modes of cognition that support and bind together communities outside the mainstream of modernity. Revising DuBois's metaphor of the Negro as "a sort of seventh son, born with a veil, and gifted with second-sight in this American world," Naylor devises a family tree of black Days culminating in a contemporary conjure woman, Miranda, who springs from the seventh son of a seventh son. This "Mama Day" inherits and passes on the gift of reversing ill fortune that was possessed by her African ancestress, Sapphira, who captivated, married, and dispossessed her European slavemaster, Bascombe Wade. Naylor hints that her own narrative, *Mama Day*, might also serve as a novel means of conjury: "Think about it: ain't nobody really talking to you. We're sitting here in Willow Springs, and you're God-knows-where. It's August, 1999—ain't but a slim chance it's the same season where you are. Uh, huh, listen. Really listen this time: the only voice is your own" (10). Where really is the reader who is transported into the unvocalized and autonomous time-space of this novelistic narrative? If the reader truly attends to what Naylor's book is saying, the magic of imaginative prose can perform the implausible and assist those who live beyond the bridge to cross over into Willow Springs.

The central plot of the novel reiterates in the present generation a mythic pattern of African American genealogy—the tragically disrupted union between two cultural components that are not easily bridged. But the unconventional narrative mode works to assert the existence of a timeless communion through ancestral memory that has the power to heal wounds and psychic divisions. In the foreground the reader eavesdrops on a dialogue of mismatched lovers as they disinter their dead connection—a comedy of errors that shades off into tragic romance. But this unfolding story is constantly interrupted by the legendary history of the present-day island. Both the posthumously revived love story and the epic family saga of the black Days in Willow Springs are tales that make coded references to Afrocentric rites and Shakespearean writ.[21] Naylor's *Mama Day* thus rivals and revises the power of the British bard to reconcile history's victims to the woe that life is and, in the process, restores the folk art of conjury to its grandest life-affirming proportions.

How, then, does Naylor rewrite the history of her people in a literary microcosm? She begins with the meeting of two young African American professionals in a dingy Manhattan coffee shop. Though they are slow to realize it, they are the predestined pair of complementary opposites that constitute the stuff of romance. George Andrews typifies the urban black as history's orphan; with nothing to rely on other than his mother wit, he is raised in a benevolent Staten Island shelter for boys devoted to the disciplined Booker T. Washington school of applied practicality: "Only the present has potential, *sir*" (23). Trained to live hard-headedly with a forgettable past and no reliable future, George grows up to be a mechanical engineer with a heart murmur: "I may have knocked my head against the walls . . . but I never knocked on wood" (27). Ophelia Day, by contrast, is the historic last hope of her deep-rooted Southern island of blackness; competent and independent, she cannot get away from the knowledge that she is her family's only surviving "child of Grace," and she proudly walks through the world bearing her pet name, "Cocoa." Although George tries to battle off an irrational sense of fated attraction and Cocoa badly misreads urban signs and signals, a natural magic, assisted by Grand Aunt Miranda's interventions, draws them together. Ophelia's insistence on her Willow Springs name "Cocoa" is, for George, a constant reminder of the golden skin he first glimpsed on the nape of her neck; later, her letters from home, lavender-scented and yellow-powdered by Miranda, carry her irresistible presence to him. Naylor is, incidentally, also suggesting the power of a subliminal racial affinity—George fondly recollects the "beautiful trouble" of Cocoa's "high-behind, sway-backed walk that moved in sync with something buried deep in my gut" (101).

Despite the many irritants that separate this regionally and temperamentally divided couple, they share both a superficial and a deeply disguised identification with Shakespeare. On the surface, George melodramatically identifies with Edmund, the enraged bastard son who protests the unfairness of the world; and the orphaned Cocoa, who resists her given name, joins George in identifying with the supreme rhetoric of victimage and abandonment in *King Lear*. But what they secretly share at a deeper level is a predisposition to avoid confrontation with the tragedy inscribed in their intimate family history. Both George's prostitute mother and Cocoa's true namesake, her great-grandmother Ophelia, drowned themselves in despair over the children they lost and could not reclaim. Naylor's plot conspires to lure both George and Cocoa to cross over to Willow Springs, where there can be no forgetting of ill fortune or of the need to search for restorative measures that make it possible to live on.

Naylor's magic island in the tempestuous Atlantic is presided over not by Prospero and his books but by Miranda Day and her home remedies.[22] It is an ancient matriarchal therapy that Miranda practices, and it works not to control but to guide natural processes in ways that promote bodily and mental harmony. Rather like Almira Todd, the herb-gathering healer of Sarah Orne Jewett's *Country of the Pointed Firs*, Miranda is the childless midwife and nurturer of her community's health. But unlike Jewett's shepherdess of a dying Maine breed, Miranda has to contend with local rivals who compete for custody of her wayward and squabbling flock. Naylor's narrative carefully separates the benevolent conjury of Mama Day from the fraudulent "voodoo" of the local trickster, Dr. Buzzard, and the malevolent "root-working" of the insanely jealous beautician, Ruby. Miranda's herbal cures and deft fingers display an intimate knowledge of bodily ailments and how to ease their pain; her practice, as the mainland physician, Dr. Smithfield, admits, "was usually no different from what he had to say himself—just plainer words and a slower cure than them concentrated drugs" (84). Yet being an outsider, "he couldn't be expected to believe the other things Miranda could do."

Miranda Day also knows how to perform magical cures that depend on a griot-like invocation of ancestral wisdom that accompanies and enlightens the living. An expert egg-candler who can see through the shell the embryonic promise of new life, Miranda is associated with community rituals and secret rites that depend on "leading on with light," seeing the creative path that belief itself illuminates. Willow Springs has no visible willows, but it still draws sustenance from a surviving taproot in Africa that is very resilient. This can be seen in several inherited customs indigenous to the island. "Candle Light Night" occurs every winter solstice, when the residents come forth with some form of illumination and exchange gifts with the blessing, "Lead on with light." Although the ritual has been subject to modifications and modernizations, with flashing headlights and packaged foods replacing the original handheld candles and handmade gifts, Miranda understands that its elusive mystique will persist, rooted as it is in changing versions of a myth of origin. Some say the island was spit from the mouth of God with stars attached and when God tried to reclaim them, his hand was grasped by the greatest conjure woman on earth: "Leave 'em here, Lord. . . . I ain't got nothing but these poor black hands to guide my people, but I can lead on with light" (110). Others say that the community used to link arms and proceed with lights to the bluff facing the ocean to commemorate the slave woman who took her freedom from her master in "18 & 23" and left in a ball of fire for Africa. The evolving holiday retains a secure foundation in miracle tales that affirm the possibility of finding a way home out of dark exile.

The residents of Willow Springs also hold fast to their own distinct form of funeral service—"the standing forth." Without flowers or music, each mourner "stands forth" before the coffin and addresses it, announcing how the deceased was first seen and how he or she will look on their next meeting. As George realizes when he attends the last rites for "Little Caesar," the precious lad brought out of a barren womb by Miranda's conjury, the islanders do not observe a "Christian ritual that should have called for a sermon, music, tears—the belief in an earthly finality for the child's life" (269). It is hard for him to understand that his bride, Cocoa, comes from a deep-rooted stock of New World Africans in whose culture the deceased are never truly departed. Peace must be made with their cries for attention.

At the climax of Naylor's novel, George (and perhaps the reader) cannot quite "cross over" to unite his mind and body with the black Days and their magic island. It requires, as does Rasputin's Matyora, a capacity to believe that one can seek and hear guidance beyond the limits of secular reality. In particular, it requires assent to scenes of effective conjury and communion with the dead. To Naylor's credit, the speaking graves and the acts of therapeutic magic do not come easily; they are, as it were, earned by a painfully close attention to what genealogy and the natural elements have to say to those who are willing to confront suffering and tragedy. It is Miranda, the matriarch and guardian of Willow Springs, who struggles to induce a curative belief in herself and others that can look past the pain and the losses that are endemic to the history of her tempest-tossed island.

Alert as she is to meteorology and psychology, Miranda does not anticipate the double fury that descends on the island and threatens the next generation of her African American family. A big wind comes out of Africa cutting off the island and leaving George no bridge back to the mainland; simultaneously, Cocoa's head is braided with poisonous nightshade by the envious hairdresser, Ruby. While George flails about helplessly, bereft of his usual recourse to efficient rational solutions, Miranda withdraws to the "other place," the remote and mysterious house and garden that holds the family secrets and ancestral lore on which her wisdom has always relied. To George, that house resonates with loss, seeing it as a lasting monument to Bascombe Wade's inability to possess the slave woman he liberated; George also knows it to be the sorrowful site of the first Ophelia's loss of her tiny daughter, Peace, and of her own subsequent despair and death by drowning. But Miranda, in her distress, finds a redemptive revelation in that same house.

The childless conjure woman, "Mama Day," discovers that she is truly a daughter of all her ancestors combined and in that recognition is born an intuition about how to save the latest Ophelia and future generations of the family. Peering down into the endless well that took Peace from her mother, Miranda suddenly recognizes her own hands resemble those of her wood-carving father and her house-building great-grandfather: "Looking past the losing was to feel for the man who built this house and for the one who nailed this well shut. It was to feel the hope in them that the work of their hands could wipe away all that had gone before. Those men *believed*—in the power of themselves, in what they were feeling. And now there is that boy. . . . She needs his hand in hers—his very hand—so that she can connect it up with all the believing that had gone before" (285). Miranda comes to see the home place both as an excruciating reminder of broken connections and as a reliquary for the remains of the faithful lovers who could not let go of what they could not keep. In the "other place" Mama Day finds proof of a consoling devotion beyond the grip of death and disaffection. She finds her father's serpent-decorated walking stick ("Live on!" he used to say) and the elaborately carved rocking chair with which he sought to distract Ophelia from her suicidal brooding. In the attic she uncovers what the reader will recognize as the original bill of sale conveying the resistant and sullen slave woman, Sapphira, to Bascombe Wade "for one-half gold tender, one half goods in kind." But in its time-obliterated state, the document has been converted into a cryptic note of redemption: "**Law . . . knowledge . . . witness . . . inflicted . . . nurse.** . . . It's all she can pick out until she gets to the bottom for the final words: **Conditions . . . tender . . . kind**" (280). Miranda intuits that her vocation as a nurse and healer is calling her to save Cocoa by enlisting George to join his hand to the ancient legacy of unyielding lovers of a mysterious African ancestry.

George's heart gives out, overstrained by the physical and mental effort of making himself act on Mama Day's "mumbo-jumbo" cure for what ails Ophelia. He is instructed to take the paternal relics, the ledger and cane, to the coop where Miranda's red hen is setting and to bring back whatever he finds behind the nest of eggs. He fails to return to the "other place," but George does manage to bring his torn and bleeding hands to the bedside of his delirious and poisoned wife before he expires. The Northerner sacrifices his life, but the endangered Southern "child of Grace" is cured. Mama Day's climactic act of conjury has worked its magic. The sickened Cocoa had hallucinated that her color wasn't right and that her whole body was corrupt and worm-eaten. George's bloodied but full-hearted devotion restores her belief that she is loved. And Naylor's "magic realist" narrative concludes by reaffirming the ongoing legacy of the black Days—Ophelia, married and with children, has returned in 1999 to the "other place" where she and her deathless departed lover have spoken again and reconstructed their exemplary romance. The race is preserved by the ongoing mystique of a resilient African American soul that is constantly divided but refuses to be broken.

Rasputin and Naylor both participate, to varying degrees, in a contemporary resurgence of ethnic particularism and cultural authenticity. It is surely significant that these two writers, so widely separated by gender and nationality, both imagine their own distinctive cultural community in terms of a barrier island threatened by an invasive mainland economy that seeks to integrate it or obliterate it in the name of national progress and resource development. Moreover, the two novelists have affiliated themselves in public forums with intellectual currents (Village Prose, Afrocentrism) that drift in the direction of xenophobia and separatism.[23] And it could be argued that the popularity of *Farewell to Matyora* and *Mama Day* is symptomatic of the return of a repressed essentialism among Russians and African Americans traumatized by the pressures of modernity and the fractures of postmodernism. Yet the textual parallels that can be drawn are more topographical than ideological, and the two novels display some crucial distinctions between the current revivals of ancestral "soul" among Russians and black Americans.

   In its narrative form and its fundamental plot *Farewell to Matyora* is profoundly ethnocentric; its literal and symbolic levels are built exclusively on Russian literary and folkloric foundations. The author's mentality is that of a cultural preservationist, and his text actively represents, in its linguistic and ideological dimension, a regressive quest for communion with an authentic origin, an ethnic purity that seems about to be erased from visibility and legibility. In Rasputin's cataclysmic fable of a Russian Atlantis overwhelmed by the tide of modern progress, there is no accommodation with or adjustment to historic change. The traditional folkways of Matyora are lyrically presented as perfectly adapted to the natural environment and the seasonal rhythms of agrarian life. The nearly vanished voice of Rasputin's rural Russia utters an appealing challenge to the reader to recover the "natural tongue" of the ancestral motherland. The true voice of Russia is imagined to inhere in certain changeless verities whispered by the forests and fields. In Rasputin's conservative mystique of the Russian soul, there is a natural supernaturalism in which the landscape utters to the reverent listener both ecological and ethnic values. The novel exudes a desperate faith that the timeless words and ways of the Russian folk cannot finally be drowned out.

The profoundly ahistoric essentialism of Rasputin's reactionary cultural nationalism bears little resemblance to Naylor's far more supple and less sentimental myth of black American ancestry in *Mama Day.* Although there are readers who presuppose that Willow Springs is an idyllic representation of a timeless African American culture that is at its core matriarchal and Afrocentric, the narrative disruptions and the contested meanings of the novel's events defy such straightforward summary.[24] The cultural custodian of Naylor's island, Miranda Day, is buffetted by the shifting winds of history, and she knows that her family tree rests on gnarled roots. As a result, the novel and its central figure are laboring to conjure into being an evolving cultural and genealogical order that can effectively nurture the wide-branching African American family.[25] The saga of the black Days has obscure origins in a troubled ancestry and unfolds in mysterious fragments with many painful ruptures and puzzling gaps. Like the double-ring quilt that Miranda and her sister make and pass on to Cocoa, Naylor's family narrative requires an artful stitching of seemingly incompatible materials. To be complete it must incorporate into the body of the text the spurned European slave master and the resistant Northern black who have both refused to let go of their tragic romance with a non-Western blackness they do not comprehend. Naylor's novel is as broad as Joseph's amazing multicolored coat. It weaves elegant variations of the Shakespearean canon into a highly oral text that speaks up in the vernacular for an African wisdom that survives and thrives on the margins of the American South. Without actively promoting cosmopolitanism or hybridity, Naylor's version of the African American story is very much a dialogic work in progress—her narrative features a woman-centered and African-derived art of conjury that is ethnically and environmentally specific yet also open to cultural synthesis with those who have crossed over and become part of the "home place."

In the final analysis, *Farewell to Matyora* and *Mama Day* embody very different strategies for preserving an ancestral essence in modern literary culture. Rasputin's novel flows with the desperate nostalgia of much contemporary Russian cultural nationalism. It represents the search to retrieve a perfectly embalmed ethnically pure identity from the endangered natural landscape that shields the graves of the ancestral agrarian folk of Russia. Authentic Russian culture is thus "naturalized" not as a biological essence but as an ecological given that has been squandered and spoiled but is not beyond resuscitation. Naylor's novel, on the other hand, participates fully in the rich polyphony and inventive conjury currently practiced by many African American literary "root-workers." It represents the multicolored and multicultural improvisations that must be woven into the shifting kaleidoscopic design of a quilted identity that holds strong over time and through troubles. It is notable, however, that this culture-sustaining activity tends to be imaged as an African survival passed on through sensitive mediums whose hands and minds are in touch with ancestral guidance. Given the brutal disruptions of spatial continuity and racial purity that figure in Naylor's American chronicle of black Days, her notion of cultural preservation depends on a mystique of spirit rather than of place. In Naylor's version, black cultural nationalism relies in essence on a historically transmitted African genius for creative adaptation rather than on a reactionary conservation of environmental and ethnic purity. Essentialism, no less than pluralism, is culturally various and shaped by historically situated crises of identity that cry out for home remedies.

EPILOGUE

Response and Call:

The African American Dialogue with Bakhtin

During the last few decades a talented and highly educated generation of African American intellectuals and artists has revived the call of the Harlem Renaissance for public recognition of a literature that adequately expresses the culture of the American Negro. To a large extent this second generation of sophisticated writers and critics has succeeded in transforming the canon of African American literature as it is now taught in schools and universities. In a remarkably rapid reassessment of cultural capital, once spurned or marginalized writers like Zora Neale Hurston, Jean Toomer, and Ralph Ellison have become the chief historical exhibits in a rearranged display of literary Black power that reaches its contemporary climax with authors like Morrison and Naylor. To put it bluntly, university-trained readers have shifted the center of gravity of African American writing away from a heavily sociological and representational literature of protest toward an artfully crafted performative literature that features the sly words and alternative rhythms of black vernacular culture.

Once again, however, as in the 1920s, a forceful proclamation of the cultural distinctiveness of African American artistic expression has been accompanied by an attentive and appreciative sideward glance at Russian precedent. It is no accident that the revision of the canon of significant African American writing coincided with the belated arrival of the "sociological poetics" of Mikhail Bakhtin in Western academic circles. The linguistic theories and discourse analysis of the Russian thinker have rightly been seen as pertinent aids in demonstrating the textual presence of that "double consciousness" that DuBois claimed was so deeply embedded in African American cultural life. The eager reception and creative appropriation of Bakhtin's thought by leading contemporary theorists of "African American cultural expressivity" is a recent phenomenon that reflects once more the strong and often problematic affinity that has long existed between these two geographically distant native literatures that both have risen up from bondage to Western literacy. How is it, though, that Bakhtin's erudite theorizing became so instrumental in making the underlying "soul" of African American literature more visible? And why did the response to Bakhtin's writings eventually lead to a call for a revised version of African American cultural nationalism? An adequate response to such questions requires a bit of background.

Beginning in 1968 with the English translation of *Rabelais and His World* and accelerating in 1973 with the first American editions of Bakhtin's *Problems of Dostoevsky's Poetics* and V. N. Voloshinov's *Marxism and the Philosophy of Language*, Anglo-American literary criticism began to be infiltrated by a new set of terms borrowed from an embattled circle of unorthodox Soviet semioticians known as "the Bakhtin school."[1] This infiltration—aided and abetted by the glossary of terms appended to a widely influential collection of Bakthin's essays, *The Dialogic Imagination*—has resulted in a now-familiar critical lingo that is served up in many academic courses and discourses despite its off-putting proliferation of polysyllabic neologisms. In retrospect, the fifty-year delay in the transmission to America of Bakhtin's "dialogical" analysis of language and cultural signs could not have been more timely. The introduction of the Russian thinker's particular theories about the restless interaction of cultural discourses coincided with a pervasive discontent directed at the failure of fashionable modes of literary analysis to acknowledge the expressive power of marginalized or noncanonical forms of writing.

In an American intellectual culture belatedly coming to terms with the nation's disruptive signs of cultural pluralism, the critical texts of the Bakhtin school played a useful role in the developing discussion. As the central writings became better known, it was increasingly clear that these Russian accounts of effective verbal meaning provocatively opposed both the established Anglo-American tradition and the newest continental fashions in literary analysis. To put it in academic terms, the works of Bakhtin and his colleagues, Voloshinov and Medvedev, were explicitly post-Formalist and anti-Structuralist and, perhaps most interestingly, they were prophetically critical of Deconstructionism, too. Although the specific arguments advanced in Bakhtin's major books on

Rabelais, Dostoevsky, and novelistic discourse have not gone unchallenged in their migration westward, it is the orientation of Bakhtin's own discourse, his radically different understanding of how words actually signify in cultural communication, that has mattered most.[2] As we shall see, Bakhtin's books have come into solid alliance with critical voices that seek to contest the overrefined literary attitude that textual meaning must be either definitive or infinitely deferred. Or, to reaccent the same point, no matter how folks speak, they be signifyin' all along.

The basic writings of the Bakhtin school occupy a strategic position within contemporary discourse about discourse. They stand in clear opposition to Russian Formalist and Anglo-American New Critical practices, which attempt to corral effective meaning within a self-sufficient verbal artifact that is, supposedly, a finished work—nothing but the sum of its internal devices and the unified tension of its calculated ambiguities. The Bakhtin school also rejects the enclosure of the effective meaning of words and texts within the stable codes of binary oppositions so systematically pursued by linguistic and literary Structuralists. Thus a Bakhtinian analysis of verbal signification insists on freeing cultural signs from the "prison houses" of language constructed by doctrines that uphold either the autonomy of the text or the inevitable operation of structural codes that determine what a text signifies. Yet—and this is crucial—despite the Bakhtin school's partiality toward "unfinalized" signification in actual cultural interchange, there is not the least inclination toward the radical Deconstructionist move toward "the endless play of signifiers."[3] Bakhtin manages to rein in the infinite deferrals of signification by insisting that any utterance, at any given moment of enunciation and/or reception, is projected into a delimited "field of answerability": "Semantic phenomena can exist in a concealed form, potentially, and be revealed only in semantic cultural contexts of subsequent epochs that are favorable to such disclosure."[4] Thus Bakhtin's socially positioned, contextualized understanding of signs and communication takes on a reassuring rather than an abysmal open-endedness. Bakhtinian "dialogics" offer a way to open out and ventilate texts in the complex crosswinds of social life while keeping at bay the heavy weather of a chaotic relativism. But how is this distinctive feat achieved in theory and in practice?

As Bakhtin's translators and explicators have noted, the starting point for his particular analysis of verbal signification is the notion that all speech and writing is "utterance." In Russian, the term *(vyskazyvanie)* is freighted with its own special semantic weight. Normally translated as "expression," it literally denotes the active process of speaking out and having one's say, of (ex)postulating to or with an interlocutor. In the beginning Bakhtin's notion of the word is "utterance," which is to say the basic verbal sign is already an act of articulation. What is emphatically within an utterance is a propulsive energy directed at pronouncing a heard, or overheard, message. In short, articulation is a primary act of cultural intervention, but it inserts itself into a prevailing discourse; it orients itself toward an anticipated respondent. In Bakhtin's understanding, speaking out is not simply to be outspoken; self-expression is ever mindful of the already spoken and necessarily attentive to an internalized other, the projected co-respondent. Consequently, we all struggle to intone in speech and writing a comprehension by others of what we aim to signify through our words. We do this by reaccenting, as best and as shrewdly as we can, the linguistic rules and cultural codes that inhabit our socialized consciousness. The actual word that gets communicated is for speaker, writer, listener, and reader a contextually embedded, socially constituted, interpersonal event that allows for unfinalized but not indeterminate meaning.

This perspective insists on the pragmatic and performative aspect of each word's delivered meaning. As Voloshinov puts it, "The actual reality of language—speech—is not the abstract system of linguistic forms . . . and not the psychophysiological act of its implementation, but the social event of verbal interaction implemented in an utterance."[5] By the same token, the actual significance of individual texts is always and necessarily transactional. As Bakhtin reminds us, any discourse is inherently double-voiced: "Within the arena of almost every utterance an intense interaction and struggle between one's own and another's word is being waged, a process in which they oppose or dialogically interanimate each other. The utterance so conceived is a considerably more complex and dynamic organism than it appears when construed simply as a thing that articulates the intention of the person uttering it."[6] The long and the short of it—and by far the most culturally influential side of it—is that Bakhtinian discourse analysis presumes that utterances come into the world showing and voicing the fact that they are markers of social contestation. Texts display themselves as linguistic arenas in which perceptible cultural negotiations are acted out or acting up. This position accorded well with the growing conviction among a new generation of African American writers and readers that the nation's literary culture had not begun to register what black expression was actively signifying.

A major turn in the perception of the cultural work being performed by African American modes of expression coincided with the gradual transmission of Bakhtin's "sociological poetics." What first emerged, however, was a polyvocal chorus of revisionist scholars who were adamant about the need to hear all the voicings present in the expressive discourses of African American people.[7] A new generation of "Negro youth" reclaimed and built on the excluded, rejected, or ignored dimensions of black American literature. Not by accident, what was retrieved and brought to notice was primarily the "impure" legacy of tricky, artfully evasive, obviously hyphenated "Afro-American" writing. Well-trained readers literally sounded out the verbal texts of black American predecessors whose works had seemed politically irrelevant and found in them a subtle transcription of the slave culture's crafty oral traditions. The irreverent double-talk that American blacks had gotten away with in their spirituals, blues, and tall tales was discovered in abundance within the most obviously "literary" texts in African American writing. Once that redemption of artistic prose had occurred, it became possible to celebrate black texts that engaged in all manner of verbal play and cross-cultural duplicity.

By 1983 two young critics had articulated ambitious theories positing in linguistic terms the existence of a culturally distinct African American expressive difference. In different but equally effective ways, Henry Louis Gates Jr. and Houston Baker Jr. reached the conclusion that African American writing displayed an inherent "double-voicedness." Both argued strenuously to restore an ear for the vernacular accents within the literate texts of black Americans. Their separate projects each entailed a long-overdue foregrounding of the rhetorical and expressive values encoded in African American writings. Both called for an end to the tone-deaf and word-blind bleaching and blanking out of Negro texts. The traditional reading of American black texts as the protest literature of "humans like us" had trivialized performances of cultural contestation and reduced them to an "indentured" discourse that seemed to be subjecting itself to an imposed definition of universal sameness. As Gates indignantly announced: "Because of this curious valorization of the social and polemical functions of black literature, the structure of the black text has been repressed and treated as if it were transparent."[8] Baker put it somewhat differently but no less strongly: "The only means of negotiating a passage beyond this underclass [status] . . . is expressive representation. Artful evasion and illusion are equally traditional black expressive modes in interracial exchange" (195–96). What was being called for was a theory of African American literature that finally allowed for the duplicitous slippage of stable meaning, for the "critique oblique" that prevails in trickster discourses and acts of cultural survivalism.[9]

Bakhtin would have delighted in the significant crossover that has occurred between book-smart definitions of "signification" and street-smart appreciations of "signifyin(g)." Finding useful a truly dialogical pun, Gates has devised a mature theory of African American discourse patterns that depend on rapid, context-specific apprehension of "signifyin(g)" significations. He has in mind a whole range of verbal behaviors ranging from the behind-the-back double-talk so joyously celebrated in the slave tales of the Signifying Monkey to the in-your-face intertextual allusions of Ishmael Reed's postmodern pastiches of literary blackness. Gates's core argument is that African American expression has traditionally cultivated a high degree of "metaphoric literacy" because public articulation within earshot of a master discourse requires "monkeyshines" and the "aping" of rhetorical figures. Signifyin(g) is, then, "essentially, a technique of repeating inside quotation marks in order to reverse or undermine pretended meaning, constituting an implicit parody of a subject's complicity"; it is repetition heard as revision in one deft discursive act.[10] By this definition, signifyin(g) is one prime instance of Bakhtin's "internally polemical discourse—the word with a sideward glance at someone else's hostile word."[11]

Though more embedded in a nonlinguistic vocabulary, Baker, too, draws from a theorized vernacular base to argue for a singular process that constitutes "Afro-American expressive culture." For him, cultural specificity is audible; American black discourse is figured and refigured in a blues matrix, a performed locomotion of cultural commodities: "the blues stanzas . . . roll through an extended meditative repertoire with a steady train-wheels-over-track-junctures guitar back beat. . . . If desire and absence are driving conditions of blues performance, the amelioration of such conditions is implied by the onomatopoetic *training* of blues voice and instrument. Only a *trained* voice can sing the blues" (8).

As Baker hears it, this blues matrix extends northward to literacy in the founding text of Harlem Modernism, *The New Negro*. Locke's anthology collects, we are told, "the fullest extensions of a field of sounding possibilities; it serves as both the speaking manual *and* the singing book of a pioneering civilization freed from the burden of nonsensically and polemically constrained expression." [12] It might be noted, however, that this discourse of an emerging civilization on the march could easily become a music unheard if the auditors lack an appreciation for its mode of "sounding" reality and signifyin(g) resistance to dominant cultural associations.

As both Baker and Gates demonstrate, an ear for Bakhtinian "heteroglossia" seems to come readily to well-attuned African American literary scholars. That said, it must also be said that there has been a rather selective hearing of Bakhtin's available words, a hearing that has been particularly receptive to the empowering and emancipatory implications of the Russian's polyphonic discourse analysis, but only gradually and reluctantly attentive to the problematic and double-edged aspects of Bakhtin's theory of the utterance as a site of unavoidable semantic contestation.

Gates, for instance, is fond of citing and reciting one particular passage from Bakhtin's influential essay, "Discourse in the Novel." It stands beside Frederick Douglass's famous description of how he secretly copied Master Thomas's writing book as a symptomatic epigraph to Gates's discussion of the origins of African American literature. The excerpt from Bakhtin is worth repeating in full:

> Language, for the individual consciousness, lies on the borderline between oneself and the other. The word in language is half someone else's. It becomes "one's own" only when the speaker populates it with his own intention, his own accent, when he appropriates the word, adapting it to his own semantic and expressive intention. Prior to this moment of appropriation, the word does not exist in a neutral or impersonal language (it is not, after all, out of a dictionary that the speaker gets his words!), but rather it exists in other people's mouths, in other people's contexts, serving other people's intentions: it is from there that one must take the word, and make it one's own. [13]

In this selection, Gates's Bakhtin appears to speak in confident monologue asserting the possibility of successful subversion, through creative "take over," of the alien implications resident in any discourse. But in the complete passage, Bakhtin goes on to make his characteristic emphasis on the resistance of all language to confident appropriation: "Language is not a neutral medium that passes freely and easily into the private property of the speaker's intentions; it is populated—overpopulated—with the intentions of others. Expropriating it, forcing it to submit to one's own intonations and accents, is a difficult and complicated process" (294). This raises the possibility that some of the most influential applications of Bakhtinian analysis in the present-day reconstruction of African American letters may not do full justice, in their celebratory mood, to the endless contestation of utterances and what they signify.

With justifiable pride, Gates has claimed that his generation of black and feminist critics elevated Zora Neale Hurston to her rightful place in the African American literary canon. His own powerful argument for Hurston's centrality rests on a "dialogical" reading of *Their Eyes Were Watching God* that proclaims it the first example of a "speakerly text" in the African American tradition. In making this argument Gates builds a case for seeing an innovative form of intertextuality within Hurston's mode of writing. It is a type of intertextuality that Gates correctly associates with Russian Formalist studies of literary ventriloquisms of orality (known as *skaz*) and with Bakhtin's studies of a hidden dialogicality scripted inside particular narrative forms. It is once again noteworthy that Russian literary theory and practice seem especially pertinent in careful discussions of how black texts actually signify.

The crucial point for Gates, though, is that Hurston's narrative procedure in her novel dramatizes and enacts the "voicing" of a culturally muted expressivity. A previously hidden outspokenness is finally given its tongue in public print. In Hurston's text a Southern black female sensibility and sensuality inserts itself forcefully into prior discursive structures (white and black, literate and oral) that had little or no room for such expression. But whose language is it that finally speaks up for the newly heard heroine, Janie Starks?

Gates emphasizes that the narrative of personal emergence we read in the novel is made of a composite language that blends dialectic speech patterns and formal lyrical transcriptions of ineffable interior experience: "It is a bivocal utterance . . . that no one could have spoken, yet which we recognize because of its characteristic 'speakerliness,' its paradoxically written manifestation of the aspiration to the oral" (208). This mode of articulation, which Bakhtin understands to be an unstable amalgam of an author's intentional monologue and a character's zone of speech, is inherently problematic. To Bakhtin's perception, such "quasi-direct discourse" exemplifies the unceasing struggle of novelistic narrators to obliterate the linguistic boundaries between authorial and characterized speech that nonetheless remain in hidden dialogue with one another. Gates, however, chooses to celebrate, in Hurston's name, the achievement of a utopian resolution of contending languages.

Their Eyes Were Watching God becomes for Gates "a paradigmatic Signi-fyin(g) text" precisely because its narrative strategies "resolve the implicit tension between the literal and the figurative . . . between standard English and black dialect" (192–93). But this claim calls a willful halt to dialogical tensions in order to acclaim Hurston's victorious inscription of a mythical African American speech essence. Ultimately, Gates sees *Their Eyes Were Watching God* as a canonical text engraved in an "oral hieroglyphic," in an African American "third language" that records the "thought pictures" commonly transmitted by black discourse (215). This is an odd terminus for a theory of expression that had envisaged a sympathy between the destabilizing cultural work of "signifyin(g)" and Bakhtin's dialogical model of unfinalized literary utterance. Sadly, it appears as if Gates has merely re-dressed the stubborn doctrine of American exceptionalism by giving it African American clothing, cloaking it in Hurston's gorgeous mantle.

In the actual text, Hurston's complex narrative begins and ends by underlining a strong anxiety concerning mouth-to-mouth resuscitations of life stories. As Janie Starks passes the village "bander log" on which the "porch monkeys" hold forth with their tall tales, she observes: "Ah see Mouth-Almighty is still sittin' in de same place. And Ah reckon they got *me* up in they mouth now." [14] This remark offers a startling image of folktalk as Moloch, but it also serves as fair and ironic warning that any act of external characterization threatens to consume Janie whole in its double-voiced mouth. In the end, Hurston's Janie knows that speaking for others is always a pretense: "Let 'em consolate theyselves wid talk. . . . It's uh known fact, Phoeby, you got tuh *go* there tuh *know* there" (285). Janie's struggle to speak for herself arises from her author's understanding that the impulse to articulate experience is the dramatic result of not knowing how to mix interior monologue with available outside discourses.¹⁵ Looked at this way, we can situate Hurston's text in close proximity with Bakhtin's theoretical stance: all utterance at its core is the motivated sign of a self-difference struggling to insert itself and make its intention known within a given repertory of speech genres.

Whereas the notion of a distinctive African American expressivity remains rather self-enclosed and literary in Gates's writings, others among the reconstructionist critics have moved more boldly toward the sociological and ideational intertextuality envisaged by Bakhtin's dialogic theory of cultural process. Houston Baker, for instance, has advanced a sophisticated argument that presents the Trueblood episode from Ralph Ellison's *Invisible Man* as a "meta-expressive commentary on the incumbencies of African American artists" (175). Jargon aside, Baker persuasively locates Ellison's notoriously "race-y" public confession of a poor black man's involuntary incest in active "dialogic" relation with a number of signifying systems. Baker is especially keen on that aspect of Bakhtin's thought conveyed by Julia Kristeva—the subversive implanting of multiple referents and multiple tones of address in premediated acts of "carnivalized" discourse. As a result, Baker appreciates both the performance value and the ideological tensions within the black sharecropper's elaborate act of "bluesy" confession to eager white ears. And Baker shrewdly suggests that Trueblood's remunerative bad-ass riff allegorically stands in for the profitable yield harvested by that supremely literary sharecropper, Ellison. What is made visible in this risible, scandalous scene is the problematics of entertainment as the culturally favored mode of black expression. Playing up and acting out benightedness is both scam and angst; the exchange between a black performance artist and the patronized patron is no simple or cost-free transaction. Having seen all this, Baker, too, calls a halt to the endless dialogic tension by suggesting that Ellison implies that "Afro-Americans, in their guise as entertainers, season the possum of black expressive culture to the taste of the Anglo-American audience maintaining, in the process, their integrity as performers" (194). The integrity of masking is, at best, a dubious concept pointing to an achievement made necessary by an unresolved and inexpressible clash of cultural assumptions. Ultimately, Baker chooses to celebrate Trueblood's bluesy trickster discourse as a victorious paradigm of "Afro-American expressive culture." But to ears (like Ellison's) well accustomed to the defi-

ant yet defensive "voicings" of self-conscious and class-conscious Russian narrators, what also surely resonates in Trueblood's performance
is that special pathos heard in the protective obliqueness of all culturally denigrated speakers and communities. Indeed, Ellison's memorable
phrasing in expressing his sense of the blues— "an impulse to keep the
painful details and episodes of a brutal experience alive in one's aching
consciousness, to finger its jagged grain, and to transcend it . . . by
squeezing from it a near-tragic, near-comic lyricism"—applies equally
well to Turgenev's depiction of Yasha's painfully throbbing and soaring
vocal technique in "The Singers." The soul music performed by Russian
serfs and black slaves left their descendants with a keen ear for polyphony and tonal shifts. Both traditions evolved a musical speech and a
speaking music that was first an eloquent "orature" before it was translated into an eloquent literature of "speaking books."

The ongoing African American dialogue with Russian dialogism has
produced a number of challenges to the newly revised versions of a single
literary canon or linguistic essence. Not surprisingly, this critique has
been most effectively advanced by black female writers and feminist critics.[16] These corrective measures against "master narratives" have occurred with some timely assistance from the writings of the Bakhtin
school. In the current reconstruction of previously stable cultural para-
digms, the very idea of a textual representation of black discourse or
African American expressivity has been dissolved in a torrent of socio-
linguistic variables. To cite Hazel Carby's sobering words: "The struggle
within and over language reveals the nature of the structure of social
relations and the hierarchy of power, not the nature of one particular
group. The sign, then, is an arena of struggle and a construct between
socially organized persons in the process of their interaction. . . . we
must be historically specific and aware of the differently oriented social interests within one and the same sign community." [17] This repri-
mand is obviously directed at those who continue to assert the existence
of one standard inflection within a speech community. In the struggle
with a dominant literacy, there can be no alternative discourse without
its own conflicting and contentious accents striving to rephrase its signifying difference. Here we have dialogism extended into critical discourse
itself, and, as Carby generously acknowledges, her argument rests on
Voloshinov's pioneering work in contextual linguistics. It would seem,
then, that the sociolinguistic theories of the Bakhtin school, in potent

combination with feminist analysis, have had the happy effect of ending rhetorical appeals to a single authentic "Afro-American tradition."[18]

Yet the temptation for each newly articulate socially subordinated group to claim for itself a specially privileged multiculturalism and polyvocalism is difficult to resist. Feminist theorists of the discursive difference in African American women's writing have tended toward a revisionism that amounts to "one-upspersonship" of the primarily male theorists of dialogism and double-voicedness. Michael Awkward, for instance, has argued that the tradition of black female writing in America has been built on a special form of intertextuality and revisionism; unlike the "ritualistic verbal jousting" of the male novelists signifying on one another, African American women writers are said to seek out "inspiriting influences" in a nonexpropriating refiguration of foremother texts.[19] Intriguingly, this gender-linked capacity for "noncompetitive revision" is made compatible with Bakhtin's "discussion of the necessity of discursive appropriation" and then construed to be representative of African American expressive systems in general. In an odd turn of events what starts out as an explication of the distinctive narrative features of black women's writing ends up as a treatise on African American female novels as paradigmatic of the "interactive unity" that is the essence of black culture.

In an equally lively creative appropriation of Bakhtin's thought, Mae Henderson has argued that the doubly excluded social positionality of black women has privileged them as writers, giving them access to the full range of discourse—the racist, patriarchal, ethnic, and domestic "heteroglossia"—that inheres in the complex subjectivity of African Americans.[20] In effect, the black female literary tradition is culturally situated to activate the entire repertory of internalized social dialects and to place them in dialogue with one another. Being familiar with the dominant and multiple subdominant discourses in a racialized and gendered society, black women are thus uniquely endowed with the burden and the gift of "speaking in tongues." Henderson means to imply by that term both a learned ability to speak in diverse identifiable language codes and an intuitive capacity to testify to the interanimating spirit that moves among all the incomprehensible and excluded "others" of the normative cultural order. This reasoning may help explain the phenomenal affective power of recent fiction by black American women, but it may also explain too much, stretching black female subjectivity so wide that it becomes one more all-inclusive variety of that mythic American "imperial self" that contains and speaks for multitudes.

Recent African American literary and cultural theorists have rightly identified a suggestive analogy between DuBois's psychological account of Negro "double consciousness" and Bakhtin's linguistic account of "double-voiced" discourse in culturally embedded speech-acts. The resulting shift of critical attention from speculations about inner cognition to analyses of complex utterances has been productive and clarifying. It has become possible to examine the socially constructed self-alienation of African Americans—the mixed blessing of "second sight"—as it has historically expressed itself in the linguistic forms of articulate speech.[21] Abstractions about a Negro mentality or black culture now tend to be located and localized in the actual "voicings" of African American texts, oral and written. Even the "Afrocentric idea" about the primacy of an African substratum undergirding the culture of black Americans is predicated on communicative patterns and a linguistic code. Asante's "metatheory" of African American "orature" holds that an ancestral Africa is responsible for the tonal styling, the improvisatory rhetoric, and the antiphonal form that is the "soul" of signifying black speech.[22]

Whenever and wherever Bakhtin's dialogical thought has been directly applied to the sociopolitical situation of colonized and subordinated communities, there seems to be a rush to proclaim the subversive and "carnivalesque" power of their disruptive "double-voiced" speech-acts. What is quickly envisioned is "an underground self with the upper hand."[23] That would be, indeed, a consummation much to be desired. But, in all fairness, neither DuBois nor Bakhtin can be associated with anything so simple as a celebration of the triumph of the countercultural discourses invented by people who have been treated as the vassals of a master civilization. Both understood that double-voiced performances and periodic parodies could not easily vanquish the resistance of a dominant culture nor swiftly liberate a denigrated community from the burden of an inner dualism and duellism.

The deepest affinity between the thought of DuBois and Bakhtin can be felt in their sensitive appreciation for the *striving* in the speech and the inner being of people who experience their own subjectivity under a veil of alien language and a curtain of cultural stereotypes. Surely the special responsiveness of African American literary critics to Bakhtin's discourse analysis has been grounded in a sympathetic and historically conditioned understanding of the strife that is at the core of his definition of "speech-acts": "Our speech, that is, all our utterances (including creative works) are filled with others' words, with varying degrees of otherness and 'our-own-ness,' with varying degrees of familiarity and of alienation. These words of others bring with them their own expression, their own intonational value, which is assimilated, reworked, and reaccented by us."[24] Given such an understanding, the very language by which "we" hope to articulate our being must express itself in a pitched contest, a coded dialogue with a resistant set of received signs and significations. Whereas Bakhtin's account of the inescapable dialogics of self-expression may seem theoretically acute or even generally valid, there can be no doubt that it does apply, practically speaking, to the situation of literary discourse in the Russian and African American cultural context.

As we have seen, the concept of a national literature was a European cultural-historical institution imposed on the expressive traditions of Russians and African Americans as an exclusive and elite norm of their articulate collective identity. As such, forms of Western literacy were bound to be experienced as both alien and authenticating. Under these circumstances, Russian and African American literary texts were from their inception simultaneously performing and contesting the established genres of Western literacy. It is no accident, then, that the most influential texts of Russian and African American literature have tended toward formal anomaly and "hidden polemic," departing strategically and willfully from the expected conventions of good form while also self-consciously adhering to the protocols of high culture—the letter of the European literary laws. No wonder, then, that Bakhtin's socio-linguistic theory of literature as utterance writ large, as a contextually formed struggle to disrupt or modify operative cultural conventions, found a particularly warm reception among the present generation of well-read and theoretically informed African American intellectuals. Given all that we know about the uncomfortable dialogue of emerging nationalisms with the ruling assumptions of European civilization, it makes sense that Russian and African American thinkers have been engaged in a never-complete (ex)postulation of a similar difference from the standards of Western literacy.

Toni Morrison, with her usual acuity, has defined the basic terms of African American literariness in a manner that evokes the restless re-constitution of relative difference so pervasive in the shaping of the Rus-sian literary tradition: "Now that the Afro-American artistic presence has been 'discovered' actually to exist . . . [w]e are not, in fact, 'other.' We are choices. And to read imaginative literature by and about us is to choose to examine centers of the self and to have the opportunity to com-pare these centers with the 'raceless' one with which we are, all of us, most familiar." [25] It is an unfortunate reality that this acceptance of stra-tegic design and artistic choice in a national literature of cultural plural-ism and internal heteroglossia has not been affirmed of late in Bakhtin's homeland, even after the collapse of centralized state authority. The re-luctance of post-Soviet writers and philosophers to deconstruct a holis-tic and separatist notion of "Russianness" is perhaps due to an under-standable wish to preserve the solidarity of a canonical national tradition that has been invoked by the intelligentsia to promote cultural resistance to the violence of state power. We have also seen, however, how diffi-cult it is for a racial group or nationality that has constructed its essen-tial identity or "soul" in terms of a non-European alternative discourse to accept any erosion of its hard-won claim to singularity.

What is most hopeful about the recent response of African Ameri-can thinkers to Bakhtin's language-sensitive and constantly recontex-tualized analysis of cultural voicings is that it is, in effect, a call to Russians (and other groups actively justifying their marginality) to ac-knowledge their long-denied kinship with the souls of black folk. It is a kinship that few Russians have cared to think about and many African Americans have lost sight of. But there has been, in fact, a long-standing historic sense of relatedness that, if fully acknowledged, may foster a mutual recognition of what was required to utter the strange meanings of being black or Russian in a world that measured civilization by a single standard of literacy. If read with patience, the double-souled struggle of Russians and African Americans with the burden and privilege of bi-culturalism can, perhaps, finally be unveiled.

NOTES

1 Alain Locke, *The New Negro: An Interpretation* (New York: Albert and Charles Boni, 1925), 48 (hereafter cited in the text).

2 Houston J. Baker Jr. employs this phrasing in describing *The New Negro* as a collective project dedicated to the sounding and imaging of an emergent black culture that would no longer be relegated to the margins of modern consciousness: "Locke's compendium . . . serves as both the speaking manual *and* the singing book of a pioneering civilization." See Baker, *Modernism and the Harlem Renaissance* (Chicago: University of Chicago Press, 1987), 84.

3 Henry Louis Gates Jr., *The Signifying Monkey: A Theory of Afro-American Literary Criticism* (New York: Oxford University Press, 1988), xxiv (hereafter cited in the text).

4 For a recent anthology of this dismal science of rational racism as practiced by the leading Western philosophers of the Age of Reason, including Hume and Kant, see Emmanuel Chukwudi Eze, *Race and Enlightenment: A Reader* (Oxford: Blackwell Publishers, 1997). A classic synopsis of the origins and development of Western race theory, now in its second edition, is George L. Mosse, *Toward the Final Solution: A History of European Racism* (Madison: University of Wisconsin Press, 1985).

5 The quote is taken from an anonymous English translation of l'abbé Chappe d'Auteroche, *Journey into Siberia* (London, 1770), 330–31. The original two-volume French edition (Paris, 1768) bore a title that better indicated its true contents: *Voyage en Siberie: fait par ordre du Roi en 1761, contenant des moeurs, les usages des Russes.*

6 The translation is by James A. Snead, who gives a thorough analysis of Hegel's negative concept of "Africanicity" in his essay, "Repetition as a Figure of Black Culture" in *Black Literature and Literary Theory*, ed. Henry Louis Gates Jr. (New York: Methuen, 1984), 59–79. Hegel's entire discussion of Africa as "Unhistorical, Undeveloped Spirit" occupies a mere nine pages in the J. Sibree translation of Hegel's *The Philosophy of History* (New York: Dover, 1956), 91–99.

7 Johann Gottfried von Herder, *Outlines of a Philosophy of the History of Man*, trans. T. Churchill (New York: Bergman Publishers, 1969), 482–83. The original four-volume work was finally published in 1791, and the English translation quoted dates from 1800.

8   For an invaluable intellectual history of the construction of Eastern Europe as the "first model of underdevelopment" and the "complementary other half" of Western civilization, see Larry Wolff, *Inventing Eastern Europe: The Map of Civilization on the Mind of the Enlightenment* (Stanford, Calif.: Stanford University Press, 1994).

9   The evolution and significance of this concept is discussed in Robert C. Williams, "The Russian Soul: A Study in European Thought and Non-European Nationalism," *Journal of the History of Ideas* 31 (1970): 573–78.

10 See the entry for *dusha* in Vladimir Ivanovich Dal', *Tolkovyi slovar' zhivogo velikorusskogo iazyka* (Moscow: Gosizdat, 1955), 1:503—the authoritative nineteenth-century Russian lexicon. For a valuable account of the intellectual evolution of the ideology of Russian "soul" see Wayne Dowler, *Dostoevsky, Grigor'ev and Native Soil Conservatism* (Toronto: University of Toronto Press, 1982). As the concept matured, especially in Dostoevsky's thought, it came to connote the innate capacity of the entire nationality for dynamic cultural evolution.

1 CIVILIZING THE RACE

1   Herzen's much-quoted tribute to the prime mover who "shook all thinking Russia" can be found in Dwight Macdonald's English abridgment of *My Past and Thoughts: The Memoirs of Alexander Herzen* (Berkeley: University of California Press, 1982), 294–95.

2   Douglass's remark was precipitated by the publication in 1862 of Crummell's first book, *The Future of Africa*, and his prominent role in recruiting African Americans to colonize and evangelize Liberia—see Wilson Jeremiah Moses's major biography, *Alexander Crummell: A Study in Civilization and Its Discontent* (New York: Oxford University Press, 1989), 142.

3   The leading role of Chaadaev in instituting the Russian intellectual penchant for teleological and theological readings of history was acknowledged by Nikolai Berdyaev in his own major contribution to the genre, *The Russian Idea* (1946; rpt. Boston: Beacon Press, 1962), 34. The tribute to Crummell as the chief progenitor of pan-Africanist thought is offered by Kwame Anthony Appiah, *In My Father's House: Africa in the Philosophy of Culture* (New York: Oxford University Press, 1992), 5.

4   Quoted from a photographic reproduction of the Russian text as first published in P. Ya. Chaadaev, *Polnoe sobranie sochinenii i izbrannye pis'ma* (Moscow: Nauka, 1991), 1:659–61. All further translations from that Russian text, abbreviated as PS, are my own. There are two available English translations of the complete French manuscript of eight letters: Raymond T. McNally, *The Major Works of Peter Chaadaev* (Notre Dame, Ind.: University of Notre Dame Press, 1969); and Mary-Barbara Zeldin, *Peter Yakovlevich Chaadayev: Philosophi-*

cal Letters and Apology of a Madman (Knoxville: University of Tennessee Press, 1969)

5   Alexandre Koyré, *Études sur l'histoire de la pensée philosophique en Russie* (Paris: Librairie Vrin, 1950), 21.

6   Alexander Crummell, "Civilization, the Primal Need of the Race" (1898), reprinted in *Destiny and Race: Selected Writings, 1840–1898*, ed. Wilson Jeremiah Moses (Amherst: University of Massachusetts Press, 1992), 285.

7   As V. Y. Mudimbe has shrewdly observed, "One might consider that missionary speech is always predetermined, pre-regulated, let us say *colonized*"; the missionary's discourse promotes a mandate for the conversion of the world in terms of a universal cultural and sociopolitical regeneration. See the discussion of missionary speech and Africa's conversion in Mudimbe, *The Invention of Africa: Gnosis, Philosophy, and the Order of Knowledge* (Bloomington: University of Indiana Press, 1988), 45–49.

8   Raymond T. McNally provides a translation of Panova's letter of appeal in the "Explanatory Notes to the Philosophical Letters" appended to his 1969 edition of Chaadaev's *Major Works*, 233–34.

9   A useful summary of the complicated publication history of Chaadaev's widely circulated letters is provided in the commentary and notes attached to the Russian edition of the complete works and selected letters (PS, 1:690–91).

10   Cited in Charles Quénet, *Tchaadaev et les lettres philosophiques* (Paris: Librairie Champion, 1931), 245.

11   A famous premodern example of this genre, the disguised "epistle to the King" written anonymously and/or in a foreign language, exists in the Latin correspondence between Prince Kurbsky and Tsar Ivan IV of Russia (1564–1579). This remarkable sequence of covert letters has been translated and edited by J. L. I. Fennell (*The Correspondences between Prince A. M. Kurbsky and Tsar Ivan IV* [Cambridge, Mass.: Harvard University Press, 1955]).

12   Unfortunately, there is no evidence that Chaadaev was aware of this family secret, but it is difficult to imagine he was not fully apprised of Prince Shcherbatov's well-known defense of aristocratic and religious traditions against the disruptive despotism and *volupté* of Catherinian Russia. The fascinating history of the original manuscript is given in the scholarly introduction by A. Lentin to his English translation of M. M. Shcherbatov, *On The Corruption of Morals in Russia* (Cambridge: Cambridge University Press, 1969), 103–6.

13   William Mills Todd III, *The Familiar Letter as a Literary Genre in the Age of Pushkin* (Princeton, N.J.: Princeton University Press, 1976), 41.

14   The most recent of many accounts of Chaadaev's centrality in initiating the "pathos of self-criticism" in Russian cultural thought appeared at the height of perestroika, soon after the publication of the complete letters renewed the old struggle to claim Chaadaev either as a prophet of Russian Western-

ization or as a champion of cultural and religious particularism. See V. Kantor's article on "the spiritual legacy of P. Ya. Chaadaev in Russian culture," "Imia rokovoe," *Voprosy literatury*, no. 3 (1988): 62–85; and the polemical response to it by Boris Tarasov on "the scope of Peter Chaadaev's thought," "Prostranstvo mysli Petra Chaadaeva," *Literaturnaia gazeta*, 11 March 1992, 6.

15 After elaborating my own comparison, I encountered one brief mention of Voltaire's precedent and Chaadaev's "peculiarly Russian Romantic answer" in Raymond T. McNally, "Chaadaev's Letters to Viazemsky," in *The Golden Age of Russian Literature and Thought*, ed. Derek Offord (New York: St. Martin's, 1992), 76–83. It is ironic that the appearance in France of the original *Lettres philosophiques* also led to a famous case of legal proscription; the Parisian high tribunal condemned them and their author as "capable of inspiring dangerous free thinking concerning religion and the order of civil society." Surely Chaadaev was aware of the notoriety and acclaim achieved by Voltaire's subversive work.

16 For a succinct overview of the biographical context and polemical thrust of Voltaire's "manifeste des lumières," consult Dennis Fletcher's critical guide, *Voltaire: Lettres philosophiques* (London: Grant and Cutler, 1986).

17 Raymond T. McNally makes an especially persuasive presentation of the shared perspective between Chaadaev and this leader of the "spiritual" Catholic universalists in *Chaadaev and His Friends* (Tallahassee: University of Florida Press, 1971), 157–58.

18 Many unresolved questions still surround Chaadaev's sudden request for demission from the Imperial honor guard in 1821 and his simultaneous withdrawal from pietistic Masonry. Clearly, some offense to his personal honor had occurred in the wake of his informing the emperor at the Congress of Troppau of the rebellion in the ranks of the Semenovsky Regiment in the late autumn of 1820. The best account of the early years up to Chaadaev's departure for Europe in 1823 is still to be found in the opening biographical chapter of Quénet's study. Even before Chaadaev sat down to compose the *Lettres philosophiques*, he had etched his personality into Russian literature, fashioning himself into a neoclassical paragon of probity, impressing his contemporaries as the very type of the "hussar-sage" whose proven courage and relentless civic-mindedness terrorized the custodians of polite salon society and the status quo—see Iurii M. Lotman, "The Decembrist in Daily Life," in *The Semiotics of Russian Cultural History*, ed. Alexander D. Nakhimovsky and Alice Stone Nakhimovsky (Ithaca, N.Y.: Cornell University Press, 1985), 138.

19 A particularly alert reading of the French sources for Chaadaev's mapping of world history is offered in Quénet, *Tchaadaev*, 140–53. Guizot's depiction of Spain's marginality clearly inspired Chaadaev's litany of Russia's woes: "Look for one great idea or a major social reform, a single philosophical system or one productive institution that Europe has taken from Spain—there isn't any." See the William Hazlitt translation of F. Guizot, *History of Civili-*

zation in Europe (London, 1884) — a text well known to Alexander Crummell, who cited it frequently in his writings.

20 To cite but a few examples of Russian spirituality's aspiration to stand at the forefront of a sanctified and harmonious Christian civilization, this vision was proclaimed in the nineteenth century in Prince V. F. Odoevsky's *Russian Nights* (1844) and in Nikolay Gogol's *Selected Passages from a Correspondence with Friends* (1847), and in the twentieth century by Nikolay Berdyaev's *The New Middle Ages* (1924).

21 Quénet expresses this view unambiguously: "What one sees is a new intellectual manifesto, a new statement of his thesis. . . . It is as the defendant in his own case that the author of the Apology comes forward" (*Tchaadaev*, 263–64). Quénet also documents Chaadaev's own activism and complicity in bringing about the publication of the scandalous "First Letter," noting with amusement the author's distribution of nineteen copies to friends while boasting proudly of his lack of concern for the "whist-playing salon" that constituted the Russian public (224–30).

22 Claire Cavanagh, "Synthetic Nationality: Mandel'shtam and Chaadev," *Slavic Review* 49 (winter 1990): 597–610. The argument is that Chaadaev served as "Virgil" to Mandel'shtam's "Dante," helping guide a native (even nativist) culture toward a cosmopolitan, hybridized sense of its national essence and historic destiny.

23 "The Responsibility of the First Fathers of a Country for Its Future Life and Character," in Crummell, *Africa and America: Addresses and Discourses* (1891; rpt. New York: Negro Universities Press, 1969), 129–31 (hereafter cited in the text).

24 Moses cites the importance of David Walker's *Appeal in Four Articles* (1829) for promoting this widespread faith in a prophetic racial destiny (*Crummell*, 80).

25 As Stanley Mellon has pointed out in the introduction to his edition of Guizot's *Historical Essays and Lectures* (Chicago: University of Chicago Press, 1972), the characteristic feature of the French liberal historian's progressivism was his conciliatory understanding of obstructions to liberty. Crummell surely noted an early passage in Guizot's *History of Civilization in Europe*: "Even facts, which from their nature are odious, pernicious, which weigh heavily upon nations . . . if they have contributed in some way to civilization, if they have enabled it to make an onward stride, up to a certain point we pardon them . . . wherever we recognize civilization, whatever the facts which have created it, we are tempted to forget the price it has cost" (6).

26 Alexander Crummell, "The Duty of a Rising Christian State" (Monrovia, 1855), reprinted in *The Future of Africa: being Addresses, Sermons, delivered in the Republic of Liberia* (Detroit, Mich.: Negro History Press, 1960), 90–92.

27 Sacvan Bercovitch, *The American Jeremiad* (Madison: University of Wisconsin Press, 1978), 4–5.

28 Much as Chaadaev's legacy remains in active dispute between those who see

him as a "Westernizer" and those who claim him as the prophet of Russia's particular national mission, Crummell's historic significance is still subject to argument between those like Appiah who emphasize his precocious "pan-Africanism" and those like Moses who stress his "Negro Saxon" cultural and religious conservatism. In the biographical sketch that follows I rely heavily on details culled from two additional sources which themselves display two different ways of reading Crummell's legacy. Compare Gregory U. Rigsby, *Alexander Crummell: Pioneer in Nineteenth-Century Pan-African Thought* (New York: Greenwood Press, 1987) with J. R. Oldfield, *Alexander Crummell and the Creation of an African-American Church in Liberia* (Lewiston, Colo.: Mellen, 1990).

29   Alexander Crummell, "The Relations and Duties of Free Colored Men in America to Africa" (1860), reprinted in *Negro Social and Political Thought, 1850–1920: Representative Texts*, ed. Howard Brotz (New York: Basic Books, 1966), 171–80.

30   The "Thanksgiving Discourse" is reprinted in Crummell, *Destiny and Race*, 194–205.

31   "Eulogium on the Life and Character of Thomas Clarkson, Esq. of England," in Crummell, *Africa and America*, 265.

32   In *Nationalism: Five Roads to Modernity* (Cambridge, Mass.: Harvard University Press, 1992), Greenfeld takes issue with Benedict Anderson's influential theory of modern nationalism as the invention of "imagined communities" constructed to unify limited, culturally particular political sovereignties. Her argument is that national identity derives from imagined membership in a historic "people" perceived as a collective solidarity, but that any such collectivity may identify itself as a civic or religious entity that participates in a world system.

33   McNally, *Chaadaev and His Friends*, 222.

2   CONSERVING THE RACE

1   On the peculiar family circumstances shared by the six "old world landowner" thinkers who are considered the original Slavophiles, see N. L. Brodskii, *Rannie slavianofily* (Moscow, 1910), x–xx.

2   This emphasis on Kireevsky's early affiliation with the self-consciously aristocratic defenders of literature's high calling and its autonomy from state and commercial imperatives is well made in Abbott Gleason, *European and Muscovite: Ivan Kireevsky and the Origins of Slavophilism* (Cambridge, Mass.: Harvard University Press, 1972), 45–51.

3   The most complete account in English of the biographical details, on which I have relied, is Peter K. Christoff, *Introduction to Nineteenth-Century Slavophilism*, vol. 2 (The Hague: Mouton, 1972). On the neglected figure of Elagina and her importance in stimulating a native literary language, see Lina Bern-

stein, "Avdot'ia Petrovna Elagina and Her Contribution to Russian Letters," *Slavic and East European Journal* 40 (1996): 215–35. The umbilical connection between the "Lovers of Wisdom" group and the later Slavophiles is delineated in Koyré, *Études*, 137–52.

4 See Boris Groys, "Russia and the West: The Quest for Russian National Identity," *Studies in Soviet Thought* 43 (1992): 186.

5 On this unresolved question, Koyré (*La philosophie et le problème national en Russie au début du XIXe siècle* [Paris: Champion, 1929]) inclines toward the party of Chaadaev and Christoff (*Nineteenth-Century Slavophilism*) entertains the possibility of the influence flowing as much from the younger to the older writer. A good summary of the dispute is given in Gleason, *European and Muscovite*, 112–14.

6 In *The Slavophile Controversy: History of a Conservative Utopia in Nineteenth-Century Russian Thought* (Oxford: Clarendon Press, 1975), 48. Andrzej Walicki makes this claim for Pogodin's *Historic Aphorisms* published in Moscow in 1827. The specific French source is Augustin Thierry, *Histoire de la conquête de l'Angleterre par les Normands* (Paris, 1825). In *Conservative Nationalism in Nineteenth-Century Russia* (Seattle: University of Washington Press, 1964) Edward C. Thaden documents the popularity in the 1820s of European "historicist" accounts of the germination of distinctive national cultures—just at the time when Russians were developing the concept of *samobytnost'*, or national particularity.

7 From a letter to Koshelev of October 1, 1828, cited in *Polnoe sobranii sochinenii I. V. Kireevskogo*, vol. 1 of Ivan Kireevsky, *Complete Works*, 2 vols. ed. M. O. Gershenzon (Moscow, 1911), 1:12. All further translations of Kireevsky's writings (hereafter cited in the text) are from these volumes and are my own.

8 This sentiment is forcefully expressed by Koyré, *Études*, 180–93; Gleason, *European and Muscovite*, 114, concurs that "one feels the presence of conversations with Chaadaev" in the shaping of the argument.

9 Christoff quotes the following extraordinary tirade from a letter of Peter Kireevsky to N. M. Yazykov, dated July 17, 1833: "This cursed [Chaadaevism] which in its senseless self-adoration makes mockery of the graves of our fathers and strives to exterminate all the great storehouse of folk memories . . . so enrages me, that it often seems to me, that the whole great life of Peter I gave birth to more evil than good fruits" (*Nineteenth Century Slavophilism*, 63).

10 Gleason, *European and Muscovite*, 165.

11 A curious document in the handwriting of the family friend and fellow Slavophile, A. I. Koshelev, relates how Arbeneva persuaded her husband that "what had so enraptured him in Schelling was all in the Church Fathers." A full account of this "Story of the Conversion of Ivan Kireevsky" and of the closer intimacy with his brother and Khomiakov is presented in Gleason, *European and Muscovite*, 137–53.

12 Christoff speculates that Peter Kireevsky may have been the source of his brother's ideological reading of the importance of the *mir*, the village com-

mune, as a distinctive ethnic institution (*Nineteenth-Century Slavophilism*, 202). In a later article of 1845, Peter Kireevsky demonstrated his close attention to the massive *History of Slavic Laws* (1832) by the Polish scholar, W. A. Maciejowski.

13 The Russian terms in these paired oppositions are *razdvoenie* versus *tsel'nost'* and *rassudochnost'* versus *razumnost'*. They have rather distinguished European intellectual credentials behind them. The latter two are perhaps best understood as Kireevsky's Russian adaptation of the Kantian distinction between *Verstand* and *Vernunft*, between the intellect's capacity to draw distinctions and the intuitive power by which the mind grasps first principles a priori. As for the former pairing, Christoff (*Nineteenth-Century Slavophilism*, 226) believes that Kireevsky probably found inspiration in Herder's attack on the faulty faculty psychology of the Enlightenment with its division of the human mind into "compartments"; from the German Romantic philosophers Kireevsky acquired his predisposition toward organicism and a holistic epistemology that integrated faith, reason, and emotion. Dostoevsky, too, readily associated the Westernized mind with a disabling reflexivity and dividedness; Raskolnikov is a later literary embodiment of Kireevsky's *razdvoenie*.

14 Here as elsewhere the biographical details are derived from David Levering Lewis's invaluable, utterly reliable *W. E. B. Du Bois: Biography of a Race, 1868–1919* (New York: Henry Holt, 1993). See especially his clarification of the intrigue around the never-received German doctorate (143–45). DuBois's insistent and remarkably undeferential correspondence with former president Rutherford B. Hayes, the chair of the Slater Fund, is reprinted in full in Herbert Aptheker's edition of *The Correspondence of W. E. B. Du Bois* (Amherst: University of Massachusetts Press, 1973), 1:10–17 (hereafter cited in the text).

15 Lewis, *Du Bois*, 134–35.

16 Ibid., 145.

17 See, for instance, DuBois's unpublished essay on "Carlyle" (c. 1890), which was intended to invigorate young Negro men and women: "We are the architects & builders of a new nation—the hesitating blacksmiths of a unique and burning idea. . . . he stood on the mountain top and stretched and screamed, swore and called names . . . all in order to rouse a listless generation" (reel 80, nos. 28–30, Du Bois Papers, W. E. B. Du Bois Library, University of Massachusetts, Amherst). On DuBois's attraction to Wagner and to "Germanic muscular civilizationism," see Wilson Jeremiah Moses, "Dark Forests and Barbarian Vigor: Paradox, Conflict, and Africanity in Black Writing before 1914," *American Literary History* 1 (1989): 650–51. In *The Age of Energy* (New York: Viking Press, 1971), 200–213, Howard Mumford Jones cites numerous late-nineteenth-century American purveyors of the popular theory that the Teutonic North had spawned both parliaments and manly virtue. The social

Darwinist John Fiske was particularly fond of contrasting a vigorous Saxon democracy to effete Roman hierarchies: "We shall discover a grand and far-reaching Teutonic idea of political life overthrowing and supplanting the Roman idea" (Jones, *Age of Energy*, 206).

18 Reel 80, nos. 8–9, Du Bois Papers.

19 The text of the Harvard commencement speech has been reprinted in the New American Library edition of W. E. B. Du Bois, *Writings* (New York: Library of America, 1986), 811–13 (hereafter cited in the text).

20 This shrewd observation and an excellent three-page appreciation of DuBois's rhetorical accomplishment may be found in Kim Townsend, *Manhood at Harvard: William James and Others* (New York: Norton, 1996), 251–53.

21 See Wilson Jeremiah Moses, "The Conservation of Races and Its Context," *Massachusetts Review* 34 (1993): 275–94, for a forceful, strong-minded reading of the essay as the work of an understudy to "Father" Crummell. In *The Crucible of Race: Black-White Relations in the American South since Emancipation* [New York: Oxford University Press, 1984], 402–13, Joel Williamson makes an extensive case for reading DuBois as early as 1897 as a Hegelian nationalist thinker. And in *To Wake the Nations: Race in the Making of American Literature* (Cambridge, Mass.: Harvard University Press, 1993), 461–63, Eric J. Sundquist specifically connects the "Conservation" essay to the burgeoning "volksgeistian" argument of *The Souls of Black Folk*.

22 See Appiah, *In My Father's House*, 28–34, for a strict and stringent critique of DuBois's racialism as being logically rooted in a biologically determined theory of descent.

23 The quote is taken from DuBois's address before the American Academy of Political and Social Science in January 1898. That text, "The Study of the Negro Problems," is probably the most comprehensive statement of DuBois's multidisciplinary methodology as an innovative social scientist. It is reprinted in Herbert Aptheker's edition of DuBois's *Writings in Periodicals Edited by Others* (Millwood, N.Y.: Kraus-Thomson, 1982), 1:40–52.

24 "The Afro-American" is among the unpublished materials preserved in the Du Bois Papers (reel 82, no. 1232). The text dates from 1894–96 and is signed by DuBois as "A.M. Professor of Ancient Classics at Wilberforce University."

25 For this perspective see Vincent Harding, "W. E. B. Du Bois and the Black Messianic Vision," *Freedomways* 9, no. 1 (1969): 44–58.

26 This comment comes from a neglected essay, "The Problem of Amusement" (1897), which takes to task the latter-day Protestant Negro churches for "forgetting to recognize for their children the God-given right to play." Originally published in *The Southern Workman*, it is reprinted in Aptheker, *Writings*, 1:32–39.

27 Lewis, *Du Bois*, 39.

28 Ibid., 148.

3 NOTES FROM THE UNDERWORLD

1 Stepto's influential argument holds that DuBois achieves a major revision of the canonical slave narrative's movement northward toward literacy and freedom by fashioning a representative spiritual autobiography of a northern Negro intellectual as a "weary traveller" who finds sustenance and *communitas* in the "deeper recesses" of the historic southern slave culture. See his chapter on DuBois's "generic narrative" in *From behind the Veil: A Study of Afro-American Narrative* (Urbana: University of Illinois Press, 1979), 53–81.

2 Robert Louis Jackson offers a particularly forceful reading of the true accomplishment of Dostoevsky's book as "the raising of the Russian people": "The spiritual and broadly ideological plane of action . . . finds its summation [as] . . . the restoration of the image of a 'lost people,' the justification of a pariah people, the symbolic redemption of the Russian people" (*The Art of Dostoevsky: Deliriums and Nocturnes* [Princeton, N.J.: Princeton University Press, 1981], 34–41).

3 For a thoroughly researched account of Dostoevsky's crucial years in Omsk prison and of his fluctuating and tormented responses to that experience, see Joseph Frank's definitive biography, *Dostoevsky: The Years of Ordeal, 1850–1859* (Princeton, N.J.: Princeton University Press, 1983), 69–162.

4 Frank is content to understand Dostoevsky's masking as little more than a convenient device to skirt the risk of censorship of remarks by former political prisoners, but he has to concede that the text is replete with awkward incongruities that require elaborate "artistic" explanations or else acceptance as a somewhat clumsy convention made necessary by external circumstances. See *Dostoevsky: The Stir of Liberation, 1860–1865* (Princeton, N.J.: Princeton University Press, 1986), 218–20.

5 F. M. Dostoevsky, *Sobranie Sochinenii*, vol. 3 of *Collected Works* (Moscow: Gosizdat, 1956), 394. All further quotations are my translations from this edition of the standard Russian text and are cited in the text. The recommended English translation is by David McDuff, *The House of the Dead* (New York: Viking Penguin, 1985).

6 This populist-redemptive reading of *The House of the Dead* is frequently encountered among Russian and Western critics, but nowhere more eloquently or systematically expressed than in Jackson's 1981 study: "A man dies, the one-time representative of a ruling class separated from the people by the 'profoundest of gulfs.' But by means of his 'Scenes' he crosses that gulf and a whole people is reborn" (*Art of Dostoevsky*, 41).

7 V. A. Tunimanov, *Tvorchestvo Dostoevskogo, 1854–1862* (Leningrad: Nauka, 1980), 93–95. The most important predecessor of this approach to Dostoevsky's compositional strategy was Viktor Shklovsky, whose once heretical ideas about a "wholeness of consciousness" embedded in the text's deliberately featured contradictions may be found in *Za i protiv: zametki o Dostoevskom* (Moscow: Soverskii pisatel' 1957), 97–125. For an influential exploration of

Dostoevsky's "aesthetics of disorder," see Gary Saul Morson, *The Boundaries of Genre* (Austin: University of Texas Press, 1981)

8 In *Dostoevsky* (Oxford: Clarendon Press, 1983), 129–73, John Jones has deconstructed many such instances of the narrator's "I/We/They/Everybody flexibility" in his sensitive reading of Dostoevsky's radically destabilizing inscriptions of uncertainty in *The House of the Dead*. He discusses the text's "contradictory universals" and what he refers to as Dostoevsky's "deliberate craft of authorial unaccountability."

9 Julie de Sherbinin, "Transcendence through Art: The Convicts' Theatricals in Dostoevskij's *Zapiski iz mertvogo doma*," *Slavic and East European Journal* 35 (1991): 339–51. This article closely examines the specific folk traditions within the four "theatricals" presented by the convict population, reading each secular play as comprising a variant on the ancient "mystery" dramas that staged, like the parable of the mustard seed, a sacrificial death presaging rebirth.

10 Dostoevsky was polemicizing with contemporary literary idealizations of criminal "unfortunates" and asserting the active presence of a "convulsive selfhood" among the imprisoned Russian people generally. See, in particular, Il'ya Serman, "Tema narodnosti v 'Zapiskakh iz mertvogo doma,' " *Dostoevsky Studies* 3 (1982): 101–44.

11 On the origins of this Russian identification with the biblical precedent of the ancient Hebrews, see Daniel B. Rowland, "Moscow—The Third Rome or the New Israel?" *Russian Review* 55 (1996): 591–614. Like the American Puritan theocrats, the Orthodox tsardom of medieval Moscow read its position in human history typologically, as a divinely ordained latter-day analogue to the Old Testament history of the chosen people of Israel. This prophetic conviction that the events befalling one's people were a reiteration of the redemptive suffering of the Jews became a mainstay of Russian (and African American) religious tradition and popular consciousness.

12 In this regard, consult M. H. Abrams's characterization of the apocalyptic "line of change in Christian history" with its decidedly noncyclical, abrupt, and cataclysmic hope for the advent of a restored age of felicity. His discussion in *Natural Supernaturalism: Tradition and Revolution in Romantic Literature* (New York: Norton Library, 1973), 35–46, specifically links Christian apocalyptic history to the eschatological prophecy enunciated in Judaism in the Book of Isaiah. This same linkage is surely present in Dostoevsky's dramatic focus on Russian gentiles paying rapt attention to a praying "Isaiah."

13 A useful summary of the compositional blending of published and unpublished material in *The Souls of Black Folk*, based on Herbert Aptheker's research, can be found in Arnold Rampersad, *The Art and Imagination of W. E. B. Du Bois* (New York: Schocken, 1990), 301 n. 9. It is Rampersad who also points out the play on words in the title's reference to "souls," indicating the "twoness" as well as the individuality of black folk (74).

14 In *Double-Consciousness/Double-Bind: Theoretical Issues in Twentieth-Century Black*

Literature (Urbana: University of Illinois Press, 1994), 11–27, Sandra Adell advances the proposition that DuBois's formulation of double consciousness establishes an "ontology of blackness" that is doubly rooted in Herder's folk-based aesthetic and Hegel's metaphysics of development, thus immersing *The Souls of Black Folk* as much in Western philosophical traditions as in the cultural specifics of the black experience in America.

15 In *The Black Atlantic: Modernity and Double Consciousness* (Cambridge, Mass.: Harvard University Press, 1993), 138–40 Paul Gilroy takes strong exception to Stepto's influential reading of *The Souls of Black Folk*. Just as Stepto sought to recruit DuBois as the forefather of a sophisticated modern cultural essentialism, Gilroy enlists the same DuBois in his project to identify the emergence of an "intercultural, anti-ethnocentric construction" of black "soul" in modernity (117).

16 The complaint was voiced in an important essay that began the exploration of the structural and allegorical features of DuBois's "fourteen essays in the form of a neo-Hegelian dialectic"; see Stanley Brodwin, "The Veil Transcended: Form and Meaning in W.E.B. Du Bois's 'The Souls of Black Folk,' " *Journal of Black Studies* (March 1972): 303–21.

17 All citations are taken from the impressive 1997 Bedford Books edition of *The Souls of Black Folk*, edited and meticulously annotated by David W. Blight and Robert Gooding-Williams (hereafter cited in the text). "The Forethought" appears on pages 34–35.

18 All scholars are indebted to the assiduous research and subtle interpretation that informs the reading of DuBois's musical epigraphs in Sundquist's *Wake the Nations*. He argues persuasively that DuBois's published text "mimicked the history of the spirituals by putting black music back at the center of black history" (470–83) and offers an invaluable identification of all the "sorrow songs" and their lyrics (492).

19 On the Hegelian derivation of DuBois's philosophy of history, see Williamson, *Crucible of Race*, 401–11. A true consciousness of Hegelian Freedom can only occur when self-knowledge is achieved through a shared participation in the emerging ideational system of a cultural nation, or *Volksgeist*. A further elaboration of DuBois's book as a generic offshoot of Hegelian historiosophy is offered in Robert Gooding-Williams, "Philosophy of History and Social Critique in *The Souls of Black Folk*," *Social Science Information* 26 (1987): 99–114.

20 Robert Gooding-Williams has devoted particular attention to the melancholy chapters concerning the Reverend Crummell and black John, the fictional would-be "baptist." In each case, a heroic pilgrim of Negro progress has fallen tragically out of sympathy with the religion and culture of slavery —a flaw that DuBois is rectifying by aligning his prophetic voice with the cultural legacy of the suffering slaves. The "eulogies" thus function as critiques of past and bypassed examples of race leadership superseded by a new vision of uplift that carries with it the souls of black folk. See Gooding-

Williams, "Du Bois's Counter-Sublime," *Massachusetts Review* 35 (1994): 203–24.

21 In "Soul Texts and the Blackness of Folk," *Modernism/Modernity* 2 (1995): 71–95, Ronald M. Radano presents an eloquent defense of DuBois's embrace of musical transcriptions of black performance art: "Far from upholding fixed notions of folkness, Du Bois celebrated hybridity."

4 RECOVERING THE NATIVE TONGUE

1 *"To Be an Author": Letters of Charles W. Chesnutt, 1889–1905*, ed. Joseph R. McElrath Jr. and Robert C. Leitz III (Princeton, N.J.: Princeton University Press, 1997), 213. In this letter, dated June 29, 1904, to Walter Hines Page, Chesnutt was responding to suggested revisions for what would be his last novel, *The Colonel's Dream.*

2 Richard H. Brodhead, *Cultures of Letters: Scenes of Reading and Writing in Nineteenth-Century America* (Chicago: University of Chicago Press, 1993), 190. Chesnutt emerges in this study as an exemplar of the rising class of black professionals who were compulsively self-improving and determined to make a disciplined success of themselves in highly competitive occupations.

3 Clifford, "On Ethnographic Allegory," in *Writing Culture: The Poetics and Politics of Ethnography*, ed. James Clifford and Steven Marcus (Berkeley: University of California Press, 1986), 98–121.

4 To Alexandra Bakunina, April 20–29, 1842, in I. S. Turgenev, *Pis'ma* [Letters] (Moscow: Akademiia Navk, 1961), 1:224.

5 My paraphrase of a valuable point made by Elizabeth Cheresh Allen, *Beyond Realism: Turgenev's Poetics of Secular Salvation* (Stanford, Calif.: Stanford University Press, 1992), 143. As will become clear, I do not share Allen's "progressive" reading of the narrator's increasing authority and control as the album continues. Turgenev's structural ironies consistently exceed the mental grasp of his limited and self-limiting narrator.

6 For a fuller version of the argument that the narrative syntax of *Zapiski okhotnika* is based on conjoined antonyms, see Dale E. Peterson, "The Origin and End of Turgenev's *Sportsman's Notebook*: The Poetics and Politics of a Precarious Balance," *Russian Literature* 16 (1984): 347–58.

7 A typical statement of this ideological account of *Notes of a Hunter* may be found in V. A. Kovalev, "Zapiski okhotnika," in I. S. Turgeneva: *Voprosky genezisa* (Leningrad, 1980), 1–19.

8 "That's what it means to attach oneself to the land and the folk—in an instant, you gain strength!" exuded K. S. Aksakov in his review of 1847. For further details on Turgenev's relations with this prominent Slavophile family, see Andrew Durkin, *Sergej Aksakov and Russian Pastoral* (New Brunswick, N.J.: Rutgers University Press, 1983), 31–34. In *Turgenev's Russia* (Ithaca, N.Y.: Cornell University Press, 1980), 50–60, Victor Ripp also points out certain Slavo-

phile tendencies within Notes of a Hunter but attributes those features to Turgenev's general irresolution and vacillation.

9 I. S. Turgenev, Sochineniia (Moscow, 1963), 4:7. All quotations from the Russian text are my translations from this volume of the Academy edition of Turgenev's collected works (hereafter cited in the text).

10 For a full description of the characteristic features of the popular genre of the Russian physiological sketch consult Tseitlin, Stanovlenie realizma v russkoi literature (Moscow, 1965), 110–13, 259–60.

11 With his usual perceptiveness S. A. Shatalov has noted the presence of recognizably "Gogolian" formulas in the syntactical non sequiturs of the initial sketch as well as in the overdrawn symmetrical opposition of the two heroes' personal qualities. The most complete and sophisticated reading of Turgenev's text to date is Shatalov's "Zapiski okhotnika" I. S. Turgeneva (Stalinabad, 1960).

12 "The Singers" was the first story written after the 1849 publication of "Forest and Steppe"; Turgenev's manuscript ends with the handwritten note: "Describe how the boys drive the horses to pasture at night. The campfires" (Sochineniia, 4:553). Not surprisingly, "Bezhin Meadow" was the next sketch to be completed after "The Singers."

13 Yashka the Turk's song, "Little Path" [Dorozhen'ka] is identified by Richard Taruskin as a classic example of Russian folk music's "most aesthetically autonomous genre," the protiazhnaia, a sung lyric characterized by capricious rhythmic shifts, tonal ambiguity, and frequent use of "melisma" (more than one note per syllable). For more examples of these peasant "art songs" and a brief history of their importance to Russian cultural nationalists, see Taruskin's article, " 'Little Star': An Etude in the Folk Style," in Musorgsky: In Memoriam, 1881–1981, ed. Malcolm Hamrick Brown (Ann Arbor, Mich.: UMI Research Press, 1982), 57–84.

14 Andrew R. Durkin has usefully suggested a number of structural links between Turgenev's sketches and ancient pastoral, finding likely prototypes for Khor and Kalinych in the juxtaposed farmers, Tityrus and Meliboeus, of Virgil's First Eclogue and the paradigm for "Singers" in the rustic singing contests featured in the idylls of Theocritus. But he concedes that the presence of Turgenev's observer-narrator creates a conflict of modes and mentalities that wholly transforms the genre. See Durkin, "The Generic Context of Rural Prose: Turgenev and the Pastoral Tradition," in American Contributions to the Eleventh International Congress of Slavists, ed. Robert A. Maguire and Alan Timberlake (Columbus, Ohio: Slavica, 1993), 43–50.

15 A full account of Turgenev's surprising revision of his twenty-two-year-old text and a more complete reading of the strategically juxtaposed penultimate sketches may be found in Dale E. Peterson, "The Completion of A Sportsman's Sketches: Turgenev's Parting Word," in The Poetics of Ivan Turgenev, ed. David A. Lowe (Washington, D.C.: Kennan Institute Occasional Paper no. 234, 1989), 53–62.

16   For an excellent survey of, and contribution to, this critical literature on the sketches as an organized cycle, see Lebedev, *U istokov eposa: Ocherkovye tsikly v russkoi literature 1840–1860-kh godov* (Yaroslavl', 1975). In 1919 Leonid Grossman first suggested that the text was built on the device of stringing together paired portraits. An English translation, "Turgenev's Early Genre," appears in *Critical Essays on Ivan Turgenev*, ed. David A. Lowe (Boston: Twayne, 1989), 63–73.

17   *The Journals of Charles W. Chesnutt*, ed. Richard H. Brodhead (Durham, N.C.: Duke University Press, 1993), 125 (hereafter cited in the text).

18   William L. Andrews, *The Literary Career of Charles W. Chesnutt* (Baton Rouge: Louisiana State University Press, 1980), 52. I am indebted to Andrews's biography for his careful reconstruction of the publication history behind Chesnutt's first book.

19   The Uncle Julius tales that were excluded from Chesnutt's first volume are fortunately available in Richard Brodhead's new edition, *The Conjure Woman and Other Conjure Tales* (Durham, N.C.: Duke University Press, 1993) (hereafter cited in the text). Much of the recent rediscovery of Chesnutt has depended on appreciations of powerful tales like "Dave's Neckliss," "A Deep Sleeper," and "Tobe's Tribulations" that were not acceptable to Chesnutt's Boston publisher. Similarly, one of Turgenev's most directly emancipationist sketches ("The Reformer and the Russian German") was never published.

20   The analogy to the minstrel show pattern is drawn by Sundquist, *Wake the Nations*, 361; the reference to the vernacular trickster narratives is everywhere obvious if one reads an anthology of black folktales like Hurston's *Mules and Men*.

21   My phrasing of an important point made by Sandra Molyneaux in "Expanding the Collective Memory: Charles W. Chesnutt's The Conjure Woman Tales," in *Memory, Narrative, and Identity: New Essays in Ethnic American Literatures*, ed. Amritjit Singh and Joseph I. Skerrett Jr. (Boston: Northeastern University Press, 1994), 164–78.

22   The critic is Ben Slote, who compares Chesnutt's most anthologized story to a recent "blackface" television commercial in "Listening to 'the Goophered Grapevine' and Hearing Raisins Sing," *American Literary History* 6 (1994): 684–94.

23   The oral source of the story is mentioned in Andrews, *Literary Career*, 19. Robert Hemenway reveals that originally the effect of eating the goophered grapes was to make the slave's penis, not his hair, grow or shrivel along with the vines. See his important essay, "The Functions of Folklore in Charles Chesnutt's *The Conjure Woman*," *Journal of the Folklore Institute* 13 (1976): 283–309.

24   John Edgar Wideman, "Charles Chesnutt and the WPA Narratives: The Oral and Literate Roots of Afro-American Literature," in *The Slave's Narrative*, ed. Charles T. Davis and Henry Louis Gates Jr. (New York: Oxford University Press, 1985), 66–67.

25 For an attempt to rectify the lack of awareness of Chesnutt's complexity as a self-consciously political writer who understood African American folklore's subversive indirection, see Craig Werner, "The Framing of Charles W. Chesnutt: Practical Deconstruction in the Afro-American Tradition," *Southern Literature and Literary Theory* (Athens: University of Georgia, 1990), 339–65.

26 The aesthetic disappointment is registered by Andrews (*Literary Career*, 52), and the political criticism is sharpest in Slote ("Listening to 'the Goophered Grapevine,' " 690).

27 Molyneaux reads the tales as a continuous series dramatizing a "thematic shift from economic competition toward the corrective power of story as a cooperative, civilizing medium that would fulfill Chesnutt's original goal of changing feelings" ("Expanding the Collective Memory," 168).

28 See especially the eloquent and elaborate argument in Sundquist, *Wake the Nations*, 359–92, that the manner of telling itself constitutes a culturally specific resistance to the proscriptions and blindnesses of the master's discourse.

29 Brodhead suggests that Chesnutt's distinction among all local colorists was his understanding that the parties to the regionalist dialogue were antagonists, not friends, and that neither party enjoyed unlimited sway in the contest to dominate the meaning of experience: "The bleak wisdom of the conjure stories is that conjure exercises power only within situations that set limits to its power—a moral Chesnutt clearly applies to himself" (*Culture of Letters*, 200–204).

30 Two articles are particularly appreciative of Hurston's precocious anticipation of current disciplinary critiques of scientific ethnography. See Benigno Sanchez-Eppler, "Telling Anthropology: Zora Neale Hurston and Gilberto Freyre Disciplined in Their Field-Home-Work," *American Literary History* 4 (1992): 464–89; and D. A. Boxwell, " 'Sis Cat' as Ethnographer: Self-Presentation and Self-Inscription in Zora Neale Hurston's *Mules and Men*," *African American Review* 26 (1992): 605–17.

31 In "The Politics of Fiction, Anthropology, and the Folk: Zora Neale Hurston," in *New Essays on "Their Eyes Were Watching God,"* ed. Michael Awkward (Cambridge: Cambridge University Press, 1990), 71–93, Hazel Carby takes a forceful polemical stance against Hurston's discourse of folk authenticity, reading it as a nostalgic displacement of anxiety over the massive urban migration of American black folk.

32 All quotations are taken from the 1990 Harper Perennial edition of *Mules and Men* (hereafter cited in the text).

33 Barbara Johnson, "Thresholds of Difference: Structures of Address in Zora Neale Hurston," in *"Race," Writing, and Difference*, ed. Henry Louis Gates Jr. (Chicago: University of Chicago Press, 1986), 325.

34 See the letter of August 20, 1934, reprinted in Robert Hemenway's invaluable *Zora Neale Hurston: A Literary Biography* (Urbana: University of Illinois, 1980),

163. The immediately ensuing quotation from Hurston's correspondence is also taken from the same page of this reliable source.

35   Cited in Hemenway, *Zora Neale Hurston*, 91.

36   "Characteristics of Negro Expression," in Zora Neale Hurston, *Folklore, Memoirs, and Other Writings* (New York: Library of America, 1995), 834 (hereafter cited in the text). The essay was originally published in Nancy Cunard's *Negro: An Anthology*.

37   Cheryl A. Wall, "*Mules and Men* and Women: Zora Neale Hurston's Strategies of Narration and Visions of Female Empowerment," *Black American Literature Forum* 23 (1989): 661–80. And more recently, see Trudier Harris's discussion of Zora's "performing personae" in *The Power of the Porch: The Storyteller's Craft in Zora Neale Hurston, Gloria Naylor, and Randall Kenan* (Athens: University of Georgia Press, 1996), 3–50.

5   UNDERGROUND NOTES

1   William L. Andrews, *To Tell a Free Story: The First Century of Afro-American Autobiography, 1760–1865* (Urbana: University of Illinois Press, 1986) is the classic account of the founding narratives of the black experience in America.

2   See Richard Yarborough, "The First-Person in Afro-American Fiction," in *Afro-American Literary Study in the 1990's*, ed. Houston Baker Jr. and Patricia Redmond (Chicago: University of Chicago Press, 1989), 105–21, for a stimulating discussion of the delayed but powerful turn toward fictionalized autobiographies in the twentieth-century tradition of African American prose. He speculates that public exposure of the psychological tensions inherent in African American experience was secondary to the historic need for documentary accounts of self-liberation by ex-slave narrators. Ultimately, though, the need for truthful representations of the complex consciousness and self-masking of an African American persona became the cultural task of black writers, especially in what was ostensibly the land of the free.

3   Mikhail Bakhtin, *Problems of Dostoevsky's Poetics*, ed. Caryl Emerson (Minneapolis: University of Minnesota Press, 1984), 8. All further page citations refer to this translation, which is based on the much-expanded 1963 Moscow edition of Bakhtin's dissertation, *Problemy tvorchestva Dostoevskogo* (Leningrad, 1929).

4   The profound imaginative and formal impact of Dostoevsky's writing on the major works of Wright and Ellison has long been evident. For recent summaries of the active intertextual connections, see Joseph Frank, "Ralph Ellison and Dostoevsky," in *Through the Russian Prism* (Princeton, N.J.: Princeton University Press, 1990), 34–48; and Dale E. Peterson, "Richard Wright's Long Journey from Gorky to Dostoevsky," *African American Review* 28 (1994): 375–88.

5　F. M. Dostoevsky, *Polnoe sobranie sochinenii* (Leningrad: Navka, 1978), 18:35. All further references to the journalistic texts are my translations of the materials found in the thirty-volume complete collected works of Dostoevsky, abbreviated as PSS. There is a valuable selection of Dostoevsky's major articles available in English; see David Magarshack, *Dostoevsky's Occasional Writings* (New York: Random House, 1963).

6　In *Dostoevsky, Grigor'ev, and Native Soil Conservatism*, Dowler offers a discriminating account of the crucial nuances that separated the ideology of the *pochvenniki* from earlier Slavophiles and later Populist progressives. Apollon Grigor'ev (1822–1864) was a major influence on Dostoevsky's thinking, preceding him in envisaging nationality as an evolving synthesis of all classes within a historic nation and anticipating Dostoevsky's cult of Pushkin as the achieved embodiment of Russian universalism.

7　Frank draws attention to this strained tone of prophetic urgency in *Stir of Liberation*, 38. I am indebted to Frank's exhaustive and subtle literary biography for most of the details and not a few of the observations that inform my discussion of Dostoevsky's mentality prior to the composition of *Notes from Underground*.

8　Also like the Slavophiles, Dostoevsky borrowed his negative view of European statehood from French liberal historiography—in this case, from Augustin Thierry. See Frank, *Years of Ordeal*, 38, and the thorough discussion of the mediating ideological position of the Dostoevsky brothers' journal in V. S. Nechaeva, *Zhurnal M. M. i F. M. Dostoevskikh "Vremia," 1861–1863* (Moscow, 1973).

9　In "Silence and Servitude: Bondage and Self-Invention in Russia and America, 1780–1861," *Slavic Review* 51 (1992): 743–47, Nancy Ruttenburg offers an elegant critical reading of Dostoyevsky's attempt to privilege the role of the literary artist as uniquely capable of transcending the split subjectivity of a nation in distress and of unleashing a textual coherence to bring the nation into conformity with itself.

10　Bakhtin, *Problems of Dostoevsky's Poetics*, 227–28.

11　The quote is my translation from volume 5 (1973) of Dostoevsky's complete collected works (PSS, 99). Notice the narrator's evasiveness (is the speaker diseased, depraved, or merely defective in appearance?) is underlined by the shifting syntactical placement of the adjectival modifiers. In addition, the term usually translated as "spiteful" (*zloi*) also carries the more fundamental ethical implication of "wicked" or "evil."

12　Frank, *Stir of Liberation*, 314. Specifically, Frank points out that the diatribes and deliriums of the underground man's embattled consciousness are deeply awash in the successive waves of European influence that overwhelmed the Russian educated class of Dostoevsky's time.

13　Frank's chapter on *Notes from Underground* (*Stir of Liberation*, 310–47) is unsurpassed as a reading of the polemics of the narrator and as a guide to the ideological contexts that inform them. Additional detailed information on the literary and polemical contexts, as well as a chapter-by-chapter commentary on the unfolding argument and plot of the work, is usefully provided by Richard Peace, *Dostoevsky's Notes from Underground* (London: Bristol Classical Press, 1993).

14   As the translator, Richard Pevear, points out in his foreword to the 1993 Knopf edition of *Notes from Underground*, Dostoevsky's narrator employs specific words that in themselves draw attention to the logical inadequacy of his argument. Quite literally, the "most profitable profit" imaginable is that man "positively ought to" insist on acting in accordance with his own freely chosen "wanting"; the repetitively used and awkward word "wanting" (*khotenie*) emphasizes the dependency of desire rather than the assertiveness of "volition."

15   The underground man's proud embrace of "whim" (*kapriz*) and "spite" (*zlost'*) ironically indicates his compulsive attachment to uncontrolled and/or reactive behavior. See Stewart R. Sutherland, "The Philosophical Dimension: Self and Freedom," in *New Essays on Dostoevsky*, ed. Malcolm V. Jones and Garth M. Terry (Cambridge: Cambridge University Press, 1983), 169–86, for confirmation of my emphasis on the text's undermining of a viable defense of the narrator's autonomous identity. Sutherland concludes that *Notes from Underground* illustrates "the logical indeterminacy of a free choice."

16   "Preface to the Original Edition of 1912" in James Weldon Johnson, *The Autobiography of an Ex-Coloured Man*, ed. Henry Louis Gates Jr. (New York: Vintage Books, 1989), xl (hereafter cited in the text).

17   In "Passing as Autobiography: James Weldon Johnson's *The Autobiography of an Ex-Coloured Man*," *African American Review* 30 (spring 1996): 17–34, Donald C. Goellnicht makes this revelation and gives a subtle account of the preface's ironies when it is read as Johnson's performance in whiteface. Goellnicht's essay is a superb example of a Bakhtinian analysis of the many types of "double-voicedness" operating within Johnson's highly elusive and allusive sentences.

18   In *"The Singer in One's Soul": Storytelling in the Fiction of James Weldon Johnson, Richard Wright, Ralph Ellison, and Toni Morrison* (Ann Arbor, Mich.: University Microfilms, 1985), 77–89, Valerie Ann Smith pays particular attention to how the style of expression adopted by the narrator manifests a "structured pattern of defensiveness and evasion." On the ironic self-effacement of the narrator, see Howard Faulkner, "James Weldon Johnson's Portrait of the Artist as Invisible Man," *Black American Literature Forum* 19 (winter 1985): 147–51. An Adlerian reading of the narrative manner's display of neurotic "avoidance behaviors" is offered by Marvin P. Garrett, "Early Recollections and Structural Irony in *The Autobiography of an Ex-Coloured Man*," *Critique* 13 (summer 1971): 5–14.

19   In *The Hammers of Creation: Folk Culture in Modern African American Fiction* (Athens: University of Georgia Press, 1992), 12–16, Eric J. Sundquist offers a stimulating reading of chapter 10, in which the excolored man is seen as a would-be

"imperialist" exploiter of Black Belt cultural riches, acting as the obverse of DuBois and Johnson, who immersed themselves in and celebrated the legacy of the Southern slave culture.

20 For an account of Matthews's role in encouraging and promoting Johnson's manuscript, see Lawrence J. Oliver, *Brander Matthews, Theodore Roosevelt, and the Politics of American Literature, 1880–1920* (Knoxville: University of Tennessee Press, 1992), 53–55.

21 Superficially, the autobiography passes for an American success story, although it is also a rogue's progress purchased at the price of racial disguise. Stepto demonstrates that the narrative is constructed with frequent ironic variations and reversals on specific motifs from African American slave narratives; he refers to the novel as an "aborted immersion narrative," a parodic negative of DuBois (*Behind the Veil*, 95–127). In "The Interplay of Narrative Modes in James Weldon Johnson's *The Autobiography of an Ex-Coloured Man*," *Jahrbuch für Amerikastudien* 18 (1973): 173–81, Simone Vauthier points out that the larger structure of the narrative observes the Spanish picaro's journey through the strata of society, evoking a tradition the bilingual Johnson (and his academic mentor) knew well.

22 The quoted phrase is from Sundquist, *Hammers of Creation*, 45; by marrying a walking symbol of classical whiteness, the narrator has chosen "to expunge his racial heritage, to forsake race-building in both procreation and creation."

23 For an early example of the spate of articles that correct naive readings of Johnson's novel as a trustworthy, "dispassionate" reflection of the author's own opinions on race matters, see Robert E. Fleming, "Irony as a Key to Johnson's *The Autobiography of an Ex-Coloured Man*," *American Literature* 43 (1971): 83–96. Most accounts of the novel's irony, however, present it in starkly simplified form. Either the protagonist is truly a black man who masquerades as a successful white, or he is a mulatto nonentity trapped by white values—see, for instance, Stephen M. Ross, "Audience and Irony in Johnson's *The Autobiography of an Ex-Coloured Man*," *CLA Journal* 18 (1974): 198–210. In "Irony and Symbolic Action in James Weldon Johnson's *The Autobiography of an Ex-Coloured Man*," *American Quarterly* 32 (1980): 540–58, Joseph T. Skerrett Jr. presents a sophisticated biographical reading of the irony, identifying the narrator as a Jacksonville childhood friend who chose racial anonymity and functioned as an exorcised alter ego for the light-skinned racial activist Johnson.

24 There can be no doubt that the underground man and the ex-colored man serve, at specific moments, as mouthpieces for their authors. Whole paragraphs of cultural commentary from Johnson's novel were later reprinted under his signature in the preface to the first edition of his 1922 anthology, *The Book of American Negro Poetry*. And it is well known that the blistering critique of enlightened self-interest in *Notes from Underground* directly reflected

Dostoevsky's attack on "rational egoism" as presented in Nikolai Cherny-
shevsky's utopian novel, *What Is To Be Done?* (1863).

25 In "Passing as Autobiography," Goellnicht invokes to good effect Bakhtin's
concept of "parodic stylization," by which "the intentions of the representing discourse are at odds with the intentions of the represented discourse"
(*The Dialogic Imagination: For Essays*, ed. Michael Holquist [Austin: University
of Texas Press, 1981], 363–64). He offers an impressive reading of Johnson's
intertextual allusions to prior slave narratives as "a two-way conversation
between texts that interrogate one another," the notion being that the narrator's unwitting revisions of African American autobiographical motifs create a double-edged irony exposing both the original version and the devia-
tion to mutual critique.

26 To their credit several commentators have approached Johnson's text as the
ironic story of the self-effacement of an African American who is truly a dual
self. In addition to Faulkner, "James Weldon Johnson's Portrait of the Artist as Invisible Man," see Roxanna Pisiak, "Irony and Subversion in James
Weldon Johnson's *The Autobiography of an Ex-Coloured Man*," *Studies in American
Fiction* 21 (spring 1993): 83–96. In *Writing between the Lines: Race and Intertextuality* (Athens: University of Georgia Press, 1994), Alden L. Nielsen has suggested that the hidden liminality of an American identity is exposed at the
novel's end, when the narrator reads his own life as that of "a white man who
has suppressed his beginnings in blackness, suppressed them at the greatest price to his own spirit" (184).

27 Quoted as cited in Skerrett, "Irony and Symbolic Action," 557.

6 NATIVE SONS AGAINST NATIVE SOUL

1 This now-famous essay from the *Antioch Review* has been reprinted in Ralph
Ellison, *Shadow and Act* (New York: Vintage, 1995), 77–94. As its title indicates, Ellison initially attempted to align Wright's text more closely with his
own loyal affiliation to black vernacular and musical forms. In a later essay,
"The World and the Jug," Ellison retreated from this reading and conceded
Wright's hostility toward the artistic deflections of pain and suffering in the
black South's musical and oral traditions.

2 Gorky's autobiography had been translated into English as early as 1915, and
interest in it was revived by the American distribution in 1938 of Mark Donskoi's riveting film, *Gorky's Childhood*. In *The Unfinished Quest of Richard Wright*
(New York: Morrow, 1973), 97, Michel Fabre reports that Wright left his first
Left Front editorial board meeting in 1933 with recent issues of *New Masses* and
International Literature, in which articles by Gorky were prominent. Wright's
private library included the 1939 International Publishers edition of Gorky's
political and literary essays, *Culture and the People*.

3   Maxim Gorky, *On Literature* (Seattle: University of Washington Press, 1973), 104. In addition to a translation of "The Disintegration of Personality" (71–137), this collection includes Gorky's wonderful literary portraits of Tolstoy and Chekhov.

4   Cited from a letter of December 16, 1911, to Professor D. N. Ovsianiko-Kulikovsky in Maksim Gorky, *Selected Letters* (Oxford: Clarendon Press, 1997), 160.

5   There is a brief account of this public polemic with Dostoevsky in F. M. Borras, *Maxim Gorky The Writer: An Interpretation* (Oxford: Clarendon Press, 1967), 39–45.

6   For a thorough, sensitive survey of Gorky's antagonistic and conflicted relationship to his powerful predecessor, see Richard A. Peace, "Some Dostoevskian Themes in the Work of Maksim Gorky," *Dostoevsky Studies* 8 (1987): 143–54.

7   Richard Wright, "Between Laughter and Tears," *New Masses*, October 5, 1937, 22, 25. In this review, Hurston was unfavorably compared to the now unknown Waters Edward Turpin, "an honest man trying desperately to say something," as opposed to her novel's "sensory sweep" and exploitation of "quaint" Negro life to satisfy the "chauvinistic tastes" of a white audience.

8   Richard Wright, "Blueprint for Negro Writing," *New Challenge* 2 (fall 1937): 53. This same issue led off with an editorial making explicit the rejection of the Harlem-based "New Negro" movement: "We are not attempting to re-stage the 'revolt' or 'renaissance' which grew unsteadily and upon false foundations ten years ago."

9   The full text of Gorky's speech on Soviet literature was available in English translation as early as 1935. See H. G. Scott, ed., *Problems of Soviet Literature: Reports and Speeches at the First Soviet Writers' Congress* (London: Martin Lawrence), 27–69.

10   For a detailed and fully contextualized reading of Gorky's discourse as "a hymn to folklore revised by himself," see Regine Robin, *Socialist Realism: An Impossible Aesthetic* (Stanford, Calif.: Stanford University Press, 1992), 51–55, 166–78. Though a remarkably salty writer in his youth, Gorky had come to distrust and oppose the use of "local locutions" in a literature of "peasant power" that he feared would be both untranslatable and chauvinistic.

11   Wright, "Blueprint for Negro Writing," 58–60.

12   For full discussion of the genre of the Russian "pseudo-autobiography," and of Gorky's successful dislodging of the Tolstoyan prototype, see Andrew Baruch Wachtel, *The Battle for Childhood: Creation of a Russian Myth* (Stanford, Calif.: Stanford University Press, 1990), esp. chap. 4.

13   Erik Erikson's essay, "The Legend of Maxim Gorky's Youth," is included in his well-known book, *Childhood and Society* (New York: Norton, 1950), 316–58.

14   Ibid., 322–24.

15 Translations are my own from the text of *Detstvo* in volume 9 of the 1952 Moscow edition of Gorky's collected works (hereafter cited in the text). The best available English translation is by Ronald Wilks, oddly mistitled *My Childhood* (London: Penguin Books, 1966).

16 Helen Muchnic, *From Gorky to Pasternak: Six Writers in Soviet Russia* (New York: Vintage, 1966), 41. The chapter on Gorky offers the most eloquent reading of *Childhood* in English criticism to date. Muchnic unabashedly presents the grandmother as Gorky's masterpiece, holding the same sacred place in Soviet literature as Pushkin's Arina Rodionovna, the nurturing folk godmother of classic Russian literature.

17 For a summary of these disputes, see Andrew Barratt, "Maksim Gorky's Autobiographical Trilogy: The Lure of Myth and the Power of Fact," *Auto/biography Studies* 11 (fall 1996): 24–41. A particularly thorough "folkloric" analysis of the narrative Gorky himself referred to as a "grim folktale" (*surovaia skazka*) is offered in G. M. Atanov, "Avtobiograficheskaia trilogiia M. Gor'kogo," *Russkaia Literatura* 1 (1981): 65–83.

18 Fabre, *Unfinished Quest of Richard Wright*, 252.

19 Stepto, *Behind the Veil*, 132.

20 This passage (on pp. 7–8) and all following quotations are cited from the 1993 Harper Perennial edition of the newly restored complete autobiography of Richard Wright, *Black Boy (American Hunger)*.

21 Robert B. Stepto speaks honestly about this difficulty in his contribution to the collection of essays, *Chant of Saints: A Gathering of Afro-American Literature, Art, and Scholarship*, ed. Michael S. Harper and Robert B. Stepto (Urbana: University of Illinois Press, 1979), "I Thought I Knew These People: Richard Wright and the Afro-American Literary Tradition" (195–211).

22 Compare, for instance, two very appropriate but very different intertextual placements of the fundamental story Wright tells in *Black Boy*: Stepto's sensitive reading of the slave narrative background in *Behind the Veil*, 128–62, and the international literary subtexts skillfully presented by Charles T. Davis, "From Experience to Eloquence: Richard Wright's Black Boy as Art," in Harper and Stepto, *Chant of Saints*, 425–39.

23 Gorky, *On Literature*, 16–17.

7 EURASIANS AND NEW NEGROES

1 Two major multimedia exhibits of the cultural production stimulated by the New Negro movement have circulated nationally and internationally and resulted in profusely illustrated catalogues. See *Harlem Renaissance: Art of Black America* (New York: Abradale Press, 1994), based on the 1987 exhibit of the Studio Museum in Harlem; and *Rhapsodies in Black: Art of the Harlem Renaissance* (Berkeley: University of California Press, 1997), based on the traveling

exhibit organized by the Hayward Gallery in London. Both catalogues include extensive essays by academic specialists on the period and its theory
and practice of a black aesthetic.

2　In the year the Soviet Union collapsed, a spate of reprints and scholarly
articles on Eurasianism appeared in numbers 2 and 3 of the nationalist journal,
Our Contemporary (*Nash sovremennik*), and major portions of *Exodus to the
East* were republished in an anthology of Eurasian materials edited by I. A.
Isaev, *Puti evrazii* (Moscow: Russkaia Kniga, 1992). Isaev's lengthy introduc-
tion is titled, rather significantly, "Utopians or Prophets?"

3　There is no full-length biography of N. S. Trubetzkoy in any language, but
one scholar, Anatoly Liberman, has appended extensive biographical information to the two translations of Trubetzkoy's writings he has assembled.
See his introduction to Trubetzkoy's *Writings on Literature* (Minneapolis: University of Minnesota Press, 1990); and especially his postscript to Trubetzkoy, *The Legacy of Genghis Khan and Other Essays on Russia's Identity*, ed. Anatoly
Liberman (Ann Arbor: Michigan Slavic Publications, 1991).

4　My translation is from *N.S. Trubetzkoy's Letters and Notes*, ed. Roman Jakobson (The Hague: Mouton 1975), 12–14. Since all of Trubetzkoy's correspondence and papers were seized by the Gestapo in searches of his Viennese flat
in the spring of 1938 and never recovered, Jakobson's extensive collection is
an invaluable resource.

5　These quotations are taken from Kenneth Brostrom's translation of *Europe
and Mankind*, in Trubetzkoy, *Legacy of Genghis Khan*, 1–64, with the exception
of the phrasing "to rally in a united detachment," in which I have sought to
capture a militant allusion to the *druzhina*, medieval Russian defenders of the
realm. All further quotations from Trubetzkoy's essays are from the *Legacy
of Genghis Khan* (hereafter cited in the text).

6　The quotation is from Savitsky's own typescript of "Europe and Eurasia,"
the review article he published in *Russkaia Mysl'*, January 8, 1921, 119–38. The
huge archive of Savitsky's letters and papers that resides in Prague's Klementinum is probably the richest extant resource for scholars interested in
the entire history of the Eurasian movement. Savitsky regarded himself as
the lifelong custodian of the movement; fortunately, his archive survived
without being confiscated by Nazi or Soviet agents.

7　It was immediately apparent to fellow émigrés that the Eurasian manifesto
represented a true revision of "the Russian intellectuals' stock of political
and historical ideas," as D. S. Mirsky expressed it in his excellent summation, "The Eurasian Movement," *Slavonic Review* 6, no. 17 (1927): 311–19. The
first and still most thorough scholarly treatment of the movement in English
is Nicholas V. Riasanovsky, "The Emergence of Eurasianism," *California Slavic
Studies* 4 (1967): 39–72, which also makes note of its "striking disjointed-
ness" with preceding Russian views of the world.

8　*Iskhod k vostoku: Predchuvstviia i sversheniia. Utverzhdenie Evraziitsev* (Sofia: Ros-
siisko-Bolgarskoe Knigoizdatel'stvo, 1921), iii–iv. All page citations not in

reference to Trubetzkoy's articles are from the original text in my own translations.

9 This point has been forcefully emphasized by one post-Soviet researcher in the newly available Eurasian archives; see Albert Sobolev, "Kniaz' N.S. Trubetskoi i Evraziistvo," *Literaturnaia Ucheba*, no. 6 (1991): 121–31.

10 Suvchinsky contributed two articles to *Exodus to the East*: "The Strength of the Weak" (4–8), and "An Age of Faith" (14–27). Both express a religiously tinged aesthetic of mystical terror. This is especially intense at the end of the second essay: "Whenever the might of chaos is strengthened, so too strengthens the power of the Holy Spirit. . . . In terror the eyes get larger. . . . one must believe that in this conflagration a new human, Russian inspiration is aflame."

11 Florovsky bulks large in the anthology, contributing three substantial essays: "Breaks and Connections" (9–13), "The Cunning of Reason" (28–39), and "About Non-Historic Peoples" (52–70). All evidence deep learning and wide-ranging reference, including a rather surprising affinity for American pragmatism and personalism, which is process-oriented and improvisatory and part of the renewal of a metaphysic of freedom from the periphery of Western civilization: "It is not accidental that every word about the 'plasticity' of the world has been spoken outside Europe" ("Cunning of Reason," 39).

12 The first Eurasian anthology was followed by six other published symposia between 1922 and 1931, a special volume in 1923 attacking Roman Catholicism, *Russia and Latinity*, and twelve volumes of the movement periodical, *The Eurasian Chronicle*, issued between 1925 and 1937. These publications (and many other occasional writings) appeared in all the centers of the Russian emigration, especially in Prague, Berlin, and Paris. Trubetzkoy left Sofia in 1922 for Vienna, where he held a university chair and from which he maintained close relations with Jakobson and Savitsky in Prague.

13 For a lucid exposition of this innovative "culturological approach" to the contiguous "family" of Eurasian peoples, see Ladislav Matejka, "N. S. Trubetzkoj's Concepts of Language Unions and Cultural Zones," *Wiener slawistischer Almanach* 25–26 (1990): 291–98.

14 Jakobson's report, "On Phonological Linguistic Unions," was printed along with Savitsky's preface, "The Announcement of a Discovery," in *Evraziia v svete iazykoznanie* (Prague, 1931).

15 My translation from Savitsky's ecstatic letter of August 9, 1930, as published in Jindrich Toman, ed., *Letters and Other Materials from the Moscow and Prague Linguistic Circles, 1902–1945* (Ann Arbor: Michigan Slavic Publications, 1994), 130.

16 Ibid., 3.

17 W. E. B. DuBois, "Negro Writers," *Crisis* 19 (April 1920): 298–99.

18 In his review in *Crisis* 31 (January 1926) of the anthology Locke edited, DuBois acknowledged it as an epoch-making expression of "the present state

of thought and culture among American Negroes," but he also made it clear that "if Mr. Locke's thesis is insisted on too much it is going to turn the Negro renaissance into decadence" (142–43). DuBois was not ready to accept the dismissal of social responsibility for racial uplift that he detected in Locke's aestheticism and in the "ghetto realism" of the volume's literary contents.

19   Jeffrey C. Stewart, "A Biography of Alain Locke: Philosopher of the Harlem Renaissance, 1886–1930" (dissertation, Yale University, 1979), 135. There is no complete biography available, but Stewart provides a carefully researched treatment of the family background and intellectual context behind Locke's emergence to prominence. Locke's homosexuality is not broached for one hundred pages, but once mentioned it is seen as a major factor in his embrace of cultural pluralism, providing as it did "a view of reality as a conglomeration of dissimilar elements and personalities" (134).

20   See, in particular, the correspondence with the Sinhalese scholar of Eastern decorative arts, Lionel S. de Fonseka, and with C. H. Dickerman, Locke's longtime Cambridge friend and associate, in the Alain Locke papers at the Moorland-Spingarn Research Center, Howard University. A letter of May 16, 1917, from "Dickus" to "Lockus" is especially open about the international gay subculture, with references to Wilde, Havelock Ellis, and Emile Verhaeren's modernist "Europeanism": "There was a general tendency for civilizations to run together before the war. . . . All cosmopolites are like that."

21   An excellent account of Locke's transformation in the elite diasporic community of intellectuals from the British Commonwealth is provided by Jeffery C. Stewart, "A Black Aesthete at Oxford," *Massachusetts Review* 34 (autumn 1993), 411–28.

22   I have consulted the original manuscript of 9 June 1908 in box 164-159, sheaf 8, Alain Locke Archive, Moorland-Spingarn Research Center, Howard University, Washington, D.C. (hereafter cited as AL Archive). The published version appeared in *The Oxford Cosmopolitan*, vol. 1, 151–61.

23   Leonard Harris, ed., *The Philosophy of Alain Locke: Harlem Renaissance and Beyond* (Philadelphia: Temple University Press, 1989), 11–16. Harris' "rendering" of Locke's meaning helpfully points out his sophisticated commitment to both cultural pluralism and imperative values, especially among colonized and subaltern peoples who necessarily experience themselves as simultaneously real and reified, as a group solidarity in constant formation and reformation.

24   Quotes are taken from the holograph copy of the Philadelphia lecture of October 24, 1911, box 164-117, sheaf 24, AL Archive.

25   There is a detailed discussion of Johnson's intellectual allegiance to the "pragmatic sociology" of Park and Dewey, and consequently, of his sympathy for a pluralistic literary rendering of the Negro experience in George Hutchinson's impressive exercise in historical contextualization, *The Harlem*

Renaissance in Black and White (Cambridge, Mass.: Harvard University Press, 1995), 50–61.

26 For a brief account of *Opportunity* and its rivalry with *Crisis*, see Abby Arthur and Ronald Maberry Johnson, *Propaganda and Aesthetics: The Literary Politics of Afro-American Magazines in the Twentieth Century* (Amherst: University of Massachusetts Press, 1979), 48–57. A much more extensive discussion of the journal's contents and cultural politics can be found in Hutchinson, *Harlem Renaissance*, 173–208.

27 Johnson's revealing letters to Locke throughout the crucial years 1923–25 are available in Correspondence, box 164-40, sheafs 23–26, AL Archive.

28 The series was initiated on June 11, 1921, with the "Prague Number," which like all the others combined contributions by "natives" and American commentators on the socioeconomic and cultural prosperity of the "young" nations arising after the war. Interestingly, the "Irish Number" makes frequent mention of Russian precursors who helped inspire the Celtic Revival in literature. Needless to say, the Soviet issue ("Russia Today and Tomorrow") was all about the deliberate campaign to construct a people's proletarian culture. Finally, the Mexican issue included impressive portraits of "national types" by the Bavarian artist, Winold Reiss, who would be asked to illustrate the New Negro volume.

29 Quoted from a letter of February 5, 1924, Survey Associates correspondence file, box 164-88, sheaf 6, AL Archive.

30 Quoted from the *Survey Graphic* file, box 164-115, sheaf 13, AL Archive.

31 The anthology contains twenty essays, eight stories, thirty-seven poems, two folktales, a play, and an extensive bibliography, amounting to well over four hundred pages in length. Amusingly, the *Opportunity* reviewer, Robert W. Bagnall, objected to the editor's "obtruding five times upon the scene" ([February 1926]: 73–74).

32 Locke, *New Negro*, xvii (hereafter cited in the text).

33 Alain Locke, "The Concept of Race as Applied to Social Culture," *Howard Review* 1 (1924), as reprinted in Harris, *Philosophy of Alain Locke*, 188–99.

34 Alain Locke, "The Colonial Literature of France," *Opportunity* 1 (November 1923): 331–35. This article marks the beginning of Locke's long association with the Martinique-born novelist René Maran, author of the Goncourt Prize novel, *Batouala* (1921), whose attack on "the literary traducers" of Africa's real features anticipates the New Negro and Negritude movements. Locke quotes to good effect the travel sketches of Lucie Consturier, in which a fetish dance is favorably compared to Dionysiac festivals: "Everything among these Negroes was artifice and discipline, and the deeper I advanced into the forest, the more rigourous and conventionalized I found their life and ways."

35 James Clifford, "Diasporas," *Cultural Anthropology* 9 (1994): 302–38. This extensive article provides an immensely clarifying discussion of the multiple

varieties of diaspora and border discourses now current in intercultural studies.

36 Feodor M. Dostoevsky, "Pushkin: A Sketch," in *Russian Intellectual History: an Anthology*, ed. Marc Raeff (New York: Harcourt, Brace and World, 1957), 289–300. For a full account of this dramatic speech and its ideological meaning, see Marcus C. Leavitt, *Russian Literary Politics and the Pushkin Celebration of 1880* (Ithaca, N.Y.: Cornell University Press, 1989).

37 The mapping of the Russian empire since Peter the Great had profound ideological implications. The division of the vast contiguous landmass into a European and Asiatic Russia separated by the modest Ural mountains proclaimed the realm to be a European power exercising colonial suzerainty and extending civilization in central Asia and Siberia. The Eurasians no less than the Bolsheviks shifted the ground from beneath this Eurocentric conception of Russia. For a fascinating lesson in Russian geopolitics, see Mark Bassin, "Russia between Europe and Asia: The Ideological Construction of Geography," *Slavic Review* 50 (1991): 1–17.

38 For a strong critique of all cultural pluralist ideologies, including *The New Negro*, as disguised versions of "identity essentialism," see Walter Benn Michaels, *Our America: Nativism, Modernism, and Pluralism* (Durham, N.C.: Duke University Press, 1995). If the claim to a higher degree of cultural hybridity is aligned neatly to one's inherent racial identity, then cultural pluralism is an "oxymoron" and nothing more than another form of essentialist cultural nationalism.

8 PRESERVING THE RACE

1 Locke, "Concept of Race as Applied to Social Culture," in Harris, *Philosophy of Alain Locke*, 195.

2 The most complete treatment of this major movement of nationalist dissent within the Soviet literary establishment is Kathleen F. Parthé, *Russian Village Prose: The Radiant Past* (Princeton, N.J.: Princeton University Press, 1992). Her analysis of the core attributes and invariants of "village prose" texts creates, in effect, a canon of nostalgic elegies to lost local paradises: "The underlying assumption in Village Prose is that the thousand-year-old rural chain of life is being—or has already been—broken" (75). I shall be arguing that Rasputin's posture is militant rather than defeatist, as is appropriate to a literary conservationist who resurrects a rural landscape that preserves vital traces of traditional Russia's cultural ecology.

3 The rural population declined from 51.48 percent to 48.51 percent between the two official census reports. See E. Starikova, "Sotsiologicheskii aspekt sovremmenoi 'derevenskoi prozy,'" *Voprosy literatury*, no. 7 (1972): 15. By 1985 only 34.7 percent lived in rural areas, and more than one-fourth of the Soviet rural population had moved to urban areas in the last twenty-five

years. See N. N. Shneidman, *Soviet Literature in the 1980's: Decade of Transition* (Toronto: University of Toronto Press, 1989), 95.

4   The first postwar examples of these so-called kolkhoz sketchbooks were Valentin Ovechkin's *Raionnye budni* [Regional workdays] (1952) and Efim Dorosh's *Derevenskii dnevnik* [Country diary], compiled and published in installments between 1954 and 1970.

5   Gleb Zekulin has argued forcefully for this conclusion in "The Contemporary Countryside in Soviet Literature: A Search for New Values," in *The Soviet Rural Community*, ed. James R. Millar (Urbana: University of Illinois Press, 1971), 376–404. A fuller account of Solzhenitsyn's peasant sketches and their strategic evocation of classic Russian subtexts is given in Dale E. Peterson, "Solzhenitsyn Back in the USSR: Anti-Modernism in Contemporary Soviet Prose," *Berkshire Review* 16 (1981): 64–78.

6   Biographical details have been gathered from N. Kotenko, *Valentin Rasputin* (Moscow: Raduga, 1988), published in English; and Svetlana Semenova, *Valentin Rasputin* (Moscow: Sovetskaia Rossiia, 1987).

7   Rasputin's Union-wide reputation was made in 1967 with the publication in Moscow of *Money for Maria*. Although never prolific, his works have never failed to elicit a strong public response. Artistic respect and literary fame arrived with *The Last Phase* (1970), followed by *Live and Remember* (1974) and the highly controversial *Farewell to Matyora* (1976). He again fanned the flames of literary and cultural dispute with the incendiary novella, *The Fire* (1985). There are two thoughtful, well-informed surveys in English of Rasputin's career: Teresa Polowy, *The Novellas of Valentin Rasputin: Genre, Language, and Style* (New York: Peter Lang, 1989); and David C. Gillespie, *Valentin Rasputin and Soviet Russian Village Prose* (London: Modern Humanities Research Association, 1986).

8   Indeed, Rasputin virtually abandoned literature for the sake of promoting ecological ("Baikal, Baikal") and chauvinist causes, as in his prominent embrace of the campaign by the Russian Writers' Union in 1990 against cosmopolitan liberals for their alleged "Russophobia." This activism on behalf of a pristine environment and an ethnically pure nationalism is hardly inconsistent with his literary vision of a native landscape that "naturally" reinforces traditional Russian values. See, for instance, his call for a return to the nurturing "essence" of Russian womanhood, "Cherchez La Femme," *Nash sovremennik*, no. 3 (1990).

9   For an excellent reading of the psychological dimensions of Viktor's therapeutic liberation from a literal regression back to his displaced home, see John Givens, "Author and Authority: Valentin Rasputin's *Downstream*, *Upstream* as a Discourse on Writing," *Modern Language Review* 91 (1996): 427–40. Criticized for his overly psychological writing, Viktor discovers that he cannot write in proximity to his reconstructed home territory, but must flee back upstream (to Moscow) where his memories can be reflected in their purity.

10   This citation, like the following ones, is my translation from the text printed
     in a widely available collection of Rasputin's writings, *Vek zhivi—vek liubi*
     (Moscow: Molodaia gvardiia, 1988), 241. There is an English translation
     (titled "Downstream") of the 1972 sketch in *Contemporary Russian Prose*, ed.
     Carl Proffer and Ellendea Proffer (Ann Arbor, Mich.: Ardis, 1982), 379–430.

11   For an interesting reconstruction of the Old Russian cult of "moist Mother
     earth," as well as for some timely remarks about "the Mother as Russia" in
     postrevolutionary literature and culture, see Joanna Hubbs, *Mother Russia:
     The Feminine Myth in Russian Culture* (Bloomington: Indiana University Press,
     1988), esp. 52–86, 228–37.

12   My translation from the Russian text in Valentin Rasputin, *Povesti* (Moscow:
     Molodaia Gvardiia, 1978), 37. There is now available a fluent English transla-
     tion by Antonina W. Bouis: *Farewell to Matyora* (Evanston, Ill.: Northwestern
     University Press, 1991).

13   For an anthropologist's account of the freedom of personal being that cus-
     tomarily accompanies the ritualized structures of traditional societies, see
     Dorothy Lee, "Individual Autonomy and Social Structure," in *Freedom and Cul-
     ture* (Englewood Cliffs, N.J.: Prentice-Hall, 1959), 5–14.

14   John B. Dunlop, "Valentin Rasputin's *Proshchanie s Materoi*," in *Russian Litera-
     ture and Criticism: Selected Papers from the Second World Congress for Soviet and East
     European Studies*, ed. Evelyn Bristol (Berkeley, Calif.: Slavic Specialties, 1982),
     66; and also Gillespie, *Valentin Rasputin*, 41.

15   Significantly, this last sentence was excised from Soviet-era reprintings of
     Rasputin's novella. It can be found in the original version published in num-
     ber 11 (1976) of the journal *Nash sovremennik* and is restored in the English
     translation by Antonina Bouis.

16   Gloria Naylor and Toni Morrison, "A Conversation," *Southern Review* 21
     (1985): 589. This collaborative meditation on the emergence of a literature
     that does justice to the "different colors" in the family history of African
     American women was itself the result of Naylor's seeking out a direct rela-
     tionship with the older writer whose example gave her confidence in her own
     potential authority to break into prose.

17   Gloria Naylor, "Love and Sex in the Afro-American Novel," *Yale Review* 78
     (1988): 19–31. By contrast, for African American women writers, "the test of
     love is what the black woman stays through" (29).

18   Susan Willis, *Specifying: Black Women Writing the American Experience* (Madison:
     University of Wisconsin Press, 1987), 57–58.

19   Although there is no full-length biography yet, a good summary of Naylor's
     early life and of the importance of religion in her development is provided
     in Virginia C. Fowler, *Gloria Naylor: In Search of Sanctuary* (New York: Twayne,
     1996), 1–20.

20   Gloria Naylor, *Mama Day* (New York: Vintage Books, 1989), 3. All further
     page references are cited from this reissue of the original Ticknor and Fields
     edition of 1988.

21 For engaging accounts of the interplay between *Mama Day* and the Shake-spearean canon, see Peter Erickson, *Rewriting Shakespeare, Rewriting Ourselves* (Berkeley: University of California Press, 1991), 124–45; and Valerie Traub, "Rainbows of Darkness: Deconstructing Shakespeare in the Work of Gloria Naylor and Zora Neale Hurston," in *Cross-Cultural Performances: Differences in Women's Re-Visions of Shakespeare*, ed. Marianne Novy (Urbana: University of Illinois Press, 1993), 150–64. The most thorough account of the novel's grounding in West African spirituality and Southern black folk medicine is provided by Lindsay Tucker, "Recovering the Conjure Woman: Texts and Contexts in Gloria Naylor's *Mama Day*," *African American Review* 28 (1994): 173–88.

22 A very interesting reading of how Miranda's magic contrasts with Prospero's in its "egg-centric" insistence on reinforcing nature's fertile curative powers is offered by Gary Storhoff, " 'The Only Voice Is Your Own': Gloria Naylor's Revision of *The Tempest*," *African American Review* 29 (spring 1995): 35–46.

23 As already mentioned, Rasputin actively joined the nationalist-chauvinist camp of opinion at the end of the perestroika period. In an address to the Congress of People's Deputies, he denounced Gorbachev's seduction by pluralism: "You have roped the country into a pluralism of values. And that is more dangerous than bombs"—see *Nash sovremennik*, no. 3 (1989): 133–36. Naylor in several interviews has admitted she used to think of herself as a cultural nationalist with separatist tendencies, but she does not now see her work as political, although it is "just very ethnocentric" and "very female-centered." See the appendix in Fowler, *Gloria Naylor*, 143–57; and the inter-view in Mickey Pearlman and Katherine Usher Henderson, *A Voice of One's Own: Conversations with America's Writing Women* (Boston: Houghton Mifflin, 1990), 27–34.

24 Fowler, for instance, concludes that the novel's larger meanings refuse to join the Afrocentric, maternal world of Willow Springs to the other side of the bridge: "At novel's end Naylor's ideal black community remains a closed circle of women's hands" (*Gloria Naylor*, 120). See also the celebration of the female-bonded idealized community as depicted in Helen Fiddyment Levy, *Fiction of the Home Place* (Jackson: University of Mississippi Press, 1992).

25 The idea that the novel is structured around Shakespearean and African American dramatizations of violently evolving "new Days" is explicated im-pressively by Missy Dehn Kubitschek, "Toward a New Order: Shakespeare, Morrison, and Gloria Naylor's *Mama Day*," *Melus* 19 (fall 1994): 75–90.

EPILOGUE: RESPONSE AND CALL

1 It is generally accepted that Mikhail Bakhtin was the éminence grise, if not the chief author of, three influential quasi-Marxist refutations of For-malism, Freudianism, and Saussurean linguistics that were officially pub-

lished in the Soviet Union between 1927 and 1929 under the names of P. N. Medvedev and V. N. Voloshinov. The correct ascription of authorship remains a highly debatable matter. For a full discussion of the disputed texts, see Katerina Clark and Michael Holquist, *Mikhail Bakhtin* (Cambridge, Mass.: Harvard University Press, 1984). Gary Saul Morson and Caryl Emerson have helpfully suggested that the works arose out of a dialogic colloquium among the three thinkers; see their introduction to *Rethinking Bakhtin: Extensions and Challenges* (Evanston, Ill.: Northwestern University Press, 1989).

2　Caryl Emerson rehearses this litany of objections with great cogency in her judicious account, "Problems with Bakhtin's Poetics," *Slavic and East European Journal* 30 (winter 1988): 503–25. They include criticism of Bakhtin's sentimental celebration of "folk laughter" and "carnivalesque" subversion, his privileging of "novelistic" discourse and overly schematic dismissal of the lyric's "monologic" mode of expression.

3　For an excellent discussion of Bakhtin's closeness to and distance from Derrida's correction of Structuralist linguistics, see Michael Holquist, "The Surd Heard: Bakhtin and Derrida," in *Literature and History: Theoretical Problems and Russian Case Studies*, ed. Gary Saul Morson (Stanford, Calif.: Stanford University Press, 1986), 137–56. Morson sharpens the distinction (192–201) by emphasizing Bakhtin's focus on the interpretive moment as a cultural process that always strives to reconstruct perceptible codes situationally, thereby reducing the inherent indeterminacy of utterances.

4　Mikhail Bakhtin, *Speech Genres and Other Late Essays*, ed. Caryl Emerson and Michael Holquist (Austin: University of Texas Press, 1986), 5.

5　V. N. Voloshinov, *Marxism and the Philosophy of Language* (New York: Seminar Press, 1973), 94.

6　Bakhtin, *Dialogic Imagination*, 354–55 (hereafter cited in the text).

7　Perhaps the fullest account of the important generational shift between an "integrationist" and an exclusivist understanding of what constitutes "Afro-American expressive culture" appears in Houston Baker Jr., *Blues, Ideology and Afro-American Literature* (Chicago: University of Chicago Press, 1984), 64–112 (hereafter cited in the text). This crucial turn toward a vernacular and ear-oriented perception of American black texts and their complex signifying was anticipated in Stephen Henderson, *Understanding the New Black Poetry* (New York: Morrow, 1973).

8　Henry Louis Gates Jr., "Criticism in the Jungle," in *Black Literature and Literary Theory*, ed. Henry Louis Gates Jr. (New York: Methuen, 1984), 6.

9　Exactly contemporary with Gates and Baker, Michael G. Cooke was also locating a culturally specific expressivity in two vernacular forms. The blues and oral signifyin' "by their obliquity . . . enabled the culture to exist without demanding, indeed without provoking recognition" (*Afro-American Literature in the Twentieth Century* [New Haven, Conn.: Yale University Press, 1984], 21–22).

10 Henry Louis Gates Jr., *Figures in Black: Words, Signs, and the "Racial" Self* (New York: Oxford University Press, 1987), 240.

11 Bakhtin, *Dostoevsky's Poetics*, 196.

12 Baker, *Modernism*, 84.

13 Quoted in Gates, *Signifying Monkey*, 1 (hereafter cited in the text).

14 Zora Neale Hurston, *Their Eyes Were Watching God* (Urbana: University of Illinois Press, 1978), 16 (hereafter cited in the text).

15 This point is elegantly made by Barbara Johnson, "Metaphor, Metonymy, and Voice in *Their Eyes Were Watching God*," in Gates, *Black Literature*, 205–19.

16 Disappointingly, Russian women writers exercised nowhere near the same influence on the evolution of Russian cultural nationalism. They tended to subscribe to the public formulations of male theorists, whether Slavophiles or Westernizers, or to evade the issue of national particularity altogether. The one prominent exception is Marina Tsvetaeva, but her impact as a cultural force has been much delayed and is largely a phenomenon related to the post-Soviet merging of the "two Russias"—White and Red, retrograde and revolutionary—into a uniquely non-Western "third world" that resembles the revived ideology of the Eurasian group with whom she was closely affiliated, especially during her years in Prague.

17 Carby, *Reconstructing Womanhood*, 17.

18 See, however, Wahneema Lubiano, "Constructing and Reconstructing Afro-American Texts: The Critic as Ambassador and Referee," *American Literary History* 1 (1989): 432–47, for a cautionary word about the reductionist pressure to summarize the essence of racialized and marginalized literatures: "The abuse of the 'Afro-American tradition' is continual and assured."

19 Michael Awkward, *Inspiriting Influences: Tradition, Revision, and Afro-American Women's Novels* (New York: Columbia University Press, 1989), 2–9. This argument for a culture- and gender-linked privilege of "non-competitive revision" rather curiously invokes and enlists Bakhtin in its campaign to establish a nonconflictual interactive unity that "permeates Afro-American vernacular communication" (49).

20 Mae Gwendolyn Henderson, "Speaking in Tongues: Dialogics, Dialectics, and the Black Women Writer's Literary Tradition" in *Changing Our Own Words: Essays on Criticism, Theory, and Writing by Black Women*, ed. Cheryl A. Wall (New Brunswick, N.J.: Rutgers University Press, 1990), 16–37.

21 For a strong critique of contemporary theorists who invoke Bakhtin's "double-voicedness" as a redemptive means to transform "double consciousness" into a triumphant equalization of power relations through acts of racial self-expression, see Dorothy J. Hale, "Bakhtin in African American Literary Theory," *ELH* 61 (1994): 445–71. Hale's shrewd analysis too quickly assumes, however, that Bakhtin's notion of "voice" functions to elide "the paralyzing dualisms that plague philosophical accounts of subjectivity" (445). Even where Bakhtin does speak of attempts to appropriate

another's word, he is fully aware that language is an interactive and unfinal-ized phenomenon in which "the word in language is half someone else's" (*Dialogic Imagination*, 293).

22   Molefi Kete Asanti, "The Idea of a Metatheory," in *The Afrocentric Idea* (Phila-delphia: Temple University Press, 1987), 34–58. It goes without saying that the Afrocentric discourse analysis presupposes an unmodified timeless es-sentialism: "Africa is at the heart of *all* African American behavior. Commu-nication styles are reflective of the internal mythic clock, the epic memory, the psychic stain of Africa in our spirits" (48).

23   Both the phrase and the larger observation are derived from Peter Stallybrass and Allon White, *The Politics and Poetics of Transgression* (Ithaca, N.Y.: Cornell University Press, 1986), esp. 5–11.

24   My translation from Bakhtin, *Estetika slovesnogo tvorchestva*, ed. S. G. Bocharov (Moscow: Isskustvo, 1979), 269.

25   Toni Morrison, "Unspeakable Things Unspoken: The Afro-American Pres-ence in American Literature," *Michigan Quarterly Review* 28 (winter 1989): 8–9.

SELECT BIBLIOGRAPHY

GENERAL WORKS

Adell, Sandra. *Double-Consciousness/Double-Bind: Theoretical Issues in Twentieth-Century Black Literature.* Urbana: University of Illinois Press, 1994.

Andrews, William L. *To Tell a Free Story: The First Century of Afro-American Autobiography, 1760–1865.* Urbana: University of Illinois Press, 1986.

Appiah, Kwame Anthony. *In My Father's House: Africa in the Philosophy of Culture.* New York: Oxford University Press, 1992.

Asanti, Molefi Kete. *The Afrocentric Idea.* Philadelphia: Temple University Press, 1987.

Awkward, Michael. *Inspiriting Influences: Tradition, Revision, and Afro-American Women's Novels.* New York: Columbia University Press, 1989.

Baker, Houston, Jr. *Blues, Ideology, and Afro-American Literature.* Chicago: University of Chicago Press, 1984.

———. *Modernism and the Harlem Renaissance.* Chicago: University of Chicago Press, 1987.

Bakhtin, Mikhail. *The Dialogic Imagination: Four Essays.* Ed. Michael Holquist. Austin: University of Texas Press, 1981.

———. *Estetika slovesnogo tvorchestva.* Ed. S. G. Bocharov. Moscow: Isskustvo, 1979.

———. *Speech Genres and Other Late Essays.* Ed. Caryl Emerson and Michael Holquist. Austin: University of Texas Press, 1986.

Bassin, Mark. "Russia between Europe and Asia: The Ideological Construction of Geography." *Slavic Review* 50 (1991): 1–17.

Berdyaev, Nikolai. 1946. Reprint, *The Russian Idea.* Boston: Beacon Press, 1962.

Brodhead, Richard H. *Cultures of Letters: Scenes of Reading and Writing in Nineteenth-Century America.* Chicago: University of Chicago Press, 1993.

Brodskii, N. L. *Rannie slavianofily.* Moscow, 1910.

Carby, Hazel V. *Reconstructing Womanhood: The Emergence of the Afro-American Woman Novelist.* New York: Oxford University Press, 1987.

Chaadaev, Peter. *The Major Works of Peter Chaadaev.* Trans. Raymond T. McNally. Notre Dame, Ind.: University of Notre Dame Press, 1969.

———. *Peter Yakovlevich Chaadayev: Philosophical Letters and Apology of a Madman.* Trans. Mary-Barbara Zeldin. Knoxville: University of Tennessee Press, 1969.

Clifford, James. "Diasporas." *Cultural Anthropology* 9 (1994): 302–38.

———. "On Ethnographic Allegory." In *Writing Culture: The Poetics and Politics of*

Ethnography, ed. James Clifford and Steven Marcus, 98–121. Berkeley: University of California Press, 1986.

Cooke, Michael G. *Afro-American Literature in the Twentieth Century.* New Haven, Conn.: Yale University Press, 1984.

Crummell, Alexander. *Africa and America: Addresses and Discourses.* 1891. Reprint, New York: Negro Universities Press, 1969.

———. *Destiny and Race: Selected Writings, 1840–1898.* Ed. Wilson Jeremiah Moses. Amherst: University of Massachusetts Press, 1992.

———. *The Future of Africa: being Addresses, Sermons, delivered in the Republic of Liberia.* Detroit, Mich.: Negro History Press, 1960.

Dowler, Wayne. *Dostoevsky, Grigor'ev, and Native Soil Conservatism.* Toronto: University of Toronto Press, 1982.

DuBois, W. E. B. *The Souls of Black Folk.* Ed. David W. Blight and Robert Gooding-Williams. Boston: Bedford Books, 1997.

Ellison, Ralph. *Shadow and Act.* New York: Vintage, 1995.

Eze, Emmanuel Chukwudi. *Race and Enlightenment: A Reader.* Oxford: Blackwell Publishers, 1997.

Gates, Henry Louis, Jr. *Figures in Black: Words, Signs, and the "Racial" Self.* New York: Oxford University Press, 1987.

———. *The Signifying Monkey: A Theory of Afro-American Literary Criticism.* New York: Oxford University Press, 1988.

———, ed. *Black Literature and Literary Theory.* New York: Methuen, 1984.

Gilroy, Paul. *The Black Atlantic: Modernity and Double Consciousness.* Cambridge, Mass.: Harvard University Press, 1993.

Greenfeld, Liah. *Nationalism: Five Roads to Modernity.* Cambridge, Mass.: Harvard University Press, 1992.

Groys, Boris. "Russia and the West: The Quest for Russian National Identity." *Studies in Soviet Thought* 43 (1992): 185–98.

Henderson, Mae Gwendolyn. "Speaking in Tongues: Dialogics, Dialectics, and the Black Woman Writer's Literary Tradition." In *Changing Our Own Words: Essays on Criticism, Theory, and Writing by Black Women,* ed. Cheryl A. Wall, 16–37. New Brunswick, N.J.: Rutgers University Press, 1990.

Hubbs, Joanna. *Mother Russia: The Feminine Myth in Russian Culture.* Bloomington: Indiana University Press, 1988.

Hurston, Zora Neale. *Mules and Men.* New York: Harper Perennial, 1990.

Hutchinson, George. *The Harlem Renaissance in Black and White.* Cambridge, Mass.: Harvard University Press, 1995.

Isaev, I. A. *Puti evrazii.* Moscow: Russkaia Kniga, 1992.

Kireevsky, I. V. *Polnoe sobranii sochinenii I. V. Kireevskogo.* Vol. 1, ed. M. O. Gershenzon. Moscow, 1911.

Koyré, Alexandre. *Études sur l'histoire de la pensée philosophique en Russie.* Paris: Librairie Vrin, 1950.

———. *La philosophie et le problème national en Russie au début du XIXe siècle.* Paris: Champion, 1929.

Lebedev, Iu. V. *U istokov eposa: Ocherkovye tsikly v russkoi literature 1840–1860-kh godov.* Yaroslavl', 1975.

Lee, Dorothy. *Freedom and Culture.* Englewood Cliffs, N.J.: Prentice-Hall, 1959.

Levy, Helen Fiddyment. *Fiction of the Home Place.* Jackson: University of Mississippi Press, 1992.

Locke, Alain, ed. *The New Negro: An Interpretation.* New York: Albert and Charles Boni, 1925.

Lotman, Iurii M., and Boris Uspensky. *The Semiotics of Russian Cultural History.* Ed. Alexander D. Nakhimovsky and Alice Stone Nakhimovsky. Ithaca, N.Y.: Cornell University Press, 1985.

Lubiano, Wahneema. "Constructing and Reconstructing Afro-American Texts: The Critic as Ambassador and Referee." *American Literary History* 1 (1989): 432–47.

Michaels, Walter Benn. *Our America: Nativism, Modernism, and Pluralism.* Durham, N.C.: Duke University Press, 1995.

Morrison, Toni. "Unspeakable Things Unspoken: The Afro-American Presence in American Literature." *Michigan Quarterly Review* 28 (winter 1989): 8–9.

Moses, Wilson Jeremiah. "Dark Forests and Barbarian Vigor: Paradox, Conflict, and Africanity in Black Writing before 1914." *American Literary History* 1 (1989): 650–51.

Muchnic, Helen. *From Gorky to Pasternak: Six Writers in Soviet Russia.* New York: Vintage, 1966.

Mudimbe, V. Y. *The Invention of Africa: Gnosis, Philosophy, and the Order of Knowledge.* Bloomington: Indiana University Press, 1988.

Nielsen, Alden L. *Writing between the Lines: Race and Intertextuality.* Athens: University of Georgia Press, 1994.

Parthé, Kathleen F. *Russian Village Prose: The Radiant Past.* Princeton, N.J.: Princeton University Press, 1992.

Robin, Regine. *Socialist Realism: An Impossible Aesthetic.* Stanford, Calif.: Stanford University Press, 1992.

Ruttenburg, Nancy. "Silence and Servitude: Bondage and Self-Invention in Russia and America, 1780–1861." *Slavic Review* 51 (1992): 743–47.

Shneidman, N. N. *Soviet Literature in the 1980's: Decade of Transition.* Toronto: University of Toronto Press, 1989.

Snead, James A. "Repetition as a Figure of Black Culture." In *Black Literature and Literary Theory,* ed. Henry Louis Gates Jr., 59–79. New York: Methuen, 1984.

Stallybrass, Peter, and Allon White. *The Politics and Poetics of Transgression.* Ithaca, N.Y.: Cornell University Press, 1986.

Stepto, Robert B. *From behind the Veil: A Study of Afro-American Narrative.* Urbana: University of Illinois Press, 1979.

Sundquist, Eric J. *The Hammers of Creation: Folk Culture in Modern African American Fiction.* Athens: University of Georgia Press, 1992.

———. *To Wake the Nations: Race in the Making of American Literature.* Cambridge, Mass.: Harvard University Press, 1993.

Thaden, Edward C. *Conservative Nationalism in Nineteenth-Century Russia*. Seattle: University of Washington Press, 1964.

Townsend, Kim. *Manhood at Harvard: William James and Others*. New York: Norton, 1996.

Trubetzkoy, N. S. *The Legacy of Genghis Khan and Other Essays on Russia's Identity*. Ed. Anatoly Liberman. Ann Arbor: Michigan Slavic Publications, 1991.

Tseitlin, A. G. *Stanovlenie realizma v russkoi literature*. Moscow: Nauka, 1965.

Wachtel, Andrew Baruch. *The Battle for Childhood: Creation of a Russian Myth*. Stanford, Calif.: Stanford University Press, 1990.

Walicki, Andrzej. *The Slavophile Controversy: History of a Conservative Utopia in Nineteenth-Century Russian Thought*. Oxford: Clarendon Press, 1975.

Williams, Robert C. "The Russian Soul: A Study in European Thought and Non-European Nationalism." *Journal of the History of Ideas* 31 (1970): 573–78.

Williamson, Joel. *The Crucible of Race: Black-White Relations in the American South since Emancipation*. New York: Oxford University Press, 1984.

Willis, Susan. *Specifying: Black Women Writing the American Experience*. Madison: University of Wisconsin Press, 1987.

Wolff, Larry. *Inventing Eastern Europe: The Map of Civilization on the Mind of the Enlightenment*. Stanford, Calif.: Stanford University Press, 1994.

SPECIALIZED STUDIES

Andrews, William L. *The Literary Career of Charles W. Chesnutt*. Baton Rouge: Louisiana State University Press, 1980.

Bakhtin, Mikhail. *Problems of Dostoevsky's Poetics*. Ed. Caryl Emerson. Minneapolis: University of Minnesota Press, 1984.

Borras, F. M. *Maxim Gorky the Writer: An Interpretation*. Oxford: Clarendon Press, 1967.

Carby, Hazel V. "The Politics of Fiction, Anthropology, and the Folk: Zora Neale Hurston." In *New Essays on Their Eyes Were Watching God*, ed. Michael Awkward. Cambridge: Cambridge University Press, 1990.

Cavanagh, Claire. "Synthetic Nationality: Mandel'shtam and Chaadaev." *Slavic Review* 49 (winter 1990): 597–610.

Christoff, Peter K. *An Introduction to Nineteenth-Century Russian Slavophilism*. Vol. 2, *I. V. Kireevskij*. The Hague: Mouton, 1972.

Clark, Katerina, and Michael Holquist. *Mikhail Bakhtin*. Cambridge, Mass.: Harvard University Press, 1984.

Davis, Charles T. "From Experience to Eloquence: Richard Wright's *Black Boy* as Art." In *Chant of Saints: A Gathering of Afro-American Literature, Art, and Scholarship*, ed. Michael S. Harper and Robert B. Stepto, 425–39. Urbana: University of Illinois Press, 1979.

Erikson, Erik. "The Legend of Maxim Gorky's Youth." In *Childhood and Society*, 316–58. New York: Norton, 1950.

Fabre, Michel. *The Unfinished Quest of Richard Wright*. New York: Morrow, 1973.

Fowler, Virginia C. *Gloria Naylor: In Search of Sanctuary*. New York: Twayne, 1996.

Frank, Joseph. *Dostoevsky: The Stir of Liberation, 1860–1865*. Princeton, N.J.: Princeton University Press, 1986.

———. *Dostoevsky: The Years of Ordeal, 1850–1859*. Princeton, N.J.: Princeton University Press, 1983.

———. "Ralph Ellison and Dostoevsky." In *Through the Russian Prism*. Princeton, N.J.: Princeton University Press, 1990.

Gillespie, David C. *Valentin Rasputin and Soviet Russian Village Prose*. London: Modern Humanities Research Association, 1986.

Gleason, Abbott. *European and Muscovite: Ivan Kireevsky and the Origins of Slavophilism*. Cambridge, Mass.: Harvard University Press, 1972.

Goellnicht, Donald C. "Passing as Autobiography: James Weldon Johnson's *The Autobiography of an Ex-Coloured Man*." *African American Review* 30 (spring 1996): 17–34.

Gooding-Williams, Robert. "Du Bois's Counter-Sublime." *Massachusetts Review* 35 (1994): 203–24.

———. "Philosophy of History and Social Critique in *The Souls of Black Folk*." *Social Science Information* 26 (1987): 99–114.

Hale, Dorothy J. "Bakhtin in African American Literary Theory." *ELH* 61 (1994): 445–71.

Harris, Leonard, ed. *The Philosophy of Alain Locke: Harlem Renaissance and Beyond*. Philadelphia: Temple University Press, 1989.

Harris, Trudier. *The Power of the Porch: The Storyteller's Craft in Zora Neale Hurston, Gloria Naylor, and Randall Kenan*. Athens: University of Georgia Press, 1996.

Hemenway, Robert. *Zora Neale Hurston: A Literary Biography*. Urbana: University of Illinois Press, 1980.

Jackson, Robert Louis. *The Art of Dostoevsky: Deliriums and Nocturnes*. Princeton, N.J.: Princeton University Press, 1981.

Johnson, Barbara. "Thresholds of Difference: Structures of Address in Zora Neale Hurston." In *"Race," Writing, and Difference*, ed. Henry Louis Gates Jr. Chicago: University of Chicago Press, 1986.

Jones, John. *Dostoevsky*. Oxford: Clarendon Press, 1983.

Kovalev, V. A. "Zapiski okhotnika" I. S. Turgeneva: *Voprosy genezisa*. Leningrad, 1980.

Leavitt, Marcus C. *Russian Literary Politics and the Pushkin Celebration of 1880*. Ithaca, N.Y.: Cornell University Press, 1989.

Lewis, David Levering. *W. E. B. Du Bois: Biography of a Race, 1868–1919*. New York: Henry Holt, 1993.

McNally, Raymond T. *Chaadaev and His Friends*. Tallahassee: Diplomatic Press, 1971.

Mirsky, D. S. "The Eurasian Movement." *Slavonic Review* 6, no. 17 (1927): 311–19.

Morson, Gary Saul, and Caryl Emerson, eds. *Rethinking Bakhtin: Extensions and Challenges*. Evanston, Ill.: Northwestern University Press, 1989.

Moses, Wilson Jeremiah. *Alexander Crummell: A Study in Civilization and Its Discontent*. New York: Oxford University Press, 1989.

———. "The Conservation of Races and Its Context." *Massachusetts Review* 34 (1993): 275–94.

Oldfield, J. R. *Alexander Crummell and the Creation of an African-American Church in Liberia*. Lewiston, Colo.: Mellen, 1990.

Peace, Richard. *Dostoevsky's Notes from Underground*. London: Bristol Classical Press, 1993.

Peterson, Dale E. "The Completion of *A Sportsman's Sketches*: Turgenev's Parting Word." In *The Poetics of Ivan Turgenev*, ed. David A. Lowe, 53–62. Washington: Kennan Institute Occasional Papers #234, 1989.

———. "The Origin and End of Turgenev's *Sportsman's Notebook*: The Poetics and Politics of a Precarious Balance." *Russian Literature* 16 (1984): 347–58.

———. "Richard Wright's Long Journey from Gorky to Dostoevsky." *African American Review* 28 (1994): 375–88.

Polowy, Teresa. *The Novellas of Valentin Rasputin: Genre, Language and Style*. New York: Peter Lang, 1989.

Quénet, Charles. *Tchaadaev et les lettres philosophiques*. Paris: Librairie Champion, 1931.

Rampersad, Arnold. *The Art and Imagination of W. E. B. Du Bois*. New York: Schocken, 1990.

Riasanovsky, Nicholas V. "The Emergence of Eurasianism." *California Slavic Studies* 4 (1967): 39–72.

Rigsby, Gregory U. *Alexander Crummell: Pioneer in Nineteenth-Century Pan-African Thought*. New York: Greenwood Press, 1987.

Ripp, Victor. *Turgenev's Russia*. Ithaca, N.Y.: Cornell University Press, 1980.

Serman, Il'ya. "Tema narodnosti v 'Zapiskakh iz mertvogo doma.' " *Dostoevsky Studies* 3 (1982): 101–44.

Shatalov, S. E. *"Zapiski okhotnika" I. S. Turgeneva*. Stalinabad, 1960.

Stewart, Jeffery C. "A Biography of Alain Locke: Philosopher of the Harlem Renaissance, 1886–1930." Dissertation, Yale University, 1979.

Tucker, Lindsay. "Recovering the Conjure Woman: Texts and Contexts in Gloria Naylor's *Mama Day*." *African American Review* 28 (1994): 173–88.

Tunimanov, V. A. *Tvorchestvo Dostoevskogo, 1854–1862*. Leningrad: Nauka, 1980.

Yarborough, Richard. "The First-Person in Afro-American Fiction." In *Afro-American Literary Study in the 1990's*, ed. Houston Baker Jr. and Patricia Redmond. Chicago: University of Chicago Press, 1989.

INDEX

Dale Peterson is Professor of English and Russian

at Amherst College.

Library of Congress Cataloging-in-Publication Data

Peterson, Dale E.
Up from bondage : the literatures of Russian and African American "soul" /
Dale E. Peterson.
p.   cm.
Includes bibliographical references and index.
ISBN 0-8223-2526-8 (alk. paper) — ISBN 0-8223-2560-8 (pbk. : alk. paper)
1. Russian literature—19th century—History and criticism.   2. Russian litera-
ture—20th century—History and criticism.   3. Nationalism—Russia.   4. Russia
—Intellectual life—1801–1917.   5. American literature—Afro-American authors
—History and criticism.   6. Nationalism—United States.   7. Afro-American intellectuals.   8. United States—Intellectual life—1865–1918.   I. Title.
PG3012 .P48   2000
891.7'09358—dc21
99-050806